THE CANONICAL PROCEDURE IN SEPARATION CASES

THE CATHOLIC UNIVERSITY OF AMERICA
CANON LAW STUDIES
No. 325

THE CANONICAL PROCEDURE IN SEPARATION CASES

A HISTORICAL SYNOPSIS AND A COMMENTARY

BY

REVEREND JAMES PATRICK KING, J.C.L.
Priest of the Diocese of Brooklyn

A DISSERTATION

Submitted to the Faculty of the School of Canon Law of the Catholic University of America in Partial Fulfillment of the Requirements for the Degree of Doctor of Canon Law

THE CATHOLIC UNIVERSITY OF AMERICA PRESS
WASHINGTON, D. C.
1952

Nihil Obstat:

LUDOVICUS MOTRY, S.T.D., J.C.D.,
Censor Deputatus.

Washingtoni, die I Aprilis, 1952.

Imprimatur:

✠ THOMAS EDMUNDUS MOLLOY, S.T.D.,
Archiepiscopus-Episcopus Brooklyniensis.

Brooklyni, die XXII Aprilis, 1952.

Printed by
THE PAULIST PRESS
401 WEST 59TH STREET
NEW YORK 19, N. Y.
51

TABLE OF CONTENTS

PAGE

FOREWORD ix

PART ONE

HISTORICAL SYNOPSIS

CHAPTER I

THE PROCEDURE IN SEPARATION CASES IN THE EARLY CANON LAW UNTIL THE DECREE OF GRATIAN (Ca. 1140) 1

ARTICLE 1. THE ROMAN EMPIRE 1

ARTICLE 2. THE GERMANIC AGE 9

CHAPTER II

THE PROCEDURE IN CASES OF SEPARATION FROM THE DECREE OF GRATIAN (Ca. 1140) TO THE COUNCIL OF TRENT (1545-1563) 15

ARTICLE 1. THE *Decree* OF GRATIAN 16

A. The Ordinary Procedure 16

B. Separation *Propria Auctoritate* 22

ARTICLE 2. THE DECRETALS OF GREGORY IX (1234) 23

A. The Ordinary Procedure 25

1. The Competent Tribunal 27

2. The Parties in the Case 28

3. Exceptions 29

4. The *Libellus* 32

PAGE

5. Proofs and Presumptions 33
6. The Sentence 34
7. *Res Iudicata* 34
8. Alimony and the Custody of the Offspring 35

B. Separation *Propria Auctoritate* 36

ARTICLE 3. THE CONSTITUTIONS *Dispendiosam* and *Saepe* OF CLEMENT V (1305-1314) 38

CHAPTER III

THE PROCEDURE IN CASES OF SEPARATION FROM THE COUNCIL OF TRENT (1545-1563) TO THE CODE OF CANON LAW (1918) 41

ARTICLE 1. THE FORMAL PROCEDURE 45
ARTICLE 2. SEPARATION *Propria Auctoritate* 54
ARTICLE 3. THE INFORMAL PROCEDURE 57

PART II

CANONICAL COMMENTARY

CHAPTER IV

THE NATURE OF THE PROPER CANONICAL PROCESS IN SEPARATION CASES 63

ARTICLE 1. PRELIMINARY NOTIONS 63
ARTICLE 2. THE AUTHORITY FOR SEPARATION 66
ARTICLE 3. THE NATURE OF THE PROCESS 73
ARTICLE 4. THE DETERMINATION OF THE PROCESS 78

CHAPTER V

PAGE

THE JUDICIAL PROCESS 80

ARTICLE 1. ORGANIZATION OF THE COURT 80

A. Competency 80

B. The Judge 83

C. The Promoter of Justice 86

ARTICLE 2. INTRODUCTORY STAGE OF THE TRIAL 88

A. The Parties 88

B. Actions and Exceptions 90

C. The *Libellus* and *Litis Contestatio* 96

ARTICLE 3. PROBATORY STAGE OF THE TRIAL 99

A. Proofs 99

B. Presumptions 101

ARTICLE 4. CONCLUDING STAGES OF THE TRIAL 105

A. Sentence 105

B. Publication of the Sentence 110

COROLLARY: Some Salient Points on the Juridical Effects of a Canonical Separation 111

ARTICLE 5. THE APPEAL AND THE COURT OF SECOND INSTANCE 114

CHAPTER VI

THE ADMINISTRATIVE PROCESS 119

ARTICLE 1. NATURE AND CHARACTER OF THE ADMINISTRATIVE PROCESS 121

ARTICLE 2. THE PROPER AUTHORITY FOR THE ADMINISTRATIVE HEARING OF SEPARATION CASES 123

PAGE

Article 3. The Process ... 127
A. Introductory and Probatory Stages of the Process ... 127
B. The Promoter of Justice ... 132
C. The Decree of Separation ... 133
Article 4. Legal Redress Against the Decree of the Ordinary ... 135

CHAPTER VII

CANONICAL SEPARATION AND CIVIL ACTION ... 138
Article 1. The Problem ... 138
Article 2. Historical Synopsis of the Question ... 142
A. Responses of the Roman Curia ... 145
B. The Opinions of the Old Authors ... 147
Article 3. Suggested Norms of Action Today ... 149
CONCLUSIONS ... 159
APPENDIX—SOME SUGGESTED INTERROGATORIES FOR THE ADMINISTRATIVE HEARING OF SEPARATION CASES ... 163
I. Request and Interrogatory of Petitioner for an Ecclesiastical Separation ... 163
II. Interrogatory for Respondent ... 168
III. Interrogatory for Witness ... 171
IV. Interrogatory for Priest Consulted ... 174
BIBLIOGRAPHY ... 177
ABBREVIATIONS ... 184
ALPHABETICAL INDEX ... 187
BIOGRAPHICAL NOTE ... 191
CANON LAW STUDIES ... 193

FOREWORD

In these words: *"Coniuges servare debent vitae coniugalis communicationem, nisi iusta causa eos excuset,"* [1] the Code of Canon Law adverts to the obligation of the married partners to live together in a common life, but at the same time signalizes the realization that because of human weakness they may at times, unfortunately, find this impossible. In the latter instance, the provision is made for a separation from this community of life, with the marriage bond, nevertheless, remaining intact.

The purpose of this dissertation, then, is to present a historical synopsis and canonical commentary of the ecclesiastical law relative to the procedural norms to be observed in these cases. The type of separation in question is what is known, not as *"separatio a tora et mensa,"* but as, *"quoad cohabitationem."* The former is more of a private matter and is often settled in the forum of conscience, but the latter affects the public good because of the interruption of family life and especially because of the impossibility relative to the fulfilling of the primary end of marriage as resulting from this disruption of the common life. Consequently, the public authority of the Church must be invoked, and this is accomplished through its procedural law.

Since the ascertainment of the proper processual regulations for these cases is the topic of this work, reference to the nature, causes and doctrine of canonical separation as such is for the most part omitted. Such reference occurs only where it serves to integrate the discussion. The treatment given here, therefore, is concerned fundamentally with the judicial and administrative processes which are proper to these suits. The inclusion of the concluding chapter, which treats of canonical separation and civil action, although not an integral part of the procedure for these cases, was thought advisable because of the intimate connection of this problem with every decree of ecclesiastical separation.

The writer takes this opportunity to express his gratitude to His

[1] Canon 1128.

Excellency, the Most Reverend Thomas E. Molloy, S.T.D., Archbishop-Bishop of Brooklyn, for the opportunity to pursue advanced studies in Canon Law and for his kind generosity in making this publication possible. The writer wishes to express his gratitude also to His Excellency, the Most Reverend Raymond A. Kearney, S.T.D., J.C.D., Auxiliary Bishop and Chancellor of the Diocese of Brooklyn, for his kind interest in suggesting the title of this work and his unfailing help and encouragement. He is also indebted to the members of the Faculty of the School of Canon Law for their kind encouragement, scholarly direction and valuable assistance in the preparation of this dissertation.

CHAPTER I

THE PROCEDURE IN SEPARATION CASES IN THE EARLY CANON LAW UNTIL THE DECREE OF GRATIAN (ca. 1140)

ARTICLE 1. THE ROMAN EMPIRE

THE moral environment that the Church entered on the first Pentecost Sunday was one completely alien to the exalted doctrine of marriage taught by our Divine Saviour. Whereas the Jews and the Romans considered marriage as a dissoluble union, Christian doctrine presented it as a permanent bond, which endures as long as the consorts should live. Although Christ had pointed out that marriage was instituted by God as indissoluble from the very beginning,[1] nevertheless, by His time, divorce was an accepted legal institute among the chosen people.[2] This was not just a mere toleration, but the rabbinical literature was replete with references to divorce. In fact, so extensive was the Talmudic doctrine on the subject, that one complete treatise, *Gittin* (Bills of Divorce), was concerned exclusively with it, and additional references are found in *Kiddushin* (Betrothals), *Yebamoth* (Sisters in law), *Kethuboth* (Marriage

[1] "Moses, by reason of the hardness of your heart, permitted you to put away your wives; but it was not so from the beginning"—Matt., XIX:8.

[2] The first recorded case of separation in the Sacred Scripture is the repudiation of Agar by Abraham—Genesis, XXI:14; but the earliest reference to any process is not found until the mention of the "bill of divorce" in the Mosaic Law—". . . he shall write a bill of divorce, and shall give it in her hand, and send her out of his house"—Deut., XXII:28, 29; this verse does not signify the institution of divorce by Moses, as some would have it, rather, it was a regulation to control an abuse, and Moses, instead of relaxing the Law, was directing the lesser of two evils—Von Hummelauer, *Commentarius in Deuteronomium* (Paris, 1901), p. 408; Joyce, *Christian Marriage* (London: Sheed and Ward, 1933), p. 283; Perrone, *De Matrimonio Christiano* (3 vols., Romae, 1858), III, 215; Knabenbauer, *Commentaria in Evangelium secundam Matthaeum* (2 vols., Paris, 1922), II, 148.

Deeds) and *Sota* (The Suspected Adulteress).[3] A study of these provisions clearly demonstrates that the procedure in divorce cases among the Jews, as compared with their contemporaries the Romans,[4] was most detailed and exacting. So itemized and particularized are the factors involved that, besides such general notions as the right of divorce belonging to the husband alone,[5] special provisions are found even for the writing material, format, special formularies and also the delivery.[6] Even with such strict and exacting norms, divorce became a common occurrence among the Jews; in fact, the leaders themselves shared in this freedom to excess.[7]

The problems facing the early Church, however, were by no means confined to the Jewish people, for even greater difficulties had to be met in view of the pagan concepts of marriage and divorce among the Romans, the world conquerors of their day. Although the basis of marriage among the Romans was *"affectio maritalis"* or mutual marital consent,[8] Unlike the consent in Canon Law, which

[3] Strack, *Introduction to the Talmud and Midrash* (Philadelphia: Jewish Publication Society of America, 1931), pp. 43 ff.; the Hebrew term for bill of divorce is *Get*. Its plural, *Gittin*, gives the title to the treatment in the Talmud.

[4] Since marriage existed and was fully entered by the parties, it was a principle of Roman Law that divorce should be just as free in dissolving the marriage—". . . Nudi consensus obligatio contrario consensu dissolvitur"—D(50.17)35; Sherman, *Roman Law in the Modern World* (2. ed., 3 vols., New York, 1924), II, n. 460; as a companion to this freedom, divorce in Roman Law was, irrespective of its form, always a private act. It needed no sanction of a court of law—Nov.(22.3); (22.4); Buckland, *A Manual of Private Roman Law* (2. ed., Cambridge: University Press, 1947), p. 70; Sherman, *op. cit.*, II, n. 485; Joyce, *op. cit.*, p. 309.

[5] *Gittin*, 23a. All citations from the Talmud in this work are taken from Epstein, *The Babylonian Talmud* (13 vols. in 8, London: Soncino Press, 1938).

[6] *Gittin*, 19a, 24b, 17a, 79b, 9b, 36a, 85a, 82a, 84b, 72a.

[7] A noteworthy example was the execution of St. John the Baptist for daring to denounce the incestuous marriage of Herod and his brother's wife, Herodias—Matt., XIV:3-5.

[8] ". . . nuptias enim non concubitus, sed consensus facit"—D.(35.1) 15; D.(50.17)30; "Concubinam ex sola animi destinatione aestimari oportet."—D.(25.7)4; ". . . non enim coitus matrimonium facit, sed maritalis affectio"—D.(24.1) (32.13); cf. also C.(5.17)11; Nov.(18.4)1; Nov.(22.3); Nov.(117.4); Roby, *Roman Private Law* (2 vols., Cambridge, 1902), I, 132; Corbett, *The Roman Law of Marriage* (Oxford: Clarendon Press, 1930), p. 95.

is of a contractual character, that of the Roman Law consisted in its factual endurance. By this it is meant that consent in Canon Law is *consensus initialis*; it must be present at the time the contract is made, or else the union is invalid. Whether or not it endures is unimportant, if once entered validly, the marriage always stands independent of any change of consent by the parties. The consent in Roman Law, however, necessarily looked to the fact of its endurance, and if at any time it ceased to exist by the will of one or of both of the parties, the marriage relationship was at an end. Marriage was freely entered, and just as freely terminated, for its permanence depended on the permanency of the *affectio maritalis,* and not in contractual promises.[9]

Divorce among the Romans then was effected with great ease, and its kinds were simply distinguished in line with the individual or mutual acts of the parties. If the divorce was effected by mutual consent, i.e., if both parties agreed to terminate the union, the term employed was *divortium*. If only one party desired to end the bond, a separation effected solely at his will was called *repudium*.[10] Although the employment of divorce was restricted somewhat by the Emperor Justinian (527-565),[11] it is nevertheless historically true that the free use of these institutes was so common that permanence in the Roman marriage bond was of very rare occurrence.[12]

It was inevitable that in such completely alien surroundings the early Christians would be influenced by the laxity of the marriage laws among the nations. In the absence of source material for these early centuries, one can only conjecture what the real state of affairs was from the writings of the Popes, the Fathers and the canons of the Councils. Christians were the few among the many. The Jews and

[9] D.(50.17)35; Nov.(22.4); (22.18); Rivier, *Précis du Droit de Famille Romaine* (Paris, 1891), p. 223.

[10] Sherman, *Roman Law in the Modern World,* II, n. 485; Muirhead, *Historical Introduction to the Private Law of Rome* (3. ed., London, 1916), p. 356.

[11] Nov.(117.8); (117.9); (117.12); (134.11).

[12] At the time of Christ, we have the testimony of Seneca (+ 65) to authenticate this sad state of affairs. He stated that some Roman matrons counted their years by the number of their marriages—*De Beneficiis,* III, 16, 2; Juvenal (ca. 60 - ca. 140) substantiated this condition by relating the story of a woman who had eight husbands in five years—*Satires,* VI, vv. 228, 229.

Romans regarded divorce as permissible with little objection, and to continue this practice after conversion, or to consider it lawful in view of such a long past tradition, was surely not difficult for the new members of the Christian community. Sufficient evidence is present, however, to indicate the position of the Church in these difficult surroundings; much of the early Christian literature manifests an unceasing struggle to control this evil, to preserve the sanctity of the home, and to insist on the indissolubility of the marriage bond.

Most of the early Fathers, concerned with the general evil of divorce, simply repeated, interpreted or emphasized the teachings of Christ and St. Paul on divorce,[13] for they wished merely to emphasize the Christian belief in the indissolubility of marriage. Several of their number discussed the obligation of the innocent spouse to dismiss the guilty party.[14] In addition the Councils of Elvira (305) [15] and Neocaesarea (314),[16] as well as the I Council of Toledo (400),[17] admonished clerics to dismiss their adulterous wives, doubtless because of the clerical state of the husband and in consequence of the scandal such behavior on the part of his wife would bring in the

[13] *Canones Apostolorum,* c. 47—Bruns, *Canones Apostolorum et Conciliorum Saeculorum IV-VII* (2 vols., Berolini, 1839), I, 8 (hereafter cited as Bruns; St. Justin, Martyr (+ ca. 165), *Apologia Prima pro Christianis,* c. 15—Migne, *Patrologiae Cursus Completus, Series Graeca* (161 vols., Parisiis, 1857-1866), VI, 350 (hereafter referred to as *MPG*); Athenagoras (fl. late 2. cent.), *Legatio pro Christianis,* c. 33—*MPG,* VI, 966, 967; Theophilus of Antioch (fl. late 2. cent.), *Ad Autolycum Libri Tres,* Lib. III, c. 13—*MPG,* VI, 1139; St. Clement of Alexandria (ca. 150 - ca. 215), *Stromata,* Lib. II, c. 23—*MPG,* VIII, 1095, 1096; Origen (ca. 185 - ca. 254), *Commentarium in Evangelium secundum Matthaeum,* Tomus XIV, c. 23—*MPG,* XII, 1243; Tertullian (+ after 220), *Liber de Patientia,* c. 12—Migne, *Patrologiae Cursus Completus, Series Latina* (221 vols., Parisiis, 1844-1855), I, 1268 (hereafter referred to as *MPL*); St. Cyprian (+ 258), *Testimonia adversus Judaeos,* Lib. III, c. 90—*MPL,* IV, 774.

[14] St. Clement of Alexandria, *loc. cit.*; St. Jerome (ca. 347 - ca. 420), *Epistolae,* Ep. LV (ad Amandum), nn. 3, 4—*MPL,* XXII, 562, 563; St. Basil (ca. 330 - ca. 379), *Epistolae, Classis Secunda,* Ep. CXCIX, c. 21—*MPG,* XXXII, 722.

[15] Canon 65—Bruns, II, 10.

[16] Canon 8—Bruns, I, 72; also incorporated in c. 11, D. XXXIV.

[17] Canon 7—Bruns, I, 204; Bruns gave the date of this Council as 398 but most of the modern authors prefer 400. Cf. Joyce, *Christian Marriage,* p. 592.

Christian community. St. Augustine (354-430) put an end to all such discussion when he asserted that Christ's words were permissive, not obligatory, that one was allowed to, but one did not need to separate from an adulterous consort. This view came to be universally accepted in the Church.[18]

Sources treating of procedural norms peculiar to this early period are difficult to find. Since the problem at the moment was the evil of divorce as such, any reference to procedure was treated in a merely incidental fashion. One finds, however, a gradually emerging form of procedure as the Church became free and won progressive recognition of its native jurisdiction over marriage.

For the first four centuries of the Christian era, the competency of the Church over marriage cases was not recognized by the civil authority. The Church's competency stood unrecognized, since the very existence of the Church as a society was not acknowledged. Needless to say, the early Christians could not, with free conscience, present their cases to the Roman Imperial Tribunals. The latter not only did not recognize marriage as a sacrament, but treated it and separation as private matters. Their jurisprudence did not even consider matrimony as a matter for court action.[19]

Moreover, even the very confession of Christianity would have been subject to persecution. How then did the early Christians settle such cases in their own communities? The Roman Law usage of private decisions and the free use of the *libellus repudii* could hardly have been practiced, since Christ had forbidden its use in every case but adultery.[20] Moreover, in separation for adultery, any remarriage was forbidden to the innocent party as well as the guilty spouse. From the context it seems that the use of the *libellus repudii* was abolished relative also to the cases of adultery, because to the Roman and Jewish mind it contained a permission for a second marriage. A determination to wipe out the evil and to forbid the practice of second marriages was emphasized in the letters of the

18 *De Conjugiis Adulterinis,* Lib. II, c. 9—*MPL,* XL, 476. This same doctrine is included in c. 5, C. XXVIII, q. 1, and c. 3, c. XXXII, q. 7.

19 Corbett, *The Roman Law of Marriage,* pp. 226-229; Joyce, *Christian Marriage,* p. 216.

20 Matt., XIX:9.

early popes, in the decrees of the Councils, and in the writings of the Fathers.[21]

To what authority then did the faithful have recourse when questions regarding marriage arose? Obviously to the Apostles and the Bishops. That this was to be the procedure, and that the Church had the right to exercise such jurisdiction over the marriage cases of the faithful, was accepted by St. Paul. He was an educated Jewish convert, he was aware that the Jewish courts were recognized by the Romans as competent in these matters. To conclude that the Christians should maintain their own judicial tribunals was a logical consequent to this.[22] We also know that the early Christians were to present their marriage plans to the bishop for approval.[23] The faithful could naturally look to the bishops for judging disputes which arose regarding marriage, especially those concerning the bond.

During the persecutions, the procedures in the hearings of the early Christian tribunals were more than likely very simple affairs

[21] Innocent I (401-417) in his Epistle to Exsuperius, Bishop of Toulouse, in 405—*Epistola VI* (ad Exsuperium), c. 6—Jaffé, *Regesta Pontificum Romanorum ab condita Ecclesia ad annum post Christum natum MCXCVIII* (2 ed. by F. Kaltenbrunner (to the year 590), P. Ewald (from 590 to 882), and S. Loewenfeld (from 882 to 1198), and so referred to as JK, JE, and JL), JK, n. 293; *MPL,* XX, 500; Leo I (440-461), *Epistolae,* Ep. CLIX (ad Nicetam), c. 1—JK, n. 536—*MPL,* LIV, 1137; The dates of the Pontificates in this work are taken from *Annuario Pontificio per l'Anno 1948* (Città del Vaticano: Tipographia Poliglotta Vaticana, 1948); Council of Elvira (305), cc. 3, 9—Bruns, II, 3; I Council of Arles (314), Canon 24—Bruns, II, 110; Council of Angers (453), Canon 6—Bruns, II, 138; St. John Chrysostom (354-407), *De Libello Repudii,* II, c. 1—*MPG,* LI, 219; idem, *Commentarius in S. Matthaeum Evangelistam,* Homilia XVII, c. 4—*MPG,* LVII, 259; St. Augustine, *Sermones,* Sermo CCCXCII, c. 2—*MPL,* XXXIX, 1710; idem, *De Nuptiis et Concupiscentia,* I, c. 10—*MPL,* XLIV, 420; St. Ambrose (333/340 - 397), *Expositio Evangelii secundum Lucam,* Lib. III, n. 5—*MPL,* XV, 1767.

[22] Prat, *The Theology of St. Paul,* translated from the eleventh French Edition by John L. Stoddard (2 vols., London, 1926), I, 104; 1 Cor., VI:5. Among the first cases to be decided were those judged by St. Paul himself, namely, that of the incestuous man (I Cor., V:3) and the Pauline Privilege (1 Cor., VII:15, 16).

[23] St. Ignatius, Martyr (+ ca. 110), *Epistola ad Polycarpum,* c. 5: "Decet vero ut sponsi et sponsae de sententia episcopali conjugium faciant . . ."—*MPG,* V, 723.

which abstracted from the formal procedure of Roman Law.[24] Moreover, they were based on scriptural principles, which discouraged the submission of cases to non-believers and discountenanced prolonged arguments about the law.[25] Evidence of this informality is even found in the Scriptures where one reads that St. Paul reached conclusions at a distance after a brief review of the matter.[26]

With the end of the persecutions the Church was able to emerge from the catacombs. Roman Law still permitted divorce, and also in other ways occasioned conflict with Christian principles regarding the indissolubility of marriage.[27] At this time, however, Constantine granted a quasi-judicial power to the bishops. Their courts were recognized as competent, and suits presented to the bishop by agreement of the parties were subject to his binding decision.[28] Although these grants were for civil suits, and marriage was not explicitly mentioned, nevertheless it seems certain that marriage cases were by the law of the Empire recognized as within the bishop's competence.[29]

24 Wernz-Vidal, *Ius Canonicum* (7 vols. in 8, Vol. I, 1938; Vol. II, 3. ed., a P. Aguirre recognita, 1943; Vol. III, 1933; Vol. IV, pars 1, 1934, pars 2, 1935; Vol. V, 3. ed., a P. Aguirre recognita, 1946; Vol. VI, 1927; Vol. VII, 1937, Romae: Apud Aedes Universitatis Gregorianae), VI, n. 2; *Didascalia,* II, cc. 45 sq.—*Didascalia et Constitutiones Apostolorum,* ed. F. X. Funk (2 vols., Paderborn, 1905), I, 138-148.

25 Matt., XVIII:15, 16; 1 Cor., VI:1, 3; Titus, III:2-9.

26 "I, indeed, absent in body but present in spirit, have already, as though present, passed judgment. . . ."—1 Cor., V:3.

27 St. Jerome, *Ep. LXXVII* (ad Oceanum), n. 3:—"Aliae sunt leges Caesarum, aliae Christi; aliud Papinianus aliud Paulus noster praecipit"—*Corpus Scriptorum Ecclesiasticorum Latinorum* (Vindobonae, 1866—*S. Eusebii Hieronymi Opera,* Vol. LV, Sect. I, Pars II, recensuit Isidorus Hilberg, Vindobonae, 1912), LV, 39; St. Ambrose, *Expositio Evangelii secundam Lucam,* Lib. VIII, n. 2—*MPL,* XV, 1765; St. Augustine, *Sermo CCCXCII,* c. 2—*MPL,* XXXIX, 1710; St. Gregory Nazianzus (329/30-ca. 390), *Epistolae,* Ep. CXLIV—*MPG,* XXXVII, 247; St. John Chrysostom, *Quales ducendae sint uxores,* n. 1—*MPG,* LI, 226.

28 This recognition was contained in a constitution of 328—C. Th. (1.27)1, and in one sent to Ablabius in 333—*Const. Sirmondiana I—Theodosiani Libri XVI* (ed. Mommsen-Meyer, 3 vols., Berolini, 1905), I, 907 sq.

29 There is a letter of Innocent I treating of a marriage case: Ep. XXXVI

The first clear inference that some procedural norm was to be followed in cases of separation is found in the canons of the Council of Vannes (465). This Council, held in Brittany, was presided over by St. Perpetuus, Archbishop of Tours. It drew up disciplinary laws for the province. In these laws was decreed excommunication for those who left their wives without furnishing proof of adultery.[30] The prohibition seemed to be directed against those who availed themselves of the civil law for divorce and remarriage. Such action was forbidden, and such a dismissal of a spouse unlawful, unless the husband first gave proof of his wife's infidelity in the bishop's court.[31]

The Council of Agde (506) was even clearer on the matter. There the ecclesiastical law required, perhaps for the first time, that the permission and judgment of the provincial bishops were necessary for a separation. This action of the bishops of the province had to precede any parting of the spouses, even on the grounds of adultery. The prohibition was fortified with the penalty of excommunication for its violators.[32] No further details were given about the procedure in such cases. We must, however, conclude that the unauthorized separating of the spouses was regarded as a very serious evil calling for severe and specific ecclesiastical regulations, which reflected not only the Church's stand on the indissolubility of marriage but also its concern for the integrity and unity of family life.

(ad Probum)—JK, n. 313—*MPL,* XX, 602; Joyce, *Christian Marriage,* p. 215. In the section of the Justinian Code known as *De Episcopali Audientia,* two special laws are contained concerning marriage, thus making more certain the competency of the bishop in these cases—C.(1.4)16, 28.

[30] Canon 2: "Eos quoque, qui relictis uxoribus suis, sicut in evangelio dicitur, excepta causa fornicationis, sine adulterii probatione alias duxerint, statuimus a communione similiter arcendos: ne per indulgentiam nostram post praetermissa peccata alios ad licentiam erroris invitent."—Bruns, II, 143.

[31] Joyce, *Christian Marriage,* p. 321.

[32] Canon 25: "Hi vero saeculares qui conjugale consortium culpa graviore dimittunt vel etiam dimiserunt, et nullas causas discidii probabiliter proponentes, propterea sua matrimonia dimittunt, ut aut illicita, aut aliena praesumant; si antequam apud episcopos comprovinciales discidii causas dixerint, et prius uxores, quam judicio damnentur, abjecerint; a communione ecclesiae, et sancto populi coetu, pro eo quod fidem et conjugia maculant, excludantur." —Bruns, II, 151; c. 1, C. XXXIII, q. 2.

Article 2. The Germanic Age

The Church was the one institution to survive the disintegration of the Roman Empire in the West. The officials of the powerful government had disappeared, their tight organization in ruins. In this new era the ecclesiastical authorities were faced with an added threat to the Christian concept of the indissolubility of marriage. The laws of all the new nations allowed divorce with legal approbation. They followed the Roman Law in this matter, permitting divorce not only by mutual consent but also at the instance of one party.[33]

The difficulty presented by this legal system was challenging, but not quite as formidable as the long standing social traditions of Rome. The bishop remained influential, yet the Frankish kings assumed judicial as well as legislative control over marriage.[34] This

[33] *Lex Burgundionum*, Tit. XXI, *de divortiis*, n. 1 "Consensu partis utriusque repudium dari et matrimonium posse dissolvi." Cf. also *ibid.*, nn. 2 and 3—*Monumenta Germaniae Historica, Leges* (5 vols. Vols. I-IV, ed. G. Pertz; Vol. V, ed. G. Pertz, G. Waitz, H. Brunner, Hannoverae, 1835-1889), III, p. 609 (hereafter cited as *MGH*); *Lex Visigothorum*, Lib. III, tit. 6, c. 2—*MGM, Legum Sectio I* (Tom. I, *Lex Visigothorum*, ed. K. Zeumer; II, pars 1, *Leges Burgundionum*, ed. L. R. de Salis; V, pars 1, ed. K. Lehmann, pars 2, *Lex Baiwariorum*, ed. E. von Schwind Hannoverae, 1888-1927), I, 167; *Lex Longobardorum, Edictus Rothari*, nn. 195-197—*MGH, Leges*, IV, 47; this sentiment was so strong at the time that even some Councils in their disciplinary statutes were tainted with this lax view and in certain cases permitted remarriage. For example, the Council of Verberie (753), cc. 5, 9, 17—Hardouin, *Acta Conciliorum et Epistolae Decretales ac Constitutiones Summorum Pontificum* (12 vols., Parisiis, 1714-1715), III, 1990-1992 (hereafter cited as Hardouin); the Council of Compiègne (756), cc. 8, 13— Hardouin, III, 2005; and many penitential books so-called. The *Poenitentiale Theodori* is a good example—*MPL*, XCIX, 933, 934. The Roman Pontiffs and many particular councils condemned this abuse in the Christian Law. Cf. Leo IV (847-855) in *Ep. ad Episcopos Brittaniae* (849)—JE, no. 2599, 5a; Council of Friuli (791), c. 10—Hardouin, III, 860; VI Council of Paris (829), Lib. III, c. 2—Hardouin, III, 1352; Council of Tribur (895), c. 46—Mansi, *Sacrorum Conciliorum Nova et Amplissima Collectio* (53 vols. in 59, Parisiis, 1901-1927), XVIII, 154 (hereafter cited as Mansi).

[34] Joyce, *Christian Marriage*, p. 218; Esmein, *Le Mariage en Droit Canonique* (2. ed., 2 tomes, par R. Genestal et Jean Dauvillier, Paris: Recueil

is quite clear from the work of Hincmar (+ 882), Archbishop of Rheims. In his *De Nuptiis Stephani,* he implied that marriage cases were heard in the royal courts.[35] He was even more explicit in his discussion of the marriage case of King Lothaire and Queen Tetberga. He held that no sentence of a bishop could deprive a spouse of conjugal rights except under certain conditions, namely, that the crime had been confessed by the guilty party, or that proof of it had been established in a court of law.[36]

Shortly after the time of Hincmar a canon of the Council of Tribur (895) lent some clarity to the problem. The canon, although concerned with a case of affinity arising from incest before marriage, is valuable in that it shows that the bishops did hear marriage cases. The canon ordered the parties to be separated, but in consideration of human frailty the bishop could, upon the performance of penance, allow the marriage to continue.[37]

To set a definite date at which the Church could effectively exer-

Sirey, 1929-1935), I, II; Daudet, *Etudes sur l'Histoire de la Jurisdiction Matrimoniale* (Paris: Recueil Sirey, 1933), p. 172.

[35] *Epistolae,* Ep. XXII: "In quibus nihil de civili judicio, cuius cognitores non debemus esse episcopi, ponere, sed quae ecclesiasticae definitioni nascuntur competere, quantum occurrit memoriae, breviter studui adnotare"—*MPL,* CXXVI, 135.

[36] *De Divortio Lotharii et Tetbergae,* Resp. IV: "Quoniam ecclesiae medici spiritales, videlicit Domini sacerdotes, de secrete sibi confessis peccatorum infirmitatibus medicinalia atque salubria possunt dare consilia: judicio autem ecclesiastico, id est separatione a communione Ecclesiae, vel a gradu, sive a consortio conjugali, neminem rationabiliter possunt secernere, nisi de criminibus aut publice sponte confessum, aut aperte convictum."—*MGH, Leges,* I, 467; *MPL,* CXXV, 653. There is much discussion among authors regarding Hincmar's exact opinions as to the precise limits of the ecclesiastical and secular authorities over marriage. Cf. Hefele-Leclerq, *Histoire des Conciles* (11 vols. in 20, Paris: Letouzey et Ané, 1907-1949), IV, Part I, 244, ftn. 1.

[37] Canon 41: "Idcirco episcopus, considerata mentis eorum imbecillitate, post poenitentiam sua institutione peractam, si se continere non possint, legitimo consoletur matrimonio, necdum sperentur ad alta sublevari, corruant in coenum."—*MGH, Legum Sect. II (Capitularia Legum Francorum),* tom. II, pars 1 (edd. A. Boretius, V. Krause, Hannoverae, 1890), p. 237. There is some doubt concerning the authenticity of the various canons of this council. The editors of this source after a very critical study have concluded that the above cited canon is to be regarded as authentic. Cf. *op. cit.,* p. 196.

cise its rightful jurisdiction over marriage is most difficult. Some authors hold the opinion that it occurred by the end of the tenth century.[38] Others incline to the view that it was only toward the middle of the eleventh century that the Church gained this judicial control.[39] There is good evidence, derivable from the writings of Regino of Prüm (+ 915), that the bishops did judge separation cases in the early tenth century. His *Libri Duo de Synodalibus Causis* was compiled for Bishop Rathbod of Treves (883-915) as a practical guide for his episcopal visitations. Among the many questions asked there was one that treated explicitly of separation. It asked whether any married couples had affected a divorce and were living in that condition, and, what was even more important, whether any man has put away his wife, even though she was guilty, without a sentence given by the bishop.[40] Regino also included among the canons that treated of marriage a capitulary indicative of a very privileged status attributed to the bishops as arbiters. The parties to any dispute could bring the matter before the bishop, who would decide it according to the canons of the Church rather than the civil law. Such a decision was final.[41]

[38] Esmein, *Le Mariage,* I, 27; Torre, *Processus Matrimonialis* (2. ed., Neapoli: D'Auria, 1947), p. 6.

[39] Joyce, *Christian Marriage,* p. 224; Goldsmith, *The Competence of Church and State over Marriage—Disputed Points,* The Catholic University of America Canon Law Studies, No. 197 (Washington, D. C.: Catholic University of America Press, 1944), p. 7; Daudet, *Etudes sur l'Histoire de la Jurisdiction Matrimoniale,* p. 172.

[40] Lib. II, cap. 15: "Deinde interrogandum de adulteriis et fornicationibus"; cap. 19: "Si interveniente repudio ab invicem separentur et sic manent"; cap. 21: "Si aliquis suam conjugem, quamvis culpabilem, sine judicio episcopi relinquit"—*MPL,* CXXXII, 282-283; Burchard of Worms (1002-1025) used source—Van Hove, *Commentarium Lovaniense in Codicem Iuris Canonici,* Vol. I, tom. 1, *Prolegomena ad Codicem Iuris Canonici* (2. ed., Mechliniae-Romas: H. Dessain, 1945), n. 313 (hereafter cited as *Prolegomena*).

[41] *Libri Duo de Synodalibus Causis,* Lib. II, cap. 122: "Statutum est ut quaecumque controversiae judicio et auctoritate ecclesiastica coeperint agitari, nequaquam ad saeculare judicium transeant, ubi iterato provocent, sed ecclesiasticis sanctionibus terminentur. Nam a judicibus quos communis consensus elegerit ad alios judices non licet provocare, nisi major auctoritas sit, secundum canonicam normam. Si autem in saeculari judicio, id est in comitis placito, causa prius fuerit ventilata, secundum legem mundanam finiatur, salvo ecclesi-

A similar stand was taken with Regino by Burchard of Worms (+ 1025). His *Decretum,* appearing early in the eleventh century (1008-1012), listed practically the same cases as Regino. He similarly denied to the secular power any authority in ecclesiastical matters.[42]

There was written at Valence before 1050 a work called the *Petri Exceptiones Legum Romanorum.* Although unorthodox in its parts, it illustrated certain procedural norms. The author expressly stated that when a separation for adultery was treated, a verdict had to be obtained from the bishop's court as well as the civil authority. Only after this was observed was the innocent party free to contract a new marriage.[43]

About this time the great reform in the discipline of the Church began to have influence. Canonical norms governing marriage are found in the writings of the great men of the times as Gregory VII (1073-1085), Anselm of Lucca (+ 1086), and Ivo of Chartres

asticae legis privilegio"—*MPL,* CXXXII, 306. This capitulary is called a *capitulare incertum,* because of some doubt concerning its authenticity. Cf. Joyce, *Christian Marriage,* p. 222; Van Hove, *Prolegomena,* n. 253. Even if spurious, it is evidence that the bishops were at least claiming and exercising this authority.

[42] Van Hove, *Prolegomena,* pp. 229, 253; *Decretum,* Lib. IX, cap. 54, 55, 57, 62, 63, 64—*MPL,* CXL, 824. Most collections of this period were tainted with the laxity of the paenitentials and permitted remarriage in certain cases, Both Burchard and Regino admitted the same series of cases as the Councils of Verberie and Compiègne; however, in principle both these authors held to the strict indissolubility of the marriage bond. Cf. Burchard, *Decretum,* Lib. VI, cap. 41 (canon 3, Verberie); Lib. IX, cap. 54 (canon 6, Verberie); Lib. XVII, cap. 10, 11 (cc. 10, 21, Verberie); Lib. XVII, cap. 17 (canon 12, Compiègne)—*MPL,* CXL, 775, 824, 921, 922; *Regino, Libri Duo de Synodalibus Causis,* Lib. II, cap. 118 (c. 5, Verberie); cap. 124 (canon 9, Verberie); cap. 127 (canon 6, Compiègne)—*MPL,* CXXXII, 307, 308, 309.

[43] Lib. I, cap. 37. This is printed as an appendix to Vol. II of von Savigney, *Geschichte des Römischen Rechts im Mittelalter* (6 vols., Heidelberg, 1815-1831), II, 314. Savigney (1779-1860) assigned the place of origin as Valence, but, according to Joyce (1864-1943), recent opinion attributes it to the school of Ravenna—*Christian Marriage,* p. 354. This statement of Joyce is very doubtful as a result of the scholarly critical study of Kantorowicz (1879-1940), which makes the place of origin as Valence practically certain. Cf. Kantorowicz, *Studies in the Glossators of Roman Law* (Cambridge: University Press, 1938), p. 117.

(+ 1117). In line with this reform there was a series of synods held in France. Two of these, the Council of Rheims (1049) and that of Chartres (1060) were notable for their legislation against divorce. The former was presided over by Leo IX (1049-1054) himself, and the latter by the papal legate Cardinal Stephen. The Council of Chartres was the more complete for the subject treated here in that it pronounced an excommunication upon those who dismissed their wives and remarried prior to an examination of the matter before the bishop.[44]

An eminent name in Canon Law in the eleventh century is undoubtedly that of Ivo, Bishop of Chartres. His two great works, the *Decretum* and *Panormia*, are most valuable on the subject of marriage during this era. In a most systematic fashion he established the indissolubility of marriage.[45] An adulterous spouse could in given cases be dismissed,[46] but the permission of the bishop was necessary for this dismissal.[47]

Although Ivo did not state it directly, it seems that some judicial procedure was necessary for obtaining episcopal permission to separate. In some of his canons he allowed separation for a false imputation of adultery. Such a wording seems to indicate a judicial procedure, even though of a very limited nature.[48] A further inference can be gathered from his statements that a separation was allowed when a man could prove that his wife had a part in a conspiracy with others to bring about his death. Prove to whom? Doubtless to the bishop, in a judicial fashion. The very use of the

[44] Canon 9: ". . . vel qui suam uxorem sine judicio episcopali dimittens, aliam duxit, vel duxerit: donec se fructuose tradat poenitentiae, a corpore et sanguine Domini Nostri Jesu, et a liminibus ecclesiae se exclusum, et alienatum, et omnibus sicut putridum membrum a sano corpore praecisum gladio spiritus, quod est verbum Dei, agnoscat"—Mansi, XIX, 928.

[45] *Decretum*, Lib. VIII, cap. 9, 12—*MPL*, CLXI, 586.

[46] *Op. cit.*, Lib. VIII, cap. 43, 104, 109—*MPL*, CLXI, 593, 605, 606.

[47] *Op. cit.*, Lib. VIII, cap. 231—*MPL*, CLXI, 633. Actually this is a recapitulation of Canon 25 of the Council of Agde (506) (cf. *supra*, p. 8, ftn. 32).

[48] *Decretum*, Lib. VIII, cap. 110—*MPL*, CLXI, 606. In this section Ivo even incorporated a judicial form for reconciliation, taken from the decrees of Innocent I (401-417), *op. cit.*, Lib. VIII, cap. 217—*MPL*, CLXI, 629.

term implies that a procedure was a necessary prerequisite for the separation.[49]

Another note of moment that Ivo incorporated in his work was the fact that the right to accuse an errant consort was not a prerogative of the husband alone. The wife was equally capable of dismissing an adulterous spouse.[50] He also emphasized that separation must have a very serious reason. Foolish and vain excuses for separation were not acceptable, nor did certain physical infirmities suffice for rupturing the marital union.[51]

With the end of the eleventh century the great abuses in the discipline of the Church were finally diminished, in consequence of this great reform in Church Law. Effective jurisdiction was now a property of the bishop's court, and marriage cases, especially those of separation, could be properly treated. The civil process seems still to have been important to a degree, but could not be compared with the weight of the bishop's tribunal. Marriage was universally held to be God's work, a sacred bond, not readily invalidated, nor could the spouses easily separate. Because of the sacred character of marriage it belonged to the jurisdiction of the Church, and not even separations were permissible without the sanction of ecclesiastical authority. The procedure, indeed, was probably very informal, but there was nevertheless some sort of process at that time. It was not until later, with the revival of Roman Law, that the more juridical and formal processes became the practice.

[49] *Op. cit.*, Lib. X, cap. 169: "Si qua mulier mortem viri sui cum aliis conciliata est, et ipse vir aliquem illorum se defendendo occiderit, et si hoc *probare* potest ille vir eam ream esse consilii, potest (ut nobis videtur) ipsam uxorem dimittere"—*MPL,* CLXI, 740.

[50] *Op. cit.*, Lib. VIII, cap. 12, 13, 41, 43, 73, 240—*MPL,* CLXI, 586, 593, 599, 636. This subject later became the topic of much dispute in view of an apparent contradiction between Gratian's c. 10, C. XXXII, q. 1, and c. 20, C. XXXII, q. 5.

[51] *Op. cit.*, Lib. VIII, cap. 237: "Dominus ad illud confirmandum, ut non facile dimittatur uxor, solam fornicationis causam excepit. . ."—*MPL,* CLXI, 655; *op. cit.*, Lib. VIII, cap. 238—*MPL,* CLXI, 655.

CHAPTER II

THE PROCEDURE IN CASES OF SEPARATION FROM THE DECREE OF GRATIAN (ca. 1140) TO THE COUNCIL OF TRENT (1545-1563)

ABOUT the middle of the twelfth century a momentous period developed in the science of Canon Law. There were great theological schools operating at the time and the scholastic method was beginning to be formed. At the same time there was a renaissance in Roman Law with the discovery of the *Digesta* of Justinian at Pisa in 1070. With this presentation to the medieval world of a document representing the exactness and elegance of Roman juridical thought, there were founded the schools of Roman Law with the medieval "glossators" of Roman Law.

Bologna was the center of Roman Law study and it was here that Gratian (+ ante 1159) flourished. It was he who made possible Canon Law as a regular science. His work, called the *Concordia Discordantium Canonum,* or simply the *Decretum,* was an organized system of juridic notions and forms, the first juridical treatise ever written which in Canon Law was both analytical and synthetical.[1]

It soon became the universal handbook of the ancient canons, a digest of ecclesiastical law superseding all previous collections, and with the later official collections of papal decretals it formed the *Corpus Iuris* until 1917. Although never an official codification, it became the universal handbook of the ancient canons, it was used by Popes and quoted in sentences. It was the best compilation of the existing ecclesiastical legislation, and therefore its individual parts partook of the authority of the ecclesiastical source from which they were taken.[2]

[1] Kuttner, "The Father of the Science of Canon Law," *The Jurist* (Washington, D. C., 1941—), I (1941), 3.

[2] Van Hove, *Prolegomena,* n. 349.

Article 1. The *Decree* of Gratian

A careful study of the various papal decretals and of the conciliar enactments contained in the Decree of Gratian fails to reveal any direct or complete statement of the rights of the Church over marriage. The evolution in practice of hearing cases in the ecclesiastical rather than in the civil courts was not established by a formal decree, but was developed through custom to the status of a recognized right. Despite this absence of any direct announcement, there is implicit evidence in Gratian's work on marriage, since he treats the sacrament at great length in the second part of his *Decretum*. Ten *Causae* (XXVII-XXXVI), in this section deal with marriage, and offer us an indirect proof in establishing the competence of the Church over the sacrament.[3]

That the Church had the right to hear marriage cases was demonstrated by Gratian in a rather clear way. In a case wherein a man had dismissed his wife under the guise that an impediment of consanguinity was present, the Pope, Alexander II (1061-1073), was firm in pointing out that no such action was permissible without the sanction of ecclesiastical authority.[4]

A. *The Ordinary Procedure*

In speaking of cases of separation, Gratian was detailed in his treatment, for he included several texts which demonstrate the firm stand of the law through the years in such matters. In his *Dictum* ad c. 1, C. XXXIII, q. 2, Gratian questioned whether a man who had left his wife without any cause having been reasonably proved by him should be forced to return to her.[5] The answer was con-

[3] Goldsmith, *The Competence of Church and State over Marriage*, pp. 3-4.

[4] C. 10, C. XXXV, q. 6: "Multorum relatione cognovimus, te propriam velle abiicere uxorem, et adhaerere alteri, pretendentem consanguinitatis occasionem. Unde apostolica auctoritate interdicendo mandamus tibi, ut hanc, quam nunc habes uxorem, nullatenus praesumas dimittere, vel aliam ducere, donec apud episcoporum religiosorum concilium causam istam examinaveris." —JL, n. 4524; Mansi, XIX, 980.

[5] "Sed quaeritur, si sine ecclesiastico iudicio, nulla causa discidii rationabiliter probata ab ab ea discessisset, an esset cogendus redire ad eam."

tained in Canon 25 of the Council of Agde (cf. *supra*, p. 8), ftn. 32), in short: *"Non licet alicui uxorem dimittere, nisi causa discidii primum ecclesiae probetur."* [6] This text was Gratian's clearest exposition of the attitude of the Church regarding separation cases.

The Glossators, however, were more complete. They clearly stated that the man who left his wife without the judgment of the Church, or on his own authority, was to be forced to return to her.[7] The judgment of the Church had reference to an ecclesiastical tribunal, where the cause for dismissal had to be proved.[8]

Adultery naturally was the primary cause for separation. But even the suspicion of adultery was sufficient as long as the justifiable warrant of it was proved. This proof had to be presented before the Church in every case before the spouse could be dismissed.[9] The justifiable warrant of a suspicion of adultery amounted to a moral certitude. The glossators referred to this suspicion as the manner of proving the crime, for if the suspicion was proved the adultery was also proven.[10] Reiffenstuel (+ 1703) writing at a much later date, expressed this suspicion in more modern terminology. He likened it to a violent presumption that was sufficient in the external forum to condemn a person of the crime.[11]

[6] C. 1, C. XXXIII, q. 2; Gratian attributed this canon to a Council of Carthage presided over by St. Augustine, but actually it was taken from the above mentioned Council of Agde.

[7] ". . . si quis dimittat uxorem sine iudicio ecclesiae, cogendus est ad illam redire . . . ideo magister annectit aliam incidentem quaestionem, scilicet an vir sit restituendus uxori a qua propria auctoritate recessit, vel e converso? Et certum est . . ."—*Glossa Ordinaria* s.v. *quod autem,* ad C. XXXIII, q. 2. The same teaching is incorporated in *Glossa Ordinaria* s.v. *sed quaeritur,* ad c. 1, C. XXXIII, q. 2.

[8] *Glossa Ordinaria* s.v. *saeculares,* ad c. 1, C. XXXIII, q. 2.

[9] *Glossa Ordinaria,* s.v. *probabiliter,* ad c. 1, C. XXXIII, q. 2; c. 3, C. XXXIII, q. 2, and the *Glossa Ordinaria* ad *loc. cit.*; *Dictum Gratiani* ad c. 4, C. XXXIII, q. 2 and the canon itself.

[10] ". . . unde pro eodem reputatur fornicatio et fornicationis suspicio. Nam probata suspicione, probata est fornicatio"—*Glossa Ordinaria* s.v. *suspicio,* ad c. 2, C. XXXII, q. 1; Rufinus explained it thus: ". . . legitima attestatione probata in iudicio ecclesiae"—*Die Summa des Magister Rufinus* (ed. Heinrich Singer, Paderborn, 1902), p. 476 (hereafter cited as Rufinus).

[11] *Ius Canonicum Universum* (5 vols. in 6, Romae, 1831-1834), Lib. IV, tit. 19, n. 95 (hereafter cited as Reiffenstuel); Rufinus distinguished between

Gratian involved himself in a slight paradox when he denied to the woman the right to dismiss an adulterous husband. He practically made her sex a cause for depriving her of the right to institute a suit. He based his stand upon the *Lex Julia* of Roman Law.[12] On the other hand, in several places he gave the woman equal rights to present accusations against an adulterous husband.[13] With the overwhelming majority of the evidence on the side of the mutual right to accuse, such can safely be said to have been the Church's stand on the matter.

The competent authority at the time of Gratian was the bishop.

a mild and a violent presumption in this matter. The first amounted to nothing, the latter was sufficient, if proved before the Church by acceptable witness—p. 476.

[12] *Dictum Gratiani* ad c. 10, C. XXXII, q. 1. The same doctrine is found in c. 17, C. XXXII, q. 7. The *Glossae* on the other hand attributed equal rights to the wife to accuse an adulterous spouse. *Glossa Ordinaria* s.v. *accusationem* and s.v. *hoc in mulieribus* ad c. 10, C. XXXII, q. 1; Rufinus, p. 477; The legal limitation on the wife to dismiss in c. 17, C. XXXII, q. 7 is called the *pseudo Ambrose.* Erasmus (1466-1536) is considered the first to establish that certain commentaries known as St. Ambrose' on the Epistles of St. Paul were written by another, known as the *pseudo Ambrose* or *Ambrosiaster*—Altaner, *Patrologie* (Freiburg im Breisgau: Herder, 1938), p. 248. The *Dictum Gratiani* ad c. 17, C. XXXII, q. 7 showed a suspicion of this and the *Glossa Ordinaria* s.v. *uxor a viro discedat* ad *loc. cit.* declared that this canon was abrogated and either inserted by falsifiers or never written by St. Ambrose. Peter Lombard (+ 1164) called it spurious and attributed it to Hilary the Deacon—*Libri IV Senteniarum,* studio et cura PP. Collegii S. Bonaventurae (2. ed., 2 vols., ad Claras Aquas, 1916), Lib. IV, D. XXXV, c. 3; Cappello writes that Gratian held that the right to dismiss an adulterous consort belonged exclusively to the man—*Summa Iuris Canonici* (3 vols., Vols. I and II, 4. ed., 1945; Vol. III, 3. ed., 1948, Romae: Apud Aedes Universitatis Gregorianae), III, 321; Wernz held the same opinion—*Ius Decretalium* (6 vols., Vol. I, 3. ed., 1913; Vol. II, 3. ed., 1915; Vol. III, 2. ed., 1908; Vol. IV, 2. ed., 1911; Vol. V, 1914; Vol. VI, 1913; Romae et Prati), IV, n. 728.

[13] After a quotation from St. Jerome he stated: "Apud nos quod non licet feminis, aeque non licet viris et eadem servitus pari conditione censetur"—c. 20, C. XXXII, q. 5. Several other canons expressed the same view in permitting the wife an essential parity with the husband in this regard—c. 4, C. XXXII, q. 4; c. 19, C. XXXII, q. 5; c. 1, 2, C. XXXII, q. 6; c. 3, 4, 5, 7, 8, 18, C. XXXII, q. 7; *Dictum Gratiani* ad c. 18, C. XXXII, q. 7; c. 7, C. XXXIV, q. 1 and 2.

The canon of the Council of Agde as delineated by Gratian mentioned the provincial bishops as the judges in such cases. The *Glossa* explained the matter fully. It pointed out that this was once the case but that such a practice would be most inconvenient and difficult to maintain in the present. To assemble all the bishops of a province together for such cases, would be most impractical. In the present the *Glossa* stated even the archpriest could hear such cases, the bishop certainly was competent, but others such as abbots need to possess a special mandate or to have a similar legitimate reason.[14]

The Procedure is not clearly enunciated but it is evident that it was that procedure which developed in this period from the *cognitio* of Roman Law. Gratian's Causae I-VII gave the foundations, and the Decretists elaborated on it.[15] By this time Roman Law was known and used in the ecclesiastical courts. Such terms as *reus, accusator, actor, exceptiones, litis contestaio,* appear in the *Glossa Ordinaria* s.v. *convincitur,* ad c. 1, C. XXXII, q. 6; *sententia, in iudicio,* in the *Glossa Ordinaria,* s.v. *sicut* ad c. 1, C. XXXII, q. 1.

14 ". . . hoc olim obtinuit: quia causa matrimonii tractabatur apud episcopos provinciae. Hodie etiam archipresbyter causam huiusmodi tractare potest. Sed certe et hodie ad episcopalem iurisdictionem cognitio matrimonialis causae spectat. Unde nec abbates, nec alii possunt de matrimonio cognoscere: nisi ex concessione, vel alia causa legitima id habeant . . ."—*Glossa Ordinaria* s.v. comprovinciales, ad c. 1, C. XXXIII, q. 2. No mention was made here of the limitations on the bishop as included in c. 6, C. XV, q. 7, viz., that the bishop must not hear any case without the presence of his chapter. This limitation was given under pain of invalidity. The discussion by the Decretists on this canon presented two views, the one that the chapter had ordinary power, the other that the members served as mere consultors. Both agreed that a sentence given without their presence was null—*Glossa Ordinaria* s.v. *Episcopus,* ad c. 6, C. XV, q. 7. In the Decretals of Gregory IX, these two canons were the basis when the matter of competent ecclesiastical authority was treated—c. 5, X, *de divortiis,* IV, 19. The logical explanation seems to be that the combination of these two canons from Gratian in c. 5, X, *de divortiis,* IV, 19 was a development in the law. Gratian's c. 6, C. XV, q. 7, was concerned with the trial in the deposition of clerics since it followed immediately upon another canon taken from the same African Council, in which canon criminal trials of these persons were treated.

15 Môra, *Die Frage des Zivilprozesses und der Beweislast bei Gratian* (Pécs, 1937), p. 13 ff.

These terms were not expanded on very fully, but the matter of judicial exceptions which could be utilized in such cases were treated at greater length.

Judicial exceptions in the strict sense are the means by which a defendant is legally qualified to retard or elide an action instituted against him.[16] The exceptions mentioned here, although not taken entirely in the strict sense were means by which a defendant could protect himself against accusations of adultery. The first clearly mentioned was that an adulterer by his sin lost the right to institute a suit against an adulterous spouse, by his sin, he became incapable of accusing the other.[17] Gratian supported this view by quoting the words of Christ: ". . . first cast out the beam from thy own eye, and then wilt thou see clearly to cast out the speck from thy brother's eye." [18]

Mention was also made of an *exceptio spolii.* This had the effect that a defendant was not bound to answer in the case until the object or right in question has been restored to him.[19] Its purpose was the recovery of the possession lost before the case continued. Although here it was not a matter of defeating a suit for separation, nevertheless the defendant could enter this exception, and by it he or she was not bound to respond to the judicial action until cohabitation had been restored.[20] As has been shown, sepa-

[16] Coyle, *Judicial Exceptions,* The Catholic University of America Canon Law Studies, n. 193 (Washington, D. C.: The Catholic University of America Press, 1944), p. 1.

[17] C. 1, C. XXXII, q. 6.

[18] *Dictum Gratiani* ad *loc. cit.*; Luke, VI:42. Gratian also referred to Romans, II:1 and to St. Augustine, *De Sermone Domini in Monte,* Lib. I, cap. 16, n. 47—*MPL,* XXXIV, 1253. The *Glossa* explained it thus: ". . . adulter non potest uxorem adulteram dimittere: cum sit eodem crimine infectus et hoc probatur duabus auctoritatibus Domini"—*Glossa Ordinaria,* s.v. *ecce,* c. 1, C. XXXII, q. 6. The authorities mentioned here are John, VIII:7, and Romans, II:1.

[19] Coyle, *op. cit.,* p. 109.

[20] "Si vero causa coram ecclesia nondum fuerit preposita, per nullum modum licebit ei dimittere eam . . . potest eam lata sententia dimittere interim quantum ad reddendum debitum, sed non quantum ad cohabitandum"—Rufinus, p. 498.

ration could not take place without the intervention of ecclesiastical authority. Should the innocent consort dismiss the guilty partner before this took place, the matter could demand to be taken back again before a suit or trial could be instituted.[21]

Another exception was the quality of the act of adultery. It had to be formal. The element of consent had to enter the action; a merely material unfaithfulness was not sufficient. Thus a woman who had been raped or violated against her will was not to be considered an adulteress.[22] In general, the material act did not constitute adultery unless there was wilful cooperation.[23] A double chastity existed according to the writers of the day who borrowed this concept from the Fathers. One was of the mind, the other of the body. The fact that a woman was violated caused adultery of the body but did not obliterate the chastity of her mind. To be culpable, the unfaithfulness had to be intended or formal.[24] Consequently, a woman who had relations with another man because of mistaken identity was not to be charged with adultery as long as she was unaware that the man was not her husband, and as long as she did not intend a denial of her nuptial promises.[25] The case was also contemplated of a wife who, while under the impression that her soldier husband had been killed, married again. Upon the return of her first spouse she had to return to him, but no censures or accusations were to be invoked since her action was not culpable.[26] If on the contrary she had not married in good faith, but had entered the new contract or had remained in the second union aware of her husband's existence, she was an adulteress.[27]

[21] C. 3, C. XXXIII, q. 2.

[22] *Glossa Ordinaria* s.v. *sed ponatur,* ad C. XXXII, q. 6; Rufinus, p. 491.

[23] C. 2, C. XXXII, q. 5.

[24] C. 1, C. XXXII, q. 5; *Glossa Ordinaria* ad *loc. cit.*; Rufinus, p. 488. Gratian expanded on this idea by giving the example of St. Lucy. This chaste maiden had declared that even if she were violated, as it was threatened, her crown of purity would remain intact.—*Dictum Gratiani* ad c. 1, C. XXXII, q. 5.

[25] C. 5, 6, 7, C. XXXIV, q. 1 and 2.

[26] C. 1, C. XXXIV, q. 1 and 2.

[27] *Glossa Ordinaria* s.v. *si virgo,* c. 1, C. XXXIV, q. 1 and 2.

B. Separation *Propria Auctoritate*

Gratian himself said explicitly that separation *propria auctoritate* was not permissible. He referred to separation as a penalty. As such, only a judge could inflict it. This was the general rule whether the separation was undertaken for a good reason or for no reason at all. He added that one did not privately inflict the penalty upon a man guilty of homicide. The inflicting of a penalty belonged to the office of judges, and the same held true regarding the penalty of a separation. It was truly a penalty and therefore subject to judicial action.[28]

The use of the word *generaliter* implied that this formal procedure was not always needed. If there were any exceptions to this rule, Gratian did not mention them, yet, in the previous *Causa* he included a section of the Commentary of St. Jerome on the Gospel of St. Matthew. The Saint there declared that a wife might be freely dismissed for even the suspicion of adutery.[29] Some of the later authors proved helpful in the interpretation of the term *libere* in this passage from St. Jerome. Among these Sanchez (1550-1610) identified it with *propria auctoritate* and in its meaning made it equivalent to *latae sententiae*.[30] Reiffenstuel equated it with *sua auctoritate,* and limited its use to the internal forum.[31]

Gratian also included in a section from St. Augustine which paralleled the crimes of heresy, apostasy and schism to adultery. The innocent party had to leave the consort guilty of these delicts or else be a partaker in his sin.[32] These cases were, it appears, very

[28] ". . . tamen quia ipsa separatio poena est, et poena nulla est inferenda nisi per iudicem, *generaliter* hoc intelligendum est, ut sive ob causam premissam, sive nulla causa existente, non liceat alicui sua auctoritate uxorem dimittere. Quod etiam de poena homicidii vel qualibet alia intelligendum est"—*Dictum Gratiani* ad c. 4, C. XXXIII, q. 2.

[29] "Ubicumque est igitur fornicatio vel fornicationis suspicio, *libere* uxor dimittitur"—c. 2, C. XXXII, q. 1.

[30] *Disputationum de Sancto Matrimonii Sacramento Tomi Tres* (Antverpiae, 1626), III, Lib. X, disp. 12, n. 31 (hereafter cited Sanchez).

[31] Lib. IV, tit. 19, n. 91.

[32] C. 6, C. XXXVIII, q. 1. According to Rufinus a separation on these grounds was to follow *propria auctoritate* and was practically compulsory.—p. 453. Gasparri said: "Verior sententia est coniugem innocentem posse propria

limited. Beyond them ecclesiastical permission was necessary, especially if this spiritual adultery was not certain.

The Glossators in general were of a much more lenient position than Gratian. In treating the excerpt from the Council of Agde,[33] they admitted of three exceptions to the rule of no separation without ecclesiastical permission. No formal procedure or even episcopal authority seemed to be necessary when the adultery was public, when the wife was in great fear of her husband's rage or cruelty, or when the parties were related in a degree which as an impediment did not yield to dispensation. Besides these three cases, the spouse who had dismissed his partner on his own authority had to allow a return to cohabitation.[34]

This is by no means conclusive evidence that the Glossators held separation *propria auctoritate* to be permissible. They may have considered these reasons as sufficing for the parties to separate but to remain so permanently and legitimately required the authorization of the bishop. Their treatment was by no means exhaustive but the general interpretation seemed to favor the view that the *Glossa* in question permitted separation *propria auctoritate* in these three cases but only as a temporary measure. To live permanently separated and to refuse for all time to return required, it seems, further ecclesiastical permission.

Article 2. The Decretals of Gregory IX (1234)

With the promulgation of the collection known as the Decretals of Gregory IX (1227-1241) in 1234, the Church had a collection of authentic legal material with the force of universal law.[35] All its laws, even those which were formerly of a particular nature, possessed the force of universal law by their inclusion in this collection.[36] Although no particular section was devoted entirely to the

auctoritate, quin sententiam Ecclesiae expectet, reum delinquere, dummodo haeresis, etc. certa sit."—*Tractatus Canonicus de Matrimonio* (3. ed., 2 vols., Paris, 1904), II, n. 369 (hereafter referred to as *De Matrimonio*, 3. ed.).

33 C. 1, C. XXXIII, q. 2.

34 *Glossa Ordinaria* s.v. *sed quaeritur,* ad c. 1, C. XXXIII, q. 2.

35 Van Hove, *Prolegomena*, n. 364.

36 Cicognani, *Canon Law* (2. ed., English version by J. O'Hara and F. Brennan, Westminster: Newman, 1947), p. 303; actually this is an *opinio communior* since the fifteenth century and not found in earlier writers.

procedure for separation cases, nevertheless, the general norms for marriage cases joined with the provisions in the law for separation suits presented a clearly defined system of procedural law. Matrimonial cases followed the general pattern of contentious trials. The fact that additional particular norms for such cases were not always observed was deplored by Pope Innocent III (1198-1216) in a decretal concerned with such matters.[37]

Besides this collection of Decretals, two other lesser compilations, the *Liber Sextus* of Boniface VIII (1298-1303) and the *Constitutiones* of Clement V (1305-1314), commonly known as the *Clementinae,* complete the most important sources of canonical procedural norms in the period to the Council of Trent.[38]

Very much like the *Decretum Gratiani,* the Decretals lacked any explicit statues stating the native right of the Church to exercise jurisdiction over marriage cases; an assertion of this kind was not necessary at the time. It was in deciding questions intimately concerned with the sacrament that one finds reference made to the competency of the Church over marriage.[39]

[37] C. 1, X, *ut lite non contestata non procedatur ad testium receptionem vel ad sententiam diffinitivam,* II, 6—Potthast, *Regesta Pontificum Romanorum inde ab anno post Christum natum MCXCVIII ad annum MCCCIV* (2 vols., Berolini, 1874-1875), n. 370 (hereafter cited Potthast).

[38] Van Hove, *Prolegomena,* nn. 364-372.

[39] Pope Honorius III (1216-1227) to Louis VIII of France (1187-1226) in deciding a case of legitimacy—c. 3, X, *de ordine cognitionum,* II, 10—Potthast, n. 7099. A similar assertion was incorporated in *Glossa Ordinaria* s.v. *ad forum ecclesiasticum* ad *loc. cit.* The Decretalists declared this right quite completely. Cf. Hostiensis, *Commentaria in Quinque Decretalium Libros* (5 vols. in 3, Venetiis, 1581), Lib. II, tit. 10, c. 3, s.v. *forum ecclesiasticum*; Panormitanus, *Commentaria in Quinque Libros Decretalium* (5 vols. in 7, Venetiis, 1588), Lib. II, tit. 10, c. 3, n. 3. These works are hereafter cited as *Commentaria.* Similar statements of this right were incorporated in a letter of Innocent III to the Archdeacon of Tours—c. 11, X, *de foro competenti,* II, 2—Potthast, n. 2645 and *Glosa Ordinaria* s.v. *ecclesiasticum judicem* ad *loc. cit.* Among the great array of letters of Pope Alexander III (1159-1181), two are especially noteworthy: c. 1, *de consanguinitate et affinitate,* IV, 14—JL, 13838, and c. 7, X, *qui filii sint legitimi,* IV, 17—JL, 14002; this right was also stated indirectly by the same Pontiff in a letter to the Bishop of Exeter in c. 5, *qui filii sint legitimi,* IV, 17—JL, n. 14218.

However, in the legal provisions for cases of separation there is no doubt concerning the Church's conviction of its right to judge such suits. In answering a question from the Bishop of Amiens, Pope Alexander III was adamant in demonstrating that over and above the right of the Church to consider these matters, even in a case wherein the adultery was well known, an innocent consort could not separate without legitimate ecclesiastical recognition of the case.[40] The *Glossa* gave the basis of this doctrine as that described in the *Dictum Gratiani* ad c. 4, C. XXXIIII, q. 2 (cf. *supra*, p. 22). Separation was a penalty according to this view, and necessitated judicial cognizance to be legitimate. Just as one could not inflict penalties privately for other crimes, so separation, a penalty for a crime, demanded a judicial sentence.[41]

It is to this same Pontiff, Alexander III, that the present canonicalterminology on separation owes its original designation. It was he who first divided the concept of common marital life into the elements contemplating bed, board and cohabitation.[42] From this time onward, the same designation regarding these marital factors was incorporated in the official legal language of the Church.

A. *The Ordinary Procedure*

The Decretals were very clear in demanding a formal judicial procedure for separation cases. A consideration of the chapters treating separation leaves no room for doubt that the full judicial process was the rule. If any informal procedure was admitted, this was the exception, and was not mentioned clearly in the sources. As

[40] C. 3, X, *de divortiis,* IV, 19—JL, n. 11866. This doctrine was elaborated quite fully in *Glossa Ordinaria* s.v. *iudicio ecclesiae,* ad c. 4, X, *de donationibus inter virum et uxorem, et de dote post divortium restituenda,* IV, 20, and *Glossa Ordinaria* s.v. *porro,* ad c. 3, *de divortiis,* IV, 19, as well as by Hostiensis, *Commentaria,* Lib. IV, tit. 19, c. 3, s.v. *absque iudicio.*

[41] *Glossa Ordinaria* s.v. *separari* ad c. 3, *de divortiis, IV,* 19. A similar treatment of this view was given in the *Glossa Ordinaria* s.v. *sine iudicio ecclesiae,* ad c. 10, X, *de restitutione spoliatorum,* II, 13; in the *Glossa Ordinaria* s.v. *ex conquestione,* ad *loc. cit.* and by Panormitanus, *Commentaria,* Lib. II, tit. 13, c. 10, n. 1.

[42] C. 11, X, *de praesumptionibus,* II, 23—JL, n. 13969. A more detailed explanation is given in *Glossa Ordinaria* s.v. separari ad *loc. cit.*

would be expected, these cases followed for the most part the general rules for marriage cases; there were, however, many particular norms applicable solely to cases of separation. Because of this connection and to avoid needless and irrelevant detail, the general norms that regulated marriage procedure will be excluded from this writing, and the pertinent legislation governing separation cases will be treated more completely. Wherever some mention of marriage procedure is necessary to clarify a point or to establish a historically significant fact, the mention will be made; but the general tenor of this treatment will confine itself to the particular norms governing the process employed in cases of separation.

From the decretal provisions for marriage and separation cases, the legal necessity of a formal trial at the time is obvious. Innocent III was most emphatic in demanding the full process of law, making no concessions to an informal or summary procedure.[43] A similar stand is found in the treatment of separation cases by Hostiensis (+1271). He stated: ". . . *quod quando agitur de crimine adulterii, quoad tori separationem in omnibus ordo iudiciarius strictissime servandus est.*"[44] Very probably bishops were not unaccustomed to make use of shorter processes in marriage cases, attempting by this means tor abbreviate the rigorous formalities of the procedural law. This fact was perhaps the occasion for the Pope's insistence on the full process as well as for the emphasis placed on its necessity by Hostiensis. This fact was later admitted by Innocent III when he spoke of the necessity of the *litis contestatio*.[45] An added argument that any use of the summary process was a practice *contra legem* at the time may derive from the exclusion by Durantis (+1296) of separation cases from the lists of *causae* which might utilize the shorter or summary process of Justinian Law.[46]

[43] C. 1, X: *ut lite non contestata non procedatur ad testium receptionem vel ad sententiam diffinitivam,* II, 6.

[44] Hostiensis, *Summa Aurea* (Lugduni, 1568), Lib. IV, rub. *de divortiis,* n. 13.

[45] C. 5, X, *ut lite non contestata non procedatur ad testium receptionem vel ad sententiam deffinitivam,* II, 67; Potthast, n. 2417.

[46] *Speculum Iuris* (4 vols. in 3, Venetiis, 1577), Lib. I, Partic. I, *De Officio Judicum,* 8, n. 3.

1. The Competent Tribunal. There was a very substantial departure in the Decretals from the *Decree* of Gratian in regard to the ecclesiastical authority before whom a suit for separation had to be entered. Canon 25 of the Council of Agde was incorporated in c. 1, C. XXXIII, q. 2, and the *Glossa* to this canon permitted the bishop to hear such cases (cf. *supra*, p. 17). The Decretals were much more demanding. The bishop alone was not competent, but these cases had to be tried before a tribunal consisting of the bishop and his chapter.[47] The reason for this provision was based upon two canons drawn from the Decree of Gratian. The first element was the designation of the bishop to hear the case in c. 1, C. XXXIII, q. 2, coupled with c. 6, C. XV, q. 19, which stated: "*Episcopus nullus causam audiat absque presentia suorum clericorum; alioquin irrita erit sententia episcopi, nisi presentia clericorum firmetur.*"[48] Although the above mentioned Decretal and the *Glossae* therein did not emphasize the question of validity, the *Glossa Ordinaria* s.v. *Episcopus* ad c. 6, C. XV, q. 2, was very clear. It pointed out that a majority vote of those present sufficed for the sentence if the absent members were of a concurrent opinion. The dispute regarding the nature of the chapter's power was of little moment, despite the difference of views, as to whether it had ordinary power, or was merely a consultative board to the bishop, in any case, a sentence given by the bishop without their consultation was null. Hostiensis brought this view to apply to the Decretal and to separation. He simply stated that a sentence of separation given without the hearing of the chapter would be invalid.[49]

The remainder of the court personnel doubtless was the same as in other formal cases. It will be sufficient to say that a notary was present as prescribed by the IV General Council of the Lateran (1215) and approved by Innocent III for ecclesiastical trials. His office entailed committing to writing all the formalities of the trial.[50]

47 "Sane tu convocato capitulo tuo, et alii viris discretis, cum ex eorundem consilio utrique privatim continentiam firmiter iniunxeris observandam, ita quod caste viverent ab invicem segregati, . . ."—c. 5, *de divortiis*, IV, 19.

48 *Glossa Ordinaria* s.v. *ex litteris*, et s.v. *abinvicem segregati*, ad. c. 5, X, *de divortiis*, IV, 19.

49 *Commentaria*, Lib. IV, tit. 19, c. 5, s.v. *consilio*.

50 C. 11, X, *de probationibus*, II, 19.

It was customary to furnish advocates,[51] but there was no official corresponding to the present day *defensor vinculi.* This office as it exists today did not come into being until 1751, under Pope Benedict XIV.[52]

2. The Parties in the Case. The innocent party naturally was the plaintiff in the case and had a right to institute action for separation against an adulterous consort.[53] The basis of this concession was taken from Reg. 75, R.J., in VI°.[54] Hostiensis made a useful observation in pointing out that an action of this sort to effect a separation was of an optional nature. There was no legal compulsion upon the aggrieved party to dismiss the adulterous spouse.[55]

Similar to the laws as presented in the *Decree* of Gratian, the Decretals provided, for the most part, the case of an innocent husband dismissing or leaving an adulterous wife. However, despite the apparent imparity of rights to initiate the suit, an implicit concession was made to injured wives in c. 2, X, *de divortiis,* IV, 19. In addition to this provision, the Decretalists and Glossators were most emphatic in demonstrating the essential equality of right for either spouse to accuse an unfaithful consort. Although quite repetitious in form their views on the matter leave no doubt that this was the practice of the day.[56]

51 *Glossa Ordinaria* s.v. *advocatus* ad c. 1, X, *ut lite non contestata etc.,* II, VI.

52 Benedictus XIV, const. *Dei miseratione,* 3 nov. 1741—*Codicis Iuris Canonici Fontes* (9 vols., Vols. I-VI, ed. cura Eñi Card. Gasparri; Vols. VII-IX, ed. cura et studio Eñi Iustiniani Card. Serédi, Romae—postea Civitate Vaticana: Typis Polyglottis Vaticanis, 1923-1939), n. 318 (hereafter cited *Fontes*).

53 Cc. 4, 5, 8, X, *de divortiis,* IV, 19.

54 *"Frustra sibi fidem quis postulat ab eo servavi, cui fidem a se praestitam servare recusat."*

55 ". . . mulieri adulterae parcere potest vir."—*Commentaria,* Lib. II, tit. 24, c. 25, s.v. *titius ergo.* This doctrine was first clearly proposed by St. Augustine (cf. *supra,* p. 7).

56 *Glossa Ordinaria,* s.v. *sequantur,* ad c. 1, X, *de coniugio leprosorum,* IV, 8; Such phrases as: *"quia vir et mulier ad imparia non iudicatur"; "non ad imparia iudicatur,"* are found in the *Glossa Ordinaria* s.v. *vel alio crimine* et s.v. *quaesivit* ad c. 2, X, *de divortiis,* IV, 19, and in the *Glossa Ordinaria* s.v. *intelleximus* ad c. 6, X, *de adulteriis et stupro,* V, 16. Cf. Hostiensis, *Summa Aurea,* Lib. IV, rub. *de divortiis,* n. 5; *op. cit.,* Lib. V, rub. *de adulteriis,* n. 1; Panormitanus, *Commentaria,* Lib. IV, tit. 19, c. 2, n. 3.

3. Exceptions. The Decretals not only made mention of the exceptions as found in Gratian but also for the first time listed as further exceptions the case in which consent was given or a condonation was accorded to the act of adultery to form the basis of the law as it exists today. Since the treatment of the exceptions common to the Decretals and the *Decree* of Gratian was very similar in both Collections, rather than risk being repetitious, the writer will limit to new development the matter that is here discussed.

A clearer definition of formal adultery was expressed by the Glossators and Decretalists, they shunned lengthy examples and preferred to demonstrate the nature of unfaithfulness by explicit principles. There is no doubt that the crime of adultery had to be formal; if it were not, it could be used as an exception by the accused partner.[57] Hostiensis presented a very clear cut principle, allowing no room for doubt regarding the nature of the sin: *"adulterium sine dolo numquam committitur."*[58] An even clearer presentation of this concept was expressed in the *Glossa*. Such statements as the following are found therein: *"Praeterea adulteria sicut et alia crimina, secundum intentionem iudicantur et ex corde procedunt."*[59]

Compensation was treated at very great length. By this exception the right to plead a case against an adulterous spouse was erased by the identical offense perpetrated by the plaintiff.[60] Pope Innocent III in a letter to the Archbishop of Tours based this provision upon a very sound principle. He stated: *"Paria delicta mutua compensatione tolluntur."*[61] In a later Decretal to the Bishop of Amiens he repeated this view as the basis of his decision of the case in question.[62]

[57] *Glossa Ordinaria* s.v. *mutua compensatione,* ad c. 6, X, *de adulteriis et stupro* V, 16.

[58] *Summa Aurea,* Lib. IV, rub. *de divortiis,* n. 8; He gave a similar statement in his *Commentaria,* Lib. V, tit. 16, c. 6, s.v. *eam.*

[59] *Glossa Ordinaria* s.v. *repetere non valebit,* ad c. 4, X, *de donationibus inter virum et uxorem,* IV, 20.

[60] C. 5, X, *de divortiis,* IV, 19.

[61] C. 6, X, *de adulteriis et stupro,* V, 16—Potthast, n. 3387.

[62] C. 7, X, *de adulteriis et stupro,* V, 16—Potthast, n. 3442. The Pope again referred to the same statement in a reponse to the Bishop of Poitiers—c. 16, X, *de conversione coniugatorum,* III, 32—Potthast, n. 3698.

The Glossators in commenting on this papal provision simply completed the axiom and applied it to marital separation.[63] It seems that a certain equality of crime was necessary for the employment of this exception in a judicial fashion. Sanchez, writing much later, made the distinction of public and occult adultery. If the crime of the one party was public and the later crime of the other was occult, then the latter crime was not a matter amenable to court procedure, so that the perpetrator of the occult crime was bound in the forum of conscience to the party guilty of the public delict. He approximated this to restitution because of a crime of theft. Although not of this period, the doctrine of Sanchez proves helpful for the proper understanding of the Glossator's views.[64]

The nature of this exception was peremptory rather than dilatory. Sanchez explicitly called it such and allowed its proposal before and after the *litis contestatio* right up to the sentence. He based this stand on c. 7, X, *de adulteriis et stupro,* V, 16.[65] Ioannes Andreae (+1348) limited his statement to the fact that this exception was peremptory.[66] What if the exception of adultery performed by the plaintiff was proposed after a sentence of separation has been given? Was such procedure embraced by this exception of compensation? The Glossators were unanimous in allowing its use, "*non obstante sententia.*" [67] Hostiensis explained this view by pointing out that a separation case never became a *res iudicata* when

[63] "Non potest maritus consortium vel cohabitationem uxoris declinare propter adulterium si et ipse fuit adulteratus"—*Glossa Ordinaria* s.v. *tua fraternitatis* ad c. 7, X, *de adulteriis et stupro,* V, 16.

[64] III, Lib. X, disp. 8, n. 9; Ioannes Andreae approached this view in his explanation of the term *paria* in c. 6, X, *de adulteriis et stupro,* V, 16, saying that the mutual crime had to be equal "*in quantitate et qualitate.*"—*Commentaria Novella in Sex Decretalium Libros* (6 vols. in 5, Venetiis, 1581), Lib. V, tit. 16, c. 7, n. 1, s.v. *paria* (hereafter cited Ioannes Andreae).

[65] III, Lib. X, disp. 6, n. 12.

[66] *Op. cit.,* Lib. V, tit. 16, c. 7, s.v. *fornicationis.*

[67] *Glossa Ordinaria* s.v. *continere,* ad c. 9, X, *de sponsalibus et matrimoniis,* IV, 1; *Glossa Ordinaria* s.v. *ex litteris* ad c. 5, X, *de divortiis,* IV, 19; *Glossa Ordinaria* s.v. *fornicationis* ad c. 7, X, *de adulteriis et stupro,* V, 16.

granted for adultery, and the subsequent unfaithfulness of the earlier aggrieved party compensated for the first adultery, despite the sentence.[68] Panormitanus qualified the majority view. The exception was allowed, but he denied its use by the defendant and confined any reinstatement of marital unity to the judge acting *ex officio*.[69]

A new exception incorporated in the Decretals, as far as the writer has been able to ascertain, was the case that involved consent to unfaithfulness. This factor deprived the aggrieved party of the right to plead the case if he permitted the crime. No grievance was allowed before the law when one knowingly consented to his partner's sin. This concept was based on Reg. 27, R.J. in VI°: "*Scienti et consentienti non fit iniuria neque dolus.*" The *scienti et consentienti* was understood in the copulative and not the disjunctive sense. One had to knowingly permit the unfaithfulness, in the case wherein one was aware of it but did not consent to it, *iniuria* was present.[70] Pope Innocent III decreed that this exception was valid and even intensified if a man gave cause or was the reason for his wife's adultery.[71] Panormitanus distinguished cause and occasion as the basis of this exception. If a man was the immediate cause of his wife's adultery, she could employ this exception, but if he was merely the occasion of her crime, there was still *iniuria*. His influence upon her actions in the latter case was considered too remote to constitute consent to adultery.[72] If a wife excused her unfaithfulness and em-

68 *Commentaria,* Lib. IV, tit. 19, c. 5, s.v. *legitimam uxorem.*

69 *Commentaria,* Lib. V, tit. 16, c. 7, n. 5. Ioannes Andreae had earlier expressed this same teaching—Lib. IV, tit. 19, c. 5, n. 6, s.v. *compellas.*

70 *Glossa Ordinaria,* s.v. *scienti,* ad Reg. 27, R.J. in XI°; Reiffenstuel, Lib. V, *De Regulis Iuris in Sexto,* ad Reg. XXVII, cap. 2.

71 C. 6, X, *de eo qui cognovit consanguineam uxoris suae vel sponsae,* IV, 13—Potthast, n. 1182. This element of causality was emphasized in the *Glossa Ordinaria* s.v. *discretionem tuam* ad *loc. cit.* Cf. Hostiensis, *Summa Aurea,* rub. *de divortiis,* n. 8; Ioannes Andreae, Lib. IV, tit. 13, c. 6, n. 7, s.v. *remotum.*

72 *Commentaria,* Lib. IV, tit. 13, c. 7, n. 8. The *Glossa Ordinaria* s.v. *materiam adulterandi* ad c. 4, X, *de divortiis,* IV, 19 concurred and reasoned that if the husband was merely the occasion of the crime, then the delict was imputed to the wife, for she was responsible for her own actions, and was not to commit this crime under any circumstances.

ployed this exception because her husband failed to provide the necessities of life, it would not be acceptable. This allegation was insufficient to constitute not only a cause but even an occasion for the sin.[73]

Condonation of the unfaithful consort's action by the innocent spouse was an additional exception found in the Decretals. It amounted to a prohibition on an otherwise legitimate plaintiff, to initiate a suit if he had condoned the *iniuria* he had suffered from his spouse after its commission. This exception approximated a remission of the *iniuria* suffered by the aggrieved party and prevented him from challenging his adulterous partner at a future date.[74] Hostiensis in his usually thorough fashion pointed out a very useful condition especially of aid to an innocent wife. If the reconciliation was forced upon the innocent consort, then a suit for separation could still be instituted, and this exception proved inefficacious.[75] He also added that an explicit reconciliation was unnecessary. Tacit condonation of the crime sufficed to obviate any future right to legal action.[76]

4. The *Libellus.* Very much like the formal canonical procedure today, the suit for separation was initiated through the presentation of a *supplex libellus.* It was to be drawn up in the customary fashion, and embraced all the information pertinent to the presentation of the case. In addition to the names of the litigants, this document was to contain the name of the partner in the crime, mention of the place, the year and the month in which the adultery occurred, the name of the judge before whom the case was to be pleaded as well as the date of presentation.[77] Hostiensis in the manner of his

[73] C. 5, X, *de divortiis,* IV, 19; *Glossa Ordinaria* s.v. *compulsa ad ibidem;* Panormitanus, *op. cit.,* Lib. IV, tit. 19, c. 5, n. 2.

[74] "Sed si reconciliata fuerit, postea illam fornicationem obiicere non poterit: quia ei remisit hoc"—*Glossa Ordinaria* s.v. *nec reconciliata,* ad c. 4, X, *de donationibus inter virum et uxorem,* IV, 20.

[75] *Commentaria,* Lib. V, tit. 16, c. 6, s.v. *eam.*

[76] *Op. cit.,* Lib. V, tit. 16, c. 3, s.v. *sed non saepe.*

[77] C. 5, X, *de procuratoribus,* I, 38; *Glossa Ordinaria* s.v. *nomen;* s.v. *Locum;* s.v. *tempus;* s.v. *lege civili,* ad *loc. cit.*

day outlined all these factors in the following short verse which is reproduced below:

> Consule mense, die coram praetore professus
> To deferre reum crimen loca pone sodalem.
> Et licet hora, dies, non mensis, praetereatur.[78]

Provision was also made for the employment of proxies to represent the litigants in the trial.[79] Despite this stipulation, Hostiensis suggested that the parties would better act themselves, since in such a case their intimate knowledge of the facts in the matter would greatly facilitate the obtaining of proof.[80]

5. Proofs and Presumptions. The principal proofs mentioned as applicable properly to separation cases were two. An act of adultery was considered notorious if the guilty party made a full confession of the crime in court or if the wife became a mother, a year having elapsed since the common life was terminated.[81] Hostiensis remarked that a husband could not act on a mere suspicion, either certitude or a strong presumption of guilt was necessary. As with the Decretists, suspicion had to be so proved as to amount to a strong presumption (cf. *supra*, p. 17).[82] The Decretal Law admitted a violent presumption as sufficient to allow separation from cohabitation. Pope Alexander III admitted the use of such a presumption in a decision of a case based on violent suspicion. The wife of the plaintiff was accused of committing incest with a relative of her husband, and the testimony of the witnesses supported the accusation of adulterous intent in stating that the two were seen: *"solum cum sola, nudum cum nuda, in eodem loco iacentem . . . in multis secretis locis, et laterbris ad hoc commodis, et horis electis."* The

78 *Summa Aurea,* Lib. IV, rub. *de divortiis,* n. 3. St. Raymond of Pennafort incorporated a form filled out with names as a practical model to be observed—*Summa* (ed. nova, Veronae, 1744), Lib. IV, tit. XXII, n. 1.

79 *Glossa Ordinaria* s.v. *noluit respondere,* ad c. 1, X, *ut lite non contestata,* etc., II, 6.

80 *Op. cit.,* Lib. IV, rub. *de divortiis,* n. 3.

81 Panormitanus, *Commentaria,* Lib. IV, tit. 19, c. 4, n. 4.

82 *Commentaria,* Lib. IV, tit. 19, c. 4, s.v. *suggestum, sobalem, constaret.*

Pope ruled that such suspicions constituted a sufficient presumption to warrant a sentence of separation.[83]

6. The Sentence. The bishop pronounced the sentence but as was mentioned previously (cf. *supra*, p. 27), in accord with the conclusions of his chapter. A sentence by the bishop alone without the chapter was invalid.[84] The wording of the Decretal, ". . . *utrique privatim continentiam firmiter iniunxeris observandam, ita, quod caste viverent ab invicem segregati* . . . ," implied that this admonition was given privately after the sentence.[85] Hostiensis supported this interpretation by reasoning that if the admonition were part of the sentence, it would have to be given publicly.[86] Ioannes Andreae expressed this interpretation this: "*non sententiando, sed consulendo.*"[87] Doubtless at this time the bishop instructed the parties regarding the prohibition of remarriage. The phrase, "*quod caste viverent ab invicem segregati,*" in the Decretal, pointed this out in an indirect manner, and Ioannes Andreae explicitly attributed this meaning to these words.[88] The inclusion of this provision in the admonition was in keeping with the law of the Church. The Popes of the time were especially adamant in asserting the indissolubility of the sacrament, and especially when separations were granted. A typical example of this position was contained in a letter of Alexander III to the Bishop of Trondhjem. The Pope decreed: ". . . *quia licet separentur, semper tamen coniuges erunt.*"[89]

7. *Res Iudicata.* In a letter to the Bishop of Norwich, Pope Alexander III decided a case pleaded on the ground of an impediment of consanguinity. This Decretal simply implied it but it was the clear doctrine of the commentators that a marriage case did not

[83] C. 12, X, *de presumptionibus,* II, 23—JK, n. 14166.

[84] C. 5, X, *de divortiis,* IV, 19; *Glossa Ordinaria* s.v. *litteris,* s.v. *ab invicem segregati, ad loc. cit.*

[85] C. 5, X, *de divortiis,* IV, 19.

[86] *Summa Aurea,* Lib. IV, rub. *de divortiis,* n. 13.

[87] Lib. IV, tit. 19, c. 3, s.v. *iniunxeris.*

[88] *Loc. cit.,* s.v. *invicem.*

[89] C. 2, X, *de divortiis,* IV, 19—JL, n. 12184. The same doctrine was clearly enunciated in c. 4, X, *de eo, qui duxit in matrimonium, quam polluit per adulterium,* IV, 7; c. 5, X, *de divortiis,* IV, 19; c. 8, X, *de divortiis,* IV, 19.

become irrevocably adjudged.[90] The *Glossa Ordinaria* s.v. *lator* to this canon stated: *"Item sententia contra matrimonium lata non transit in rem iudicatem."* Thus, it presented the view on the normal marriage case. However, in treating the sentence of separation, the glossators did not make the same explicit statement. Here the glossators in discussing the concept of compensation declared that from the aforementioned decretal of Alexander III it could be seen that a *delictum superveniens* did void what had become an adjudged case but they did not assert that the sentence did or did not entail a *res iudicata.*[91]

Hostiensis pointed out that despite the fact that a sentence of separation did not destroy the marriage bond, nevertheless, such a state was contrary to marriage; consequently, the sentence did not result in a *res iudicata.* If it did, he reasoned, the exception of compensation could not have been employed. He conceded that a change of state of life such as the entering of religion or the receiving of sacred orders did allow the case to be considered irrevocably adjudged.[92] Panormitanus allowed the sentence of separation to entail a *res iudicata* after ten days unless one could demand a reinstatement of his former position against the sentence for a just cause. However, unless the exception was lodged before ten days, a new case would have to be instituted.[93] Sanchez held that the case was irrevocably adjudged, if the sentence was in favor of the innocent spouse. In his opinion, equity did not permit any presumption to favor the guilty party. Since a sentence of separation concerned the properties of marriage and not the bond itself, the sentence did not result in a *res iudicata,* but only in so far as it might favor the aggrieved party to the detriment of the unfaithful spouse.[94]

8. Alimony and the Custody of the Offspring. Disposition regarding the custody of the children of the separated parents was left to the judge and it was doubtless mentioned in the sentence.[95] Nor-

[90] C. 7, *de sententia et re iudicata,* II, 27—JL, n. 14036.

[91] *Glossa Ordinaria* s.v. *redire compellas,* ad c. 5, X, *de divortiis,* IV, 19.

[92] *Commentaria,* Lib. IV, tit. XIX, c. 5, n. 2, s.v. *legitimam uxorem.* This view was also supported by Ioannes Andreae, Lib. IV, tit. XIX, c. 5, n. 10.

[93] *Commentaria,* Lib. II, tit. 27, c. 7, n. 12.

[94] III, Lib. X, disp. 9, n. 4.

[95] Sanchez, III, Lib. X, disp. 20, n. 1.

mally the children were given over to the care of the innocent party. This practice was based on a decision of Pope Gregory IX in judging a case of a converted infidel husband who had left his wife, she remaining in infidelity. The Pope decreed that the solution must favor the Faith and gave the child into the custody of the father.[96] The *Glossa Ordinaria,* s.v. *insidientur,* to this canon applied this decision to separation cases. It stated: "... *si pater causam divortii praestitit, tunc ali debeat apud matrem. Si vero mater causam praestitit divortii, tunc ali debet apud patrem.*" A limitation on this interpretation was stated in another *Glossa.* Children under three years would better be given over to the mother, whether she was the guilty one or not; but children over this age to the father. In the latter case the general rule was applicable.[97] The support of the offspring was also provided for, the guilty party bearing the burden of their sustenance.[98] The support of the innocent wife by an unfaithful husband was the responsibility of the delinquent. He had to bear the burden of her maintenance in proportion to the quantity of the dowry he had received.[99]

B. Separation *Propria Auctoritate*

As with the legal norms contained in the *Decree* of Gratian, so with the Papal Decretals in the collection of Gregory IX there was unanimity in the demand for a judicial procedure in cases of separation. Both Popes Alexander III and Urban III (1185-1187) clearly indicated that separation on one's own authority was not permissible.[100] Moreover, in two additional decretals the above mentioned Alexander III explicitly treated this controversy. In a response to a question regarding a marriage case, the Pontiff stated that no man was permitted to leave his spouse unless he had clearly shown that she had been unfaithful.[101] He further qualified this

[96] C. 2, X, *de conversione infidelium,* III, 33.

[97] *Glossa Ordinaria* s.v. *triennium,* ad *loc. cit.;* Durantis, *Speculum Iuris,* Lib. IV, Partic. 4, n. 26.

[98] Sanchez, III, Lib. X, disp. 20, n. 2.

[99] Panormitanus, *Commentaria,* Lib. IV, tit. 19, c. 5, n. 3, 4.

[100] C. 4, X, *de divortiis,* IV, 19—JL, n. 14107; c. 6, X, *de divortiis,* IV, 19—JL, n. 15734.

[101] C. 9, X, *de sponsalibus et matrimoniis,* IV, 1—JL, n. 13872.

decision in an answer to the Bishop of Amiens. What was meant by clearly proving infidelity was here demonstrated in a very definite manner. The Holy Father declared: ". . . *quod si etiam parentela esset publica et notoria, absque iudicio ecclesiae ab ea separari non potuit.*" [102]

The Glossators apparently considered these words to be conclusive. All their comments on these statements confined any case of separation to the authority of the Church and forbade any personal decisions in the matter. In the *Glossa* concerned with term *manifesta,* this interpretation is found: "*probata scilicet et sententia subsecuta: quia alias non licet dimittere.*" The argument is based on c. 1, C. XXXIII, q. 2 (cf. *supra,* p. 17), a recapitulation of Canon 25 of the Council of Agde.[103] A later *Glossa* in treating the decretal to the Bishop of Amiens explicitly disallowed any separation on one's own initiative because of a notorious crime of adultery. It limited such a case as follows: "*in notoriis servandus est ordo iuris.*" [104] This thorough restriction on marital separation surely leaves no room for doubt on their opinion in the matter; this opinion however, was not universal among the commentators.

Hostiensis agreed with the general view of the Glossators on separation with reference to a notorious crime of adultery. However, he permitted separation to a wife, on her own authority, when it was a case of a husband who had lapsed into heresy.[105] Panormitanus admitted that the doctrine given above represented the general view, but he dissented, in part from the Glossator's general assertions. He was inclined towards permitting a spouse to leave an adulterous consort when the crime was notorious. The chief basis for his view apparently was the concluding part of c. 4, X, *de divortiis,* IV, 19. In the first part of this decretal Pope Alexander III stated that a man who had left his wife because of a reported sin of adultery should

[102] C. 3, X, *de divortiis,* IV, 19.

[103] *Glossa Ordinaria* s.v. *manifesta,* ad c. 9, X, *de sponsalibus et matrimoniis,* IV, 1.

[104] *Glossa Ordinaria,* s.v. *notaria,* ad c. 3, X, *de divortiis,* IV, 19; The *Glossa Ordinaria* s.v. *separari,* ad *loc. cit.,* repeated the reason constantly found in the Glossator's treatment of separation. It referred again to c. 1, C. XXXIII, q. 2, and described separation as a penalty demanding judicial recognition.

[105] *Commentaria,* Lib. IV, tit. 19, c. 6, s.v. *compellandum.*

return to her; in the latter part he ruled: *"si notorium est, mulierem ipsam adulterium commisisse, ad eam recipiendam praefatus vir cogi non debet."* Panormitanus interpreted this as supporting his view on the matter.[106] Again when concerned with notorious adultery, this commentator stated: ". . . *si adulterium est manifestum, propria auctoritate potest denegare debitum coniugale et eam de domo expellere, secus si occultum."* [107] He further substantiated his interpretation by permitting free separation to the innocent partner because of the notorious adultery, since the adulterer was thereby deprived of all marital rights. Because of this fact, in his opinion, separation by the aggrieved party was permissible.[108] Aside from these assertions by Panormitanus, the general view of the day seemed to have confined separation to a judgment of the ecclesiastical authority.

ARTICLE 3. THE CONSTITUTIONS *Dispendiosam* AND *Saepe* OF CLEMENT V (1305-1314)

Despite the firm emphasis on the obligation of observing formal procedural norms, the sources show traces that in practice a shorter process was being followed. As has been mentioned previously (cf. *supra*, p. 26), bishops very probably made use of shorter processes in marriage cases, and although the shorter procedure was not permitted in separation cases, it seems that the Popes wished to expedite matters at least in litigations concerning the bond. These exceptions to the general rule date from the period of the renewed interest in Roman Law. Cerchiari, in his history of the Sacred Roman Rota, pointed out that the Popes often used such terms as *simpliciter, et de plano, sine strepitu iudicii et figura*. These words were even found inserted in decretals before the end of the twelfth century and they were to become the basis of the summary procedure which was pre-

[106] *Commentaria*, Lib. IV, tit. 1, c. 9, n. 9.

[107] *Op. cit.*, Lib. V, tit. 16, c. 7, n. 6. An addition to this section of his commentary termed such action *"lata sententia."*

[108] *Op. cit.*, Lib. III, tit. 32, n. 4. He repeated his general theme in Lib. IV, tit. 20, c. 4, n. 4.

sented by Pope Clement V, and incorporated in the legislation of the Council of Vienne (1311-1312).[109]

In addition, there is a decretal of Innocent III, which decreed that a sentence of separation was permissible, even without the joining of issues if the latter proved unfeasible in view of a contumacious defendant.[110] Because of this general attitude and the exception made in a case of separation by Innocent III, it seems helpful here to consider these later provisions of Clement V and to study their possible application to the topic being treated.

Doubtless the general tendency toward the abbreviated form or summary trial was an important factor in the decision by Clement V to allow such processes. Although written beforehand, the two constitutionswere incorporated in the legislation of the Council of Vienne and were named after the initial letters of their opening sentences.[111]

The first constitution, *Dispendiosam,* reads as follows: "*Statuimus, ut in causis super electionibus . . . necnon super matrimoniis . . . procedi valeat de cetero simpliciter et de plano, ac sine strepitu iudicii et figura.*"[112] The later decretal *Saepe* merely defined the words of this earlier constitution as far as the procedure was concerned; it added nothing regarding the kind of case in and for which it was allowable to use this summary trial.[113] The important document for this the present treatise is the *Dispendiosam* and an attempt will be made here to determine whether or not separation cases were embraced under its provision, "*super matrimoniis,*" and whether a summary procedure was permitted.

Ioannes Andreae in the *Glossa* to this constitution denied that separation cases, pleaded on the ground of adultery, could partake of the benefit of this shorter trial. However, he was not particularly

[109] Cerchiari, *Capellani Papae et Apostolicae Sedis Auditores Causarum Sacri Palatii Apostolici seu Sacra Romana Rota, ab origine ad Diem usque 20 Septembris, 1870* (4 vols., Romae: Typis Polyglottis Vaticanis, 1919-1921), I, 140, n. 5 (hereafter cited *Sacra Romana Rota*).

[110] C. 1, X, *ut lite non contestata non procedatur ad testium receptionem vel ad sententiam diffinitivam,* II, 6.

[111] Cerchiari, *op. cit.,* I, 140, n. 6; Schroeder, *Disciplinary Decrees of the General Councils* (St. Louis: Herder, 1937), pp. 417, 418.

[112] C. 8, *de iudiciis,* II, E, in Clem.

[113] C. 2, *de verborum significatione,* V, 11, in Clem.; Cerchiari, *loc. cit.*

firm in his stand, as may be seen from his observations which follow. He stated: "*Quid si agatur de crimine adulterii ad separationem thori? Videtur per decretum* c. 1, *ut lite non contestata etc.,* II, 6, *quod constitutio locum non habeat: nam ut ibi patet, processus qui per iura vetera fieri poterat contumace in causa matrimoniali fieri non potest eo casu.*" [114] The use of *videtur* leads one to surmise that in actual practice the liberties as granted in this constitution were applied to separation cases. Wernz (+ 1914) remarked that this was the case, and disagreed with the Glossator, who had restricted such marriage cases as were contemplated in the constitution to cases respecting the bond.[115]

Since the later constitution, *Saepe* did not qualify the extent of the earlier constitution *Dispendiosam* in regard to marriage cases, it cannot be said that there was any authentic prohibition of the inclusion of separation cases under its provisions. Although the commentators for the most part restricted the comprehension of "*causae super matrimoniis*" to the matrimonial bond, nevertheless a contrary practice seems to have been in use. Zabarella (+ 1417) who wrote a century after the constitutions were issued, agreed with Ioannes Andreae in excluding the cases of separation from being prosecuted in a shortened procedure.[116] The commentators seemed to depend for the most part on the interpretation of Ioannes Andreae, yet, as Cerchiari pointed out, there was a general tendency to employ the summary procedure even before the Clementine legislation. The latter served only to authenticate a more or less general trend.[117] Since the prohibition derived from a doctrinal interpretation rather than from any positive law, it seems that the bishops interested in a speedier dispatch of separation cases applied the favorable view, and included them in the provisions of the two constitutions. Such a conclusion, although not supported by the teaching of the commentators at the time, seems to have some merit, especially in the light of the statements made by Cerchiari and Wernz.

[114] *Glossa Ordinaria* s.v. *matrimoniis* ad c. 2, *de iudiciis,* II, 1, in Clem.

[115] *Ius Decretalium,* IV, n. 728.

[116] *Commentarium in Clementinas* (Venetiis, 1504), Rub. *de iudiciis,* s.v. *Dispendiosam,* n. 25.

[117] *Sacra Romana Rota,* I, 140, n. 5.

CHAPTER III

THE PROCEDURE IN CASES OF SEPARATION FROM THE COUNCIL OF TRENT (1545 - 1563) TO THE CODE OF CANON LAW (1918)

THE canonical sources from the Council of Trent to the Code of Canon Law are replete in demonstrating procedural norms especially for marriage cases. Since cases of separation are included under this general heading, a complete survey of the matrimonial procedural law would be far too extensive for the purpose of this work. With this in mind, the writer will limit his treatment here to particular norms for separation cases and any treatment of the ordinary rules of marriage procedure, utilized in separation trials, will be generally omitted. This will forestall all needless repetition and unwarranted detail. However, whenever reference to the common processual regulations is necessary for the presenting of a clear and unified treatment, such mention will be made.

In the endeavor to present a uniform historical survey, the strictly chronological order will be abandoned for a rather topical treatment, inasmuch as this type of presentation seems to be more acceptable in demonstrating the evolution of already existing norms, as well as the emergence of new developments in the hearing of separation cases. In view of this distinction, the present chapter will be occupied with a study of the formal process, still the ordinary method in this period, as also with a study of the later extra-judicial and administrative procedures.

The outstanding influence for Canon Law in this period was obviously the Council of Trent. Summoned by Pope Paul III (1534-1549) in May of 1542, its primary purpose was to combat the erroneous teachings of the current Protestant revolt. As a result there were incorporated in the decrees of the Council several canons concerned with marriage, and, more important for the subject treated here, separation. The procedural norms presented in the later sessions of the Council (152-1563), although very biref, nevertheless constituted the framework for the later legislation which dealt with the contemplated reform.[1]

In the two centuries subsequent to the Council of Trent, it is clear that procedural norms for conducting marriage trials were widely neglected.[2] Poland was especially lacking in this regard. The shocking conditions there occasioned two encyclical letters of Pope Benedict XIV (1740 - 1758).[3] So strong was the language of these epistles to the Polish bishops that the Pontiff even threatened to reserve all marirage cases of that nation to the Roman Tribunals, unless improvement was soon apparent.

Authors mentioned Poland as an example of deplorable conditions, but the disregard of legal provisions was almost universal. A more general legislation was felt so very necessary that the same great Pontiff on November 3, 1741 published to the universal Church his renowned Constitution *Dei miseratione*.[4] This celebrated constitution had far reaching effect; it not only stabilized judicial procedure in marriage cases, but was to be the norm for the thenceforth intervening legislation until the enactment of the Code of Canon Law, almost two centuries later.

Further legal enactments particularly pertinent to procedural law were the Instruction of the Sacred Congregation of the Council, issued on August 22, 1840,[5] and an Instruction of the Sacred Congre-

[1] The Council was concerned with general reform rather than particular norms. Its chief concern was an insistence that matrimonial cases belonged to ecclesiastical tribunals and a recommendation for a reorganization of the different grades of tribunals—sess. XXXIV, *de matrimonio,* c. 12; Sess. XXIV, *de ref.,* c. 20.

[2] Feije, *De Impedimentis et Dispensationibus Matrimonialibus* (3. ed., Lovanii, 1885), p. 475 (hereafter referred to as *De Impedimentis*).

[3] Ep. encycl. *Matrimonii,* 11 apr. 1741—*Fontes,* n. 307; ep. encycl. *Nimiam licentiam,* 18 maii 1743—*Fontes,* n. 337.

[4] *Fontes,* n. 318; Bouix, *Tractatus de Judiciis Ecclesiasticis* (2 vols. in 1, Parisiis, 1855), II, 434 (hereafter referred to as *De Judiciis*).

[5] *Fontes,* n. 4069. This Congregation was erected on August 2, 1564 by Pope Pius IV (1559-1565) to provide for the execution of the Tridentine decrees. Its power was extended by Pope St. Pius V (1566-1572) and Gregory XIII (1572-1585). Finally Pope Sixtus V (1585-1590) in a constitution of Jan. 22, 1588, *Immensa aeterni Dei,* gave it the full faculty of interpreting the decrees of the Council, but reserved to the Pope any interpretation of dogma—

gation of the Holy Office of June 22, 1883, addressed to Oriental bishops.[6] This last directive was incorporated for the most part by the Sacred Congregation for the Propagation of the Faith in its Instruction of the same year as sent to the bishops of the United States.[7] This Instruction was incorporated along with the Constitution *Dei miseratione,* of Benedict XIV in the *Acta* of the III Plenary Council of Baltimore in 1884.[8] The assembly of the hierarchy also recommended to the attention of the American bishops the procedural norms of the Austrian Instruction of 1855. This Instruction was promulgated by Joseph Cardinal Rauscher (1797 - 1875), Archbishop of Vienna, in the meeting of the Austrian hierarchy in 1855 and it was approved by the Holy See as a particular law of the Austrian Empire.[9]

Zamboni, *Collectio Declarationum Sacrae Congregationis Cardinalium Sacri Concilii Tridentini Interpretum* (4 vols., Atrebati, 1860-1868), I, XIV (hereafter cited as *Collectio Declarationum S.C.C.*); Bouix, *Tractatus de Curia Romana* (Parisiis, 1859), p. 169. This Congregation shared the hearing of marriage cases with the Sacred Roman Rota, although the latter was not very active until the present century. Pope Pius X (1903-1914), by his constitution, *Sapienti Consilio,* of June 29, 1908, revived the Sacred Roman Rota and gave it jurisdiction to hear *"causae omnes contentiosae non maiores,"* which included cases of separation—*Fontes,* n. 682.

[6] S. C. S. Off., instr. (*ad Ep. Rituum Orient.*), a. 1883—*Fontes,* n. 1076.

[7] S. C. de Prop. Fide, instr., *Causae Matrimoniales,* a. 1883—*Fontes,* n. 4901; *Collectanea S. Congregationis de Propaganda Fide* (2 vols., Vol. I, ann. 1622-1866, Nn. 1-1299; Vol. II, ann. 1867-1906, Nn. 1300-2317, Romae: S. C. de Propaganda Fide, 1907), II, n. 1587 (hereafter referred to as *Collectanea*). Although there is no title of address prefaced to this Instruction in the *Fontes* or the *Collectanea,* it follows immediately upon another Instruction to the bishops of the United States regarding the manner of procedure in criminal and disciplinary cases of clerics. Many authors refer to it as directed to the bishops in the missionary territories of the world, but the better opinion confines it to the bishops of the United States. This view is substantiated by a response of the Sacred Congregation of the Holy Office, which refers to it as sent to the hierarchy of this country—cf. S. C. S. Off. (*Colonien*), 23 iun. 1903, n. 2—*Fontes,* n. 1266.

[8] "In agendis hisce causis pro rei gravitate exacte servetur tum Constitutio Benedict XIV, *Dei Miseratione,* 3 nov. 1741, tum Instructio a S. Cong. de Prop. Fide Nobis communicata quae incipit *Causae Matrimoniales . . .*"—*Acta et Decreta Concilii Plenarii Baltimorensis Tertii, A. D. MDCCCLXXXIV* (Baltimore: John Murphy and Co., 1886), n. 304.

[9] "Utiliter etiam consuli poterit Instructio pro judiciis acclesiasticis Imperii

Not only the Council of Trent but the Holy See through several papal letters and through Instructions of the Congregations insisted upon the right of the Church to hear marriage cases. These suits, it was pointed out, were not a matter of the mixed forum, but belonged to the exclusive jurisdiction of the Church. The reason for this declaration was based on the nature of such cases as "*causae spirituales*"; thus the Church alone was competent. The same applied to separation cases. These cases, since they affected the very status of persons, were considered "*res gravissimae*" and were to be judged solely by an ecclesiastical tribunal.[10]

It was not intended that the jurisdiction of the Church was exclusive in only vincular cases. Separation, even if it was only temporary, was considered a public matter and contrary to the nature of marriage. As a result, it not only looked to ecclesiastical recognition but also necessitated the intervention of ecclesiastical authority. Moreover, the actual hearing before the Church was to be considered not simply as a recommendation, but rather as a compulsory mandate.[11]

Austriaci in causis matrimonialibus, a. 1855 a gravis theologis et canonistis Romanis, licet solo privato suo judicio, commendata"—*loc. cit.;* cf. *Instructio Austriaca Josephi Cardinalis Rauscher,* 4 maii 1855—*Acta et Decreta Sacrorum Conciliorum Recentiorum, Collectio Lacensis* (7 vols., Friburgi Brisgoviae: Herder, 1870-1890), V, coll. 1286-1316 (hereafter referred to as *Collectio Lacensis*); *Analecta Iuris Pontificii* (Romae, 1855-1869; Parisiis, 1872-1891), II (1857), 2515-2562.

10 "Si quis dixerit, causas matrimoniales non spectare ad iudices ecclesiasticos: anathema sit."—Conc. Trident., sess. XXIV, *de matrimonio,* canon 12; Pius VI, const. *Auctorem fidei,* 28 aug. 1794, Prop. 58, 59, 60—*Fontes,* n. 475; Pius IX, *Syllabus Errorum* (a. 1864), Prop. 74—*Fontes,* n. 543; idem., litt. ap. *Ad apostolicae* 22 aug. 1852, n. 2—*Fontes,* n. 511; *Idem.,* allocut. "*Acerbissimum,*" 27 sept. 1852, n. 3—*Fontes,* n. 515; instr. S. C. De Prop. Fide (a. 1883), n. 1—*Collectanea,* II, n. 1587. The authors of this period clearly confined separation cases to the ecclesiastical forum—Schmalzgrueber, *Ius Ecclesisticum Universum* (5 vols. in 12, Romae, 1843-1845), II, tit. 1, n. 53 (hereafter cited as Schmalzgrueber); Gasparri, *Tractatus Canonicus de Matrimonio,* 3. ed., II, nn. 1457, 1458; Wernz, *Ius Decretalium,* IV, n. 731.

11 "Et propterea nefal est coniuges fideles se, propria voluntate aut arbitrio, a coniugali toro separare, nisi ex causa a sacris canonibus permissa et auctoritate ac iudicio Ecclesiae cognita et probata."—Sixtus V, const. *Ad compescendum,* 30 oct. 1586—*Bullarum Diplomatum et Privilegiorum Romanorum Pontificum*

Furthermore, this hearing before the Church was a serious matter. Even in this late post-Tridentine period the solemn process was still the ordinary mode of judging such suits. The summary and administrative methods were doubtless in use, but the law still considered the formal procedure to be the accepted practice. It was not until the latter part of this era that the more informal method received ecclesiastical sanction.[12]

Article 1. The Formal Procedure

There were in this period actually very few major changes from the law of the Decretals with respect to the procedural norms for separation cases. Because of this small degree of development, the formal process will be treated as a whole, without the various divisions of the last chapter. Emphasis, as would be expected, will be placed upon the emergence of later developments. It is to be noted that the general outline of a separation suit followed the rules of marriage trials and, as was noted in the study of the Decretals, certain special provisions were added for separation cases. These supplementary norms suffered a degree of change in the period now being treated.

The Council of Trent in its decrees on separation emphasized the evangelical teaching of the indissolubility of marriage and of the need of permission for separation on the grounds of adultery.[13] It further ruled that the causes for separation were not delineated in an exhaustive list. The unity of marital life could be broken by the Church for many causes, and this could be done permanently or just as a temporary measure.[14] However, despite the general tone of the

Taurinensis Editio (24 vols. et Appendix, Augustae Taurinorum, 1857-1872), VIII (1572-1588), 789. The III Plenary Council of Baltimore (1884) was faced with a special problem of Catholics seeking a civil separation without ecclesiastical permission. Such people were warned of the gravity of this offense and reminded of the penalty which he bishop might inflict at his own discretion—*Acta et Decreta Concilii Plenarii Baltimorensis Tertii, A.D.* MDCCCLXXXIV, n. 126.

[12] Wernz, *Ius Decretalium,* IV, n. 714.

[13] Sess. XXIV, *de matrimonio,* Canon 7.

[14] "Si quis dixerit, ecclesiam errare, cum ob multas causas separationem inter coniuges quoad thorum seu quoad cohabitationem ad certum incertumve

Tridentine legislation, the interpretation of this canon always confined permanent separation to the ground of adultery. Other causes for separation were many but permitted only a temporary separation which terminated at the cessation of the motive cause.[15]

The competent ecclesiastical authority for the hearing of separation cases was determined by the Council of Trent as belonging to the bishop alone. By this decree, all inferior prelates of the diocese were excluded from any immediate jurisdiction over these suits and no infringement upon the episcopal right to judge these cases in the first instance was to be permitted.[16] The general opinion of the authors not only admitted that the vicar general could hear these cases when empowered with a special mandate but even held it as *probabilius* that he might act without this commission. In practice they noted that this difficulty was obviated through the issuance of a special mandate or in consequence of an extant legitimate custom.[17]

If the bishop himself or the vicar general in his stead could not hear these cases, provision was to be made for delegated judges.

tempus fieri posse decernit: anathema sit"—sess. XXIV, *de matrimonio,* Canon 8.

[15] S. C. C., *Taurinen.,* 16 mart. 1726—*Thesaurus Resolutionum Sacrae Congregationis Concilii* (167 vols., Urbini, 1739-1740; Romae, 1741-1908), III, 290 (hereafter cited as *Thesaurus Resolutionum S. C. C.*); Zamboni, *Collectio Declarationum S. C. C.,* IV, 388; S. C. C., *Firmana,* 16 maii 1789—*Thesaurus Resolutionum S. C. C.,* LVIII, 99; Sacra Romana Rota, *Separationis quoad Thorum et Mensam,* 5 iul. 1910 coram Rmo. P. D. Michaeli Lega, Decano, dec. XXIV, n. 11—*S. Romanae Rotae Decisiones seu Sententiae quae . . . prodierunt ab anno 1909* (Romae: Typis Polyglottis Vaticanis, 1912—), II (1910), 238, 247 (herefter referred to as *Decisiones*).

[16] "Ad haec causae matrimoniales et criminales non decani, archidiacani aut aliorum inferiorum iudicio, etiam visitando, sed episcopi tantum examini et iurisdictioni relinquantur. . . ."—sess. XXIV, *de ref.,* c. 20.

[17] Sanchez, Lib. II, disp. 40, n. 17; Lib. III, disp. 29, n. 18; Pirhing, *Ius Canonicum in V Libros Decretalium* (5 vols., Dilingae, 1674-1678), Lib. I, tit. 18, n. 47 (hereafter cited as *Ius Canonicum*); Santi, *Praelectiones Iuris Canonici* (5 vols. in 2, Ratisbonae, Neo Eboraci et Cincinnati, 1886), Lib. IV, tit. 18, n. 10; Mansella, *De Impedimentis et de Processu Iudiciali in Causis Matrimonialibus* (Romae, 1881), p. 173, n. 3; Wernz, *Ius Decretalium,* IV, n. 729; Lega, *Praelectiones de Iudiciis Ecclesiasticis* (4 vols., Romae, 1896 - 1901), IV, 468 (hereafter cited *De Iudiciis Ecclesiasticis*); Gasparri, De Matrimonio 3. ed., II, n. 1460.

Tridentine law decreed that such judges were to be appointed in provincial and diocesan synods. Their number was to be at least four, and vacancies occurring between synods were to be filled by the ordinary with the advice of his chapter. Later enactments of the Holy See repeated these provisions.[18]

Other officers of the court worthy of mention were the notary and the defender of the bond. The former was necessary to inscribe accurately the acts of the case, as in all marriage cases.[19] The office of the *defensor vinculi* was demanded by Benedict XIV for all marriage cases involving the dissolution of the bond.[20] However, most of the authoritative authors of this period dispensed with this officer in cases of separation. They were for the most part agreed that his presence was required simply in vincular cases and therefore was superfluous in separation suits; he was regarded as the defender of a bond that was not attacked, and therefore he had nothing to defend.[21]

The general rule for competency in marriage cases, and therefore in separation suits, was that the bishop of the domicile of the husband possessed jurisdiction to hear these cases. The two rules, *"actor sequitur forum rei,"* and *"uxor sequitur domicilium mariti,"* were united in the above given general norm. Both resolved themselves into a grant of competency to the bishop of the husband's domicile.[22] An important exception to this general rule was incorporated in the Instruction of the Sacred Congregation for the Propa-

[18] Conc. Trident., sess. XXV, *de ref.*, c. 10; *Benedictus XIV*, const. *Dei miseratione*, 3 nov. 1741, n. 4—*Fontes*, n. 318; S. C. C., instr., 22 aug. 1840—*Fontes*, n. 4069; S. C. de Prop. Fide, instr. a. 1883, n. VI— *Collectanea*, II, n. 1587.

[19] Benedictus XIV, *ibid.*, n. 5; S. C. de Prop Fide, *loc. cit.*

[20] *Loc. cit.*

[21] Wernz, *Ius Decretalium*, IV, n. 730; Gasparri, *De Matrimonio*, 3. ed., II, n. 1473; Lega, *De Iudiciis Ecclesiasticis*, IV, 478; Feije, *De Impedimentis*, p. 476.

[22] S. C. C., 28 ian. 1865, III: "Uxorem forum sortiri in quo vir suum domicilium habet."—*Acta Sanctae Sedis* (41 vols., 1865-1908), II (1866), 137-141 (hereafter referred to as *ASS*); *Austrian Instruction*, Sec. 96—*Collectio Lacensis*, V, col. 1298; S. C. de Prop. Fide instr., a. 1883, n. II—*Collectanea*, II, n. 1587; Schmalzgrueber, Lib. II, tit. II, n. 12; Gasparri, *De Matrimonio*, 3. ed., II, n. 1463, ftn. 2.

gation of the Faith in 1883. This exception presented two situations in which the ordinary rule of competency was not observed. They were of particular import, since they were concerned with separation cases. The two circumstances provided for were the cause of a separation *a toro et mensa* and that of a wife maliciously deserted by her husband. In the first case each spouse had the right to present his or her case before the bishop of the diocese where the defendant had a domicile after a decree of separation had been granted. In the second case, the wife maliciously deserted by her husband had the choice of pleading her cause before the bishop of the diocese wherein she was residing or before the bishop of the domicile of her errant husband. Any change of domicile after the institution of proceedings was of no importance.[23] The replies of the Roman Congregations are ample proof that the domicile of the husband with these stated exceptions continued in the law to determine competency until the advent of the Code of Canon Law.[24]

Whether a bishop was competent to hear a separation case on the basis of quasi-domicile was not stated in the law. The concept did not develop until after the Council of Trent when authors treated

[23] S. C. de Prop. Fide, instr. a. 1883, n. II: "Exceptioni locus est si conjugale vitae consortium aut per separationem a toro et mensa, aut per desertionem malitiosam a marito patratam sublatum sit. Priori casu quaelibet pars ius accusandi contra alteram ipsi competens, coram episcopo dioecesis, ubi haecce domicilium habet, exercere debet. Posteriori casu uxor apud Episcopum intra cuius dioecesim domicilium eius situm est, actionem instituere potest. Postquam citatio iudicialis intimita est, mutatio quoad coniugum domicilium facta mutationem respectu iudicis competentis minime operatur"—*Collectanea,* II, n. 1587. This quotation is a verbatim inclusion of Sec. 96 of the *Austrian Instruction,* and is demonstrative of the great influence of this particular legislation—*Collectio Lacensis,* V, col. 1298. The III Plenary Council of Baltimore explicitly decreed that this section of the foregoing instruction of the Sacred Congregation for the Propagation of the Faith should be observed in determining the competency of a judge.—*Acta et Decreta Concilii Plenarii Baltimorensis Tertii, A. D. MDCCCLXXXIV,* n. 305.

[24] S. C. C., *Parisien.,* 14 dec. 1889—*Thesaurus Resolutionum S. C. C.,* CXLVIII, 838. The Sacred Congregation of the Holy Office, while sustaining this general juridical principle, limited its application to a case of two Catholics. In a judgment affecting a mixed marriage, the bishop of the domicile of the Catholic spouse was competent—S. C. S. Off., 30 iun. 1892—*Fontes,* n. 1157; S. C. S. Off. (*Colonien.*), 23 iun. 1903—*Fontes,* n. 1266.

of the validity of marriage in places wherein the Decree *Tametsi* of the Council of Trent was not in force. Their treatment was concerned chiefly with determining the proper pastor in cases wherein the possession of parochial jurisdiction was necessary on the part of the assisting pastor.[25]

Authors were not agreed on the adequacy of quasi-domicile as a determinant of juridical competency. Gasparri (+ 1934) made mention of this lack of concord among canonists but termed the opinion favoring its inclusion as *"probabilior."* He based his argument on the fact that one becomes a subject by quasi-domicile and, since in a positive and probable doubt jurisdiction is supplied, he concluded that this was a safe opinion to follow. His treatment was a conclusion from the views of acceptable earlier canonists.[26]

The role of plaintiff in a case of separation was limited to the innocent consort alone. For no reason was a third party allowed to plead such a suit, unless he acted for the aggrieved consort with a special mandate from the latter. As a result, the parties alone had this right antecedent to the suit, and the pleading of an actual case was the right of the injured spouse alone.[27]

The adultery postulated for the bringing of a suit of separation was still what it had been in the Decretal Law. Authors of this period discussed the formal aspect more clearly, and in their descriptions of this crime always postulated an act as fully consummated, perpetrated without the consent of the other spouse, not condoned nor compensated by the same. Actually, there were no legal enactments on this matter.[28]

[25] Reiffenstuel, Lib. II, tit. II, n. 22; Schmalzgrueber, Lib. I, tit. II, n. 16, In his letter *Paucis abhinc,* Pope Benedict XIV (1740-1758) gave official recognition to quasi-domicile as a factor in the law—*Fontes,* n. 447.

[26] *De Matrimonio,* 3. ed., II, n. 1463; Pirhing, *Ius Canonicum,* Lib. II, tit. II, n. 18; Reiffenstuel, Lib. II, tit. II, n. 39; Schmalzgrueber, Lib. II, tit. II, n. 17.

[27] S. C. de Prop. Fide, instr. a. 1883, n. III—*Collectanea,* II, n. 1587; *Austrian Instruction,* sec. 215—*Collectio Lacensis,* V, col. 1311; Schmalzgrueber, Lib. IV, tit. XVIII, n. 13; Wernz, *Ius Decretalium,* IV, n. 743, III; Gasparri, *op. cit.,* II, n. 1364.

[28] Sanchez, Lib. X, disp. V, nn. 2, 3, 13, 19, 20, 23; Schmalzgrueber, Lib. IV, tit. XVIX, nn. 98, 99, 103, 106, 107, 108, 133; Cosci, *De Separatione Tori*

From a general review of the decisions and replies of the Roman Congregations as well as the doctrine of the authors of this period, it is evident that separation cases were regarded as matters of gravity and the need for most conclusive proofs is manifest. Furthermore, judges were admonished to proceed cautiously especially because of the danger of incontinence for separated consorts, and because of the danger to the public good arising from the consequent impossibility of offspring from the broken conjugal life.[29] Proofs had to be full and conclusive. They needed at least to furnish a basis for a most violent suspicion. Naturally such a thing as adultery was difficult to prove and the law duly took cognizance of this fact. A mere probable suspicion on the one hand was insufficient; a well-founded suspicion on the other hand, with its basis duly established was admissible. This proof could take the form of presumption which, although only demonstrative and not conclusive in themselves, nevertheless, when taken collectively established the necessary moral certitude in the mind of the judge. This moral certitude was sufficient for him to pass a sentence of separation.[30]

Since eyewitnesses were practically impossible in such cases, they were not expected. However, hearsay witnesses were to be barred: they had to be "*de auditu proprio alicuius actus copulae propinquae*"

Coniugalis (Florentiae, 1855), Lib. II, cap. XVI, nn. 6, 12, 17, 23, 25; Wernz, *Ius Decretalium,* IV, n. 707; Gasparri, *De Matrimonio,* 3. ed., II, n. 1365.

[29] *Sacrae Romanae Rotae Decisiones Recentiores* (ed. Pr. Farinacius, Petrus Rubeus et Ioannes Baptista Compagnus, pro annis 1518-1684, 25 vols., Romae, 1618-1703), Pars XVI (1669), dec. XCIX, n. 3 (hereafter cited as *S. R. Rotae Decisiones Recentiores*); S. C. C. *Firmana,* 16 maii 1789: "Res porro est de separatione thori, in qua ad vitandum incontinentiae periculum, publicumque deficientis prolis damnum, caute procedendum monent"—*Thesaurus Resolutionum S. C. C.,* LVIII, 99.

[30] "Tum quia concurrunt plures actus probati per testes qui simul iuncti valde adminiculantur, et maximam adulterii praesumptionem inducant, nempe . . . secretae allocutiones de nocte, salutationes et signa amoris (etc.) . . . ex quibus omnibus simul iunctis adeo fortis et intensa resultat adulterii presumptio, ut de eo moraliter dubitari nequeat"—*S. R. R. Decisiones Recentiores,* XII (1658), CCCXXXVII; XVI (1669), XCIX, n. 3; VI (1625), CCCXXIV, n. 2; S. C. C., *Imolen.,* 11 mart. 1786—*Thesaurus Resolutionum S. C. C.,* LV, 41-43; Sanchez, Lib. X, disp. XI, n. 39; Cosci, *De Separatione Tori Conjugalis,* Lib. II, cap. XVI, nn. 20, 21; Gasparri, *De Matrimonio,* 3. ed., II, n. 1365.

at least, and above all suspicion.[31] Not only was the testimony of relatives and intimates deemed altogether suitable for evidence, but if the case warranted it even the deposition of medical men or of several matrons appointed by the judge *ex officio* to examine the woman. These latter experts were especially useful in cases wherein extreme cruelty was alleged to ascertain the existence of physical abuse. Cruelty was perhaps the most frequent cause after adultery for seeking a separation. Here again strict proof and witnesses were demanded before a separation would be granted for as the Sacred Roman Rota declared: ". . . *rari sint coniuges inter quos aliquae dissensiones non oriantur.*" [32]

Wernz pointed out a very useful recommendation which he based on Sec. 236 of the *Austrian Instruction.* He remarked that, since in cases of separation there is often animosity between the spouses and therefore a danger to soul and body, the judge may, because of the possibility of harm, permit a temporary separation from the very beginning of the suit by way of a provisional decree.[33]

With regard to the matter of alimony and of the custody of children, the law manifested little change from that of the Decretals. The authors considered these points in more detail and, as would be expected, gave their opinions on the matter in a more up to date fashion. The judge was normally to give the children over to the care of the innocent party and they were to be reared at the expense of the guilty partner. However, it was left to the discretion of the judge to make any different provisions in the individual case. In a case wherein a guilty partner despite his or her unfaithfulness proved more suitable in the mind of the judge for undertaking the care of the children, the judge could issue his decree accordingly.[34]

[31] *S. R. R. Decisiones Recentiores,* XVI (1669), XCIX, n. 1; VI (1625), CCCXXIV, n. 3; VI (1633), CCXXXIX, n. 18; Schmalzgrueber, Lib. IV, tit. XIX, n. 115; Cosci, *op. cit.,* Lib. I, cap. XIV, nn. 1, 5, 6.

[32] *S. R. R. Decisiones Recentiores,* VI (1632), CLV; IX, tom. II (1645), CCCXXII; XVI (1669), XCIX, n. 4.

[33] *Ius Decretalium,* IV, n. 744, ftn. 72.

[34] Sanchez, Lib. X, disp. XIX, n. 3; disp. XX, n. 2; Pirhing, *Ius Canonicum,* Lib. IV, tit. XIX, n. 63; Reiffenstuel, Lib. IV, tit. XIX, nn. 103, 104; Schmalzgrueber, Lib. IV, tit. XIX, n. 181; Feije, *De Impedimentis,* p. 467;

Despite the guilt of the Catholic party in a case of a mixed marriage, the general rule here was to be changed. In such a case the faith of the children was to be favored through the commitment of them to the custody of the Catholic party. The great risk of putting the children in the danger of being reared in infidelity was considered to be avoided by this means.[35]

Alimony or the support of the injured spouse and payment of the expenses for the support of the children were provided for in the law of the Decretals. The same continued to be the regular norm, although the judge could provide otherwise in particular cases.[36] Authors of the period pointed out that the civil authority at the time was accustomed to adjudicate these temporal effects of marriage. However, it was not a question here of a civil divorce or separation, but merely of a declaration of the material property settlement; permission for a civil separation or divorce, a very important matter, was then as now an entirely different element, which will be discussed in a later chapter.[37]

An important problem of the post-Tridentine period was one which continues to this day, namely, when and under what conditions was the aggrieved party of a separation suit obliged to return to the erring spouse? In the matter of perpetual separation the solution was very simple. Since adultery was the only cause recognized as sufficient to effect such a separation, the necessity of returning was never present. By his or her breach of marital fidelity, the erring spouse lost all rights to cohabitation, and the innocent party could not be forced even to effect a reconciliation. Naturally judges were advised to attempt this end by persuasion; but, with adultery as a basis for the separation, it remained the pleasure of the injured party to permit or not to permit a reunion, and a new judicial sentence

Bangen, *Instructio Practica de Sponsalibus et Matrimonio* (4 vols. in 1, Monasterii, 1858), p. 148; Gasparri, *De Matrimonio,* 3. ed., II, n. 1373.

[35] Benedictus XIV, const. *Probe,* 15 dec. 1751—*Fontes,* n. 418; S. C. C., 12 aug. 1865—*ASS,* II (1866), 136, n. IX; S. C. C., *Basileen.,* 31 iul. 1869—*Fontes,* n. 4215; *Austrian Instruction,* Sec. 236—*Collectio Lacensis,* V, col. 1313.

[36] S. C. C., *loc. cit.*; Sanchez, Lib. X, disp. XX, n. 1.

[37] *Austrian Instruction,* Sec. 244—*Collectio Lacensis,* V, col. 1314; Santi, *Praelectiones Iuris Canonici,* Lib. IV, tit. XIX, n. 16; Wernz, *Ius Decretalium,* IV, n. 714.

was not necessary if the aggrieved partner wished to allow a return of the guilty one to the common life. The latter could be recalled, and since he or she was the original cause of the separation, there was an obligation to return and the errant party could even be forced by a judicial sentence to obey the summons of the innocent consort.[38]

If one of the spouses lapsed into apostasy, heresy or schism, there was a case which approximated the effects of adultery, but nevertheless, it did not as such constitute a cause for perpetual separation. In such a case the authors distinguished two elements in treating the matter of reconciliation. Needless to say, as long as the erring spouse remained in the state of apostasy, heresy or schism, the faithful spouse did not need to allow a return to marital life. The question became a little more involved when the party guilty of these sins re-embraced the faith. In such a case the authors looked to the state of the innocent party, viz., whether he or she had entered religion or had remained in the world. By entering religion, the party effected a change of state and no reconciliation was prescribed; if the party's state had not been changed, a further distinction was made in line with the method of procedure that led to the separation. If the separation occurred *propria auctoritate* on the part of the injured consort, the latter was bound to return upon the conversion of the other. However, if the separation was granted by ecclesiastical authority, then no reconciliation was necessary unless it was ordered by a judge, and it could be ordered only if there was present a sufficient guarantee of the guilty party's real sincere return to the faith.[39]

In general the other causes for separation which permitted only a temporary disruption of the marital union could be listed under two main headings. They were dangers to the soul and dangers to the body. There was no exhaustive list stated in the law. It was

[38] S. C. C., *Taurinen.*, 16 mart. 1726—*Thesaurus Resolutionum S. C. C.*, III, p. 291; S. C. C., *Firmana*, 16 maii 1789—*op. cit.*, LVIII, p. 99; Schmalzgrueber, Lib. IV, tit. XIX, nn. 118-123.

[39] Barbosa, *Collectanea Doctorum tam Veterum quam Recentiorem in Ius Pontificium Universum* (5 vols., Lugduni, 1656), Lib. IV, tit. XIX, c. VI, n. 5; Pirhing, *Ius Canonicum*, Lib. IV, tit. XIX, nn. 30, 31; Gasparri, *De Matrimonio* 3. ed., II, n. 1371.

merely illustrative and left the determination of particular causes in individual cases to the prudent judgment of the ecclesiastical authority.[40]

Article 2. Separation *Propria Auctoritate*

As has been mentioned previously, the separation of the spouses was considered a public matter, and therefore the intervention of the ecclesiastical authority was necessary for such action to be legitimate.[41] However, in special cases wherein some real danger of spiritual or physical harm impended in consequence of any delay, separation on one's own authority was allowed. The law in this matter derived from the Decretals. The authors of the period interpreted this legislation as making provision in many very practical cases. They insisted upon the necessity of ecclesiastical recognition of these suits as a general norm but clearly pointed out that there were exceptions to the general rule.

As had been the practice through the history of canon law, the important reason for any separation *propria auctoritate* was adultery.[42] The fact of a consort's suspicion did not provide a sufficient reason for a separation. If the adultery of the other party was in any way doubtful, or if proofs of the crime did not in any way exceed the domains of mere probability, the intervention of the Church was necessary. In such an event, the hypothetically innocent party could not leave on his or her own authority, since there was not adequate basis for such action. Separation was not something arbitrary, not left to the discretion of the injured party to determine whether or not the proofs sufficed for a parting. Rather, if there was any doubt or uncertainty, the right to leave on one's own authority was denied.[43]

40 Conc. Trident., sess. XXIV, *de matrimonio,* Canon 8; Wernz, *Ius Decretalium,* IV, n. 713.

41 Cf. *supra,* p. 45.

42 S. C. C., Florentina, 29 mart. 1727—*Thesaurus Resolutionum S. C. C.,* IV, 33.

43 Sanchez, Lib. X, disp. XII, nn. 2, 3, 4; Pirhing, *Ius Canonicum,* Lib. IV, tit. XIX, n. 16; Schmalzgrueber, Lib. IV, tit. XIX, n. 110; *Austrian Instruction,* Sec. 205, 241—*Collectio Lacensis,* V, coll. 1311. 1314; Feije, *De Impedi-*

The case of a notorious and certain adultery was another matter. If such a circumstance was present, then the authors did not hinder an aggrieved spouse from leaving an unfaithful partner. This opinion was based on the evangelical provision permitting separation for adultery. The authors were of the view that since the sin was notorious and certain, no further proof was necessary and the law which allowed a separation on such grounds also allowed a separation to be effected by the innocent spouse.[44]

Another general reason allowing a separation prior to an ecclesiastical decree was the possibility of danger in delay. It was not difficult to envisage cases wherein such danger could exist. A wife in leaving an insane, cruel or immoral husband might endanger her life or spiritual well-being by remaining to await a judgment of the Church. In this type of case, a separation effected on the aggrieved party's own authority was permissible. When peaceful cohabitation was impossible, there was no necessity of prolonging the imminent danger of physical or spiritual harm. A real threat to the innocent party had to be present; mere whims and fancied notions of harm were not sufficient. There had to be present a real and well founded danger in any delay.[45]

It is to be noted, however, that the authors of this period are more clear than the earlier writers on the significance of this type of separation. There is no doubt that they considered this leaving of an erring spouse an emergency measure. It is better termed a *discessus* than a *separatio*. The innocent spouse could leave because of the earlier mentioned causes, but a permanent decree of separation had to be sought in the ecclesiastical court. This applied to

mentis, p. 464; Wernz, *Ius Decretalium*, IV, n. 711; Gasparri, *De Matrimonio* 3. ed., II, n. 1368.

[44] Sanchez, Lib. X, disp. XII, nn. 12, 13, 25; Pirhing, *op. cit.*, n. 16, not. 2; Schmalzgrueber, Lib. IV, tit. XIX, n. 111; Reiffenstuel, Lib. IV, tit. XIX, n. 89; Joder, *Formulaire Matrimonial* (3. ed., Paris, 1891), p. 242; Wernz, *loc. cit.*; Gasparri, *loc. cit.*

[45] Cosci, *De Separatione Tori Coniugalis*, Lib. II, cap. V, n. 1; De Becker, *De Sponsalibus et Matrimonio Praelectiones Canonicae* (Lovanii, 1893), p. 399; Wernz, *op. cit.*, IV, n. 714; Gasparri, *op. cit.*, II, n. 1371.

all cases but notorious adultery. The reasons given were the avoidance of the scandal which otherwise might arise from this interruption of the common marital life, and the protection of the innocent party from later blame and legal action at the behest of the guilty partner.[46]

The case of a notorious adultery was another matter. Here according to most of the authors the distinction between a *discessus* and a *separatio* was not necessary. In this situation the reason for the separation, namely the crime of adultery was superfluous. Gasparrri stressed this idea very clearly when he saids *"Ratio est quia coniunx ad divortium ius habet ex ipsa Evangelii lege, ita ut sententia iudicis tantum declaret causam, idest adulterium, vereficari: atque haec declaratio non est, quando adulterium est certum et notorium."* [47]

Wernz seemed to stand alone in his support of the stricter view. He allowed a separation for notorious adultery because of the same reason, viz., the evangelical law, but he limited it as permissible *"saltem provisorie."* He concluded that since delusions can so easily be present with regard to the notoriety of adultery a definitive and permanent separation was not to be adopted apart from a sentence rendered by an ecclesiastical judge.[48] In his well-annotated work which normally abounds in substantiating footnotes, Wernz in this instance seemed to be presenting a personal opinion. This may be inferred from the absence of any footnote by way of substantiation against the more common opinion held by the several authors cited above. It seems then, that a spouse who had left the common marital life because of notorious adultery was legally separated, and no further judicial procedure was necessary according to the common opinion of the time.

[46] Sanchez, Lib. X, disp. 11, n. 7; Schmalzgrueber, Lib. IV, tit. XIX, n. 112; Feije, *De Impedimentis,* p. 465; Wernz, *op. cit.,* II, n. 711; Gasparri, *loc. cit.*

[47] *De Matrimonio* 3. ed., II, n. 1368. Support for this view may also be found in Sanchez, Lib. X, disp. XII, n. 12; Pirhing, *Ius Canonicum,* Lib. IV, tit. XIX, n. 16; Reiffenstuel, Lib. IV, tit. XIX, n. 89; Schmalzgrueber, Lib. IV, tit. XIX, n. 11; Feije, *De Impedimentis,* p. 465.

[48] *Ius Decretalium, loc. cit.*

Article 3. The Informal Procedure

There is evidence in this post-Tridentine period of the rise in many quarters of a practice that expedited separation cases in a less formal fashion than that prescribed in the ordinary procedural law. These were doubtless the beginnings of the administrative process as it is known in the law of the present day.[49] This tendency toward a shortened process was treated in the last chapter when reference was made to the constitutions *Dispendiosam* and *Saepe* of Pope Clement V (cf. *supra*, p. 38). As was noted there, the sources did not give a clear picture of the use of these constitutions in separation cases. Some authors held to the opinion that this type of case did not benefit from the liberty granted in these constitutions, while others favored their inclusion and seemed to be supported in this view by the actual practice then current. The canonical history of the period from the Council of Trent to the Code of Canon Law shows an increasing majority favoring the latter view.

There is a difficulty, however, in determining the exact nature of the shortened process of which mention was made during this era. In some instances it was clearly judicial but of a summary type; in others it was called extrajudicial and seemed to approximate the present day administrative procedure. In order to avoid any generalities which could lead to complication, the writer will seek to distinguish the two types through examples of the few cases found in the sources and canonical commentaries of this period.

From the time of the first appearance of the Clementine legislation (1312) which permitted summary trials until the constitution *Dei miseratione* of Pope Benedict XIV in 1741, there seem not to have been any legal enactments limiting the use of the summary process. However, Cerchiari points out a development designating a proceeding *mixti ordinis,* which, so he says, consisted of an inter-

49 The Pontifical Commission for the Authentic Interpretation of the Code of Canon Law allowed the use of the administrative form of procedure in cases of separation. Cf. *Pontificia Commissio Interpretationis* (hereafter cited P. C. I.), 25 iun. 1932—*Acta Apostolicae Sedis* (Romae, 1909—), XXIV (1932), 284 (hereafter cited *AAS*).

mingling of solemn or formal procedural elements with the shortened summary process.[50]

The earliest traceable author at least in the present writer's search who explicitly treated of the summary process in separation cases for this period is Sanchez. In his treatment of the procedure to be used in mission territories in the matter of separation and in the marriage of converts from paganism, he clearly admitted of the advisability of the shortened form. He stated that missionary judges might proceed: *"simpliciter, et de plano, absque tabellione et scriptura aliqua et iuramento testium."* He based his opinion on the great expenses involved in a formal trial as compared with the poverty of these people, as well as the difficulty in arriving at any certitude with witnesses. He directed the reader's attention to the fact that this did not signify a complete abandonment of all formalities, but that it rather justified a simplified process which still preserved the quality of a careful judicial investigation.

He distinctly pointed out that missionaries in these cases were acting in the capacity of judges with various privileges of the Holy See. He did not mention the exact nature of these privileges, but it seems derivable from his statement that missionary bishops customarily received such favors and subdelegated them to their priestly coworkers in the field.[51]

Other authors of the period until Benedict XIV continued to include marriage cases among the judicial suits that enjoyed the favor of the simpler process. Their unanimity was nevertheless confined to suits regarding the bond. Some, such as Reiffenstuel, simply included marriage cases without any express exclusion of separation trials.[52] Pirhing (1606-1679), on the other hand, while he permitted the summary treatment of marriage cases, distinctly excepted cases of separation on the ground of adultery.[53] Pellegrino (+ 1678) treated the question as Reiffenstuel; he neither expressly

[50] *Sacra Romana Rota,* I, p. 145, n. 44.

[51] Lib. X, disp. XIX, disp. XIX, nn. 1, 2. It is important to note that this author explicitly mentioned separation cases and did not confine his remarks to vincular litigations.

[52] Lib. I, tit. I, s. II, n. 47.

[53] *Ius Canonicum,* Lib. II, tit. 1, n. 104.

included nor expressly excepted separation cases from the summary procedure. He merely mentioned that marriage cases were regularly treated in summary fashion.[54] Worthy of note is the fact that this edition of Pellegrino was published two years after the constitution, *Dei miseratione*, of Benedict XIV, which had appeared in 1741. This monumental enactment had revised the procedure for matrimonial cases and according to good opinion had abrogated the Clementine summary process.[55] Yet, very soon after the appearance of this constitution there was evidence of a trend toward the shortened process as granted in indults and faculties from the Holy See.[56] Although these grants concerned vincular cases, nevertheless, there is evidence from other replies of the Holy See that a shortened form was tolerated in the hearing of separation trials. The first authoritative source on this matter that the writer has been able to discover was a reply of the Sacred Congregation of the Council in 1786. This was a response to a question regarding a separation case, and, although not explicit nor containing any express grants, the general tenor of the response implied the existence of a summary process in practice, and that even of an extra-judicial type.[57]

The nineteenth century brought clearer and more explicit legislation on this matter. There is clear evidence in the *Austrian Instruction* that in a case of necessity and for other grave reasons a briefer type or administrative procedure might be used.[58] Shortly after the appearance of this Instruction there was issued a reply from the Sacred Congregation of the Council which decided the separation suit of a woman in Bavaria whose husband had deserted her and emigrated to America. The Congregation instructed the Archbishop of Munich that the ordinary procedure in separation cases was the

[54] *Praxis Vicariorum* (ed. novissima, Venetiis, 1743), Pars II, sect. II, subj. I, intersec. 1, n. 8.

[55] Kennedy, *The Special Matrimonial Process in Cases of Evident Nullity*, The Catholic University of America Canon Law Studies, n. 93 (Washington, D. C.: The Catholic University of America, 1935), p. 47.

[56] S. C. C., *Theatina*, 18 iul et 9 sept. 1761—*Thesaurus Resolutionum S. C. C.*, XXX, 129, 134; S. C. C. *in Tanuen., Matrim.*, 30 iulii 1793, 28 ian. et 15 mart. 1794—*Op. cit.*, LXII, 184; LXIII, 2, 46.

[57] S. C. C., *Imolen.*, 11 mart. 1786—*Fontes*, n. 3850.

[58] Sec. 243—*Collectio Lacensis*, V, col. 1314.

formal process of the Decretals, but in a case such as this, with one party absent, a shorter form was permissible. Reference was made in this response to the treatment by Sanchez on this matter as mentioned above. The Roman Congregation concluded its remarks by stating: "*Consuetudo in Bavaria existens circa modum procedendi in causis separationis quoad thorum et habitationem non adversatur iuri canonico.*" This is indeed clear evidence of an official recognition of the informal process by the ecclesiastical authority.[59] The explicit concession of his response served to strengthen the toleration shown in an earlier reply of the same Congregation treating of a separation case. In this prior statement, the Congregation ruled that the formal process was the ordinary method, but accepted a case for review which had been heard in the summary fashion. It even went so far as to point out the necessary elements of the summary procedure.[60]

Authors of the period were not very complete in their treatment of the summary and administrative procedures. For the most part they allowed the shortened judicial process to be used, although they pointed out that the formal method was still the ordinary legal mode of treatment. Thus Bouix (+ 1870) [61] and Feije (+ 1894) [62] limited their remarks, but Santi (+ 1885) generally demanded the regular judicial trial, although he recommended that attention be paid to the aforementioned reply to the Archbishop of Munich regarding the shorter process.[63] Wernz, however, summarized the relation of the three methods of procedure by stating: "*cum ex disciplina vigente in hisce causis nequaquam solemnis vel ordinarius processus canonicus adhiberi debeat, sed summarius usui esse possit, imo quandoque extraiudicialis procedendi modus toleretur.*" This state-

[59] S. C. C., *Monacen.*, 23 ian. 1875—*Thesaurus Resolutionum S. C. C.*, CXXXIV, p. 103. Only a reference to the title and date of issuance is made in this source. A complete copy of this response may be found in Santi, *Praelectiones Iuris Canonici*, Lib. II, tit. VI, n. 8.

[60] S. C. C., 31 iul. 1869—*AAS*, V (1869), 3, 11. A further description of this type of case was included in Appendix I of the same volume, 35 ff.

[61] *De Judiciis*, II, 441.

[62] *De Impedimentis*, p. 491.

[63] *Praelectiones Iuris Canonici*, Lib. IV, tit. XIX, n. 60.

ment clearly shows the general acceptance of the different processes in separation cases at his time.[64]

It may be noted that there is not apparent in every instance a clear distinction between the summary judicial process and what is known as the administrative process. Doubtless because of the early stages of development of the latter type, a distinct concept was now shown in canonical literature. The clearest exposition, and one important for the United States, was presented by Smith (1845-1895). He distinguished between the requirements of the letter of the law and the demands deriving through custom. According to the letter of the law, he demanded three necessary elements for a legitimate separation, namely, a just cause, a summary judicial process or trial, and a judicial sentence of the judge granting the separation. He then asserted that by custom, prevailing both in the United States and in Europe, separation cases, at least those that did not entail a permanent departure were treated more informally. In his opinion a separation for a just cause, approved by the bishop or the parish priest, and consequently without any judicial process or sentence, was legitimate. The basis for this view in his mind was clearly inferable from the fact that the Instruction which the Sacred Congregation for the Propagation of the Faith sent to the United States in 1883 made no requirement of a judicial trial in separation suits. Further support was found in the omission by the III Plenary Council of Baltimore of any definite provision on this matter, despite the custom in this country toward the informal process.[65] This argument was further supported by the recommendation of the III Plenary Council of Baltimore regarding the use of the Austrian Instruction.[66] Inasmuch as this Instruction contained provisions for the use of the administrative procedure, its recommendation as a procedural norm for the bishops of the country presented an implicit indication of the mind of the Fathers of the Council on the use of this type of procedure.

[64] *Ius Decretalium,* IV, n. 714.

[65] Smith, *The Marriage Process in the United States* (New York, 1893), nn. 79-80.

[66] *Acta et Decreta Concilii Plenarii Baltimorensis Tertii, A. D.* MDCCCLXXXIV, n. 304.

By way of summary it may be noted that, despite the provisions for a shorter process, the formal judicial procedure remained the legal norm in this period. The summary procedure in separation cases gradually began to share the benefits of the shortened process allowed to other marriage cases and soon became very general. The more informal or administrative procedure gradually developed from the need and necessity felt in mission lands for a more expeditious treatment. By force of custom in many places, it soon appeared to have the tolerance, at least, of the ecclesiastical authority.

PART II

CANONICAL COMMENTARY

CHAPTER IV

THE NATURE OF THE PROPER CANONICAL PROCESS IN SEPARATION CASES

Article 1. Preliminary Notions

The art of concise yet exact expression, so characteristic of the eminent compilers of the Code of Canon Law, reaches a full demonstration in the Code's affirmation of the unity and indissolubility of marriage. Summarizing centuries of legislation and canonical writings, the law today is succinct but accurate in defining the essential properties of the great social sacrament.[1] To emphasize the important property of unity and its accompanying element of the common life, the Code of Canon Law again in brief form, but very clearly, reminds the married partners of their mutual obligations which arise from the exchange of marital consent. It states: "*Coniuges servare debent vitae coniugalis communicationem, nisi iusta causa excuset.*"[2] This obligation is based on the natural law, since the ends of marriage could not otherwise be properly attained. Even the positive divine law enjoins this community of life, that the union might be fruitful and successful, with regard both to its sacramental purposes and to the consorts themselves.[3] Not indeed of minor import is this obligation. Gasparri pointed out that it is founded in the virtue of justice as a result of the mutually exchanged

1 Canon 1013, §2: Essentiales matrimonii proprietates sunt unitas ac indissolubilitas quae in matrimonio christiano peculiarem obtinent firmitatem ratione sacramenti.

2 Canon 1128.

3 "Wherefore a man shall leave father and mother, and shall cleave to his wife: and they shall be two in one flesh."—Gen., II:24.

marital consent,[4] and the common law demonstrates the gravity of this responsibility in demanding a just cause for a separation.

In interpreting the phrase, "just cause," found so often in the law, no absolute norm can be stated; rather, each canon wherein it is contained must be judged on its own merits. Who is to judge when it is a matter of conjugal separation? Since marriage is a social institution, the private judgment of the consorts surely does not suffice as a general norm. There is need of a higher authority. Inasmuch as cohabitation is so intimately connected with the integrity of the sacrament,[5] any breach of this mutual obligation pertains to the public good.[6] It is for this reason that the public authority of the Church must be invoked whether it be through its procedural norms or through a permission granted in the law itself. Especially important is this today when married life is considered by so many as a private matter, to be continued or disrupted at the will of the parties.

Regularly, a canonical separation, i.e., a separation from bed, board and cohabitation is subject to a hearing before the Church if it is to be final.[7] It results in either the complete cessation or at least a temporary interruption of the common life of the consorts, with the marriage bond of course remaining intact. Consequently, it is subject to the jurisdiction of the Church and is to be treated according to its processual regulations.[8] Before proceeding with the study

[4] *Tractatus Canonicus de Matrimonio,* ed. nova ad mentem Codicis Iuris Canonici, 2 vols., Romae: Typis Polyglottis Vaticanis, 1932, II, n. 1102 (hereafter referred to as *De Matrimonio*).

[5] S.R.R., *Separationis,* 3 ian. 1929, coram R.P.D. Henrico Quattrocolo, dec. I, n. 2—*Decisiones,* XXI (1929), 3; Cappello, *Tractatus Canonico-Moralis De Sacramentis* (5 vols., Vol. V, 5. ed., Romae: Marietti, 1947), V, nn. 827-828 (hereafter referred to as *De Sacramentis*); Gasparri, *loc. cit.*

[6] S.R.R., *Separationis quoad Thorum et Mensam,* 5 iul. 1910, coram R.mo.P.D. Michaeli Lega, Decano, dec. XXIV, n. 11—*Decisiones,* II (1910), 243; S.R.R., *Separationis,* 6 aug. 1930, coram R.P.D. Andrea Jullien, dec. XLVII, n. 2—*Decisiones,* XXII (1930), 524; *Normae S.R.Rotae Tribunalis,* 29 iun. 1934, Art. 27—*AAS,* XXVI (1934), 457.

[7] Canon 1960.

[8] Noval, *Commentarium Codicis Iuris Canonici,* Liber IV, *De Processibus,* Pars I, *De Iudiciis* (Augustae Taurinorum—Romae: Marietti, 1920), p. 557 (hereafter referred to as *De Iudiciis*).

of these procedural norms, and with a view to understanding better the ecclesiastical law relative to this institute, the writer deems it feasible at this point to present in outline form some of the notions used in its treatment.

The first distinction to note is that between a temporary and a permanent separation. The Church has ever recognized the sin of marital infidelity to be a just cause for a permanent separation on the part of the innocent spouse. It repeats this cause, founded in the divine law,[9] and presents it as the only legitimate reason for a perpetual separation provided it was not caused or condoned in any way by the aggrieved consort.[10]

Besides this historical ground, the Church recognizes other reasons for the discontinuance of the common life,[11] but only as a temporary measure.[12] Notwithstanding the fact that this temporary parting may be for a determinate or indeterminate time, it is of a temporary nature and never to be considered permanent, despite the possibility of the latter resulting in such. In addition to these notions, certain authors distinguish a legitimate separation and a

[9] Matt., V:32.

[10] Canon 1129, § 1: Propter coniugis adulterium, alter coniux, manente vinculo, ius habet solvendi, etiam in perpetuum, vitae communionem, nisi in crimen consenserit, aut eidem causam dederit, vel illud expresse aut tacite condonaverit, vel ipse quoque idem crimen commiserit.

§ 2: Tacita condonatio habetur, si coniux innocens, postquam de crimine adulterii centior factus est, cum altero coniuge sponte, maritali affectu, conversatus fuerit; praesumitur vero, nisi sex intra menses coniugem adulterum expulerit vel dereliquerit, aut legitimam accusationem fecerit.

[11] Con. Trident., sess. XXIV, *de matrimonio,* canon 8.

[12] Canon 1131, § 1: Si alter coniux sectae acatholicae nomen dederit; si prolem acatholicae educaverit; si vitam criminosam et ignominiosam ducat; si grave seu animae seu coporis periculum alteri fecessat: si saevitiis vitam communem nimis difficilem reddat, haec aliaque id genus, sunt pro altero coniuge totidem legitimae causae discedendi, auctoritate Ordinarii loci, et etiam propria auctoritate, si de eis certo constet, et periculum sit in mora.

§ 2: In omnibus his casibus, causa separationis cessante, vitae consuetudo restauranda est, sed si separatio ab Ordinario pronuntiata fuerit ad certum incertumve tempus, coniux innocens ad id non obligatur, nisi ex decreto Ordinarii vel exacto tempore.

legitimate departure.[13] An awareness of this difference is important when the institute of separation *propria auctoritate* is examined.

Article 2. The Authority for Separation

To understand fully the procedural norms to be observed in the canonical separation of the spouses, one must necessarily for an integral treatment determine the proper authority for the effecting of such a state, and give consideration especially to the canonically known institute of separation by the private authority of an aggrieved consort. This is important inasmuch as a separation juridically sanctioned by the Church bears with it certain canonical effects. Noteworthy among these is the fact that such a legal separation is a determinant for an independent domicile on the part of the wife, who would normally have as a necessary domicile that of her husband.[14] As a consequence, the establishment of jurisdiction both judicial and voluntary will be affected.

There has ever been much discussion and controversy among the authors on this matter as has been seen in the preceding historical synopsis. Since the law is not absolutely definite, this controversy continues today, especially in the light of a reply of the Pontifical Commission for the Authentic Interpretation of the Code of Canon

[13] Gibbons, *Domicile of Wife Unlawfully Separated from her Husband,* The Catholic University of America Canon Law Studies, n. 249 (Washington, D. C.: The Catholic University of America Press, 1947), p. 77; Hines, *De Coniugum Separatione ac de Civili Divortio in Iure Canonico et in Iure Civili Statuum Foederatorum Americae Septentrionalis* (Pontificium Institutum Utriusque Iuris, Theses ad Lauream, n. 62 (Romae: Officium Libri Catholici, 1949), p. 47 (hereafter referred to as *De Coniugum Separatione*); Regatillo, *Ius Sacramentarium* (2 vols., Santander: Sal Terrae, 1945-1946), II, n. 588; Torre, *Processus Matrimonialis,* p. 14; Sartori, *Enchiridion Canonicum* (8. ed., Romae: Pontificium Athenaeum Antonianum, 1947), p. 13, ad canon 93.

[14] Canon 93, § 1: Uxor, a viro legitime non separata, necessario retinet domicilium viri sui; amens, domicilium curatoris; minor, domicilium illius cuius potestati subiicitur.

§ 2: Minor infantia egressus potest quasi-domicilium proprium obtinere; item uxor a viro legitime non separata, legitime autem separata etiam domicilium.

It is immaterial whether the wife is the innocent or guilty spouse; once the legitimate separation takes place, the canonical effects follow—Forbes, *The Canonical Separation of Consorts,* Universitas Catholica Ottaviensis, Series

Law,[15] and of the Instruction issued by the Sacred Congregation of the Sacraments under the date of August 15, 1936.[16] Although some authors have changed their opinions as held in the past on this institute in view of the foregoing authoritative declarations, the question is far from officially settled, nor is there now any closer agreement among the authors than there was in the past.

No canonist would deny that it is regularly left to the public authority of the Church, namely the ordinary of the diocese, to render a decision whether or not in a particular case a just cause for separation is present. To the same authority it is left to decide if this separation is to be perpetual or temporary, and, if it be the latter, for a determinant or an indeterminate period of time.[17] Such unanimity is not present in any discussion of the institute of separation *propria auctoritate* as it is delineated in Canons 1130 and 1131.

Canonica—Tom. 15 (Ottawa, Ontario: The University of Ottawa Press, 1948), p. 233.

[15] P.C.I., 14 iul. 1922:—"Utrum uxor, a viro malitiose deserta, possit, ad normam canon 93, § 2, obtinere proprium ac distinctum domicilium. Resp. Negative, nisi a iudice ecclesiastico obtinuerit separationem perpetuam, aut ad tempus indefinitum."—*AAS*, XIV (1922), 526.

[16] S.C. de Sacramentis, instr. 15 aug. 1936:—

Art. 6, § 1: Uxor, etsi a viro malitiose deserta, eum convenire debet vel coram Ordinario loci in quo matrimonium celebratum est, vel coram Ordinario domicilii vel quasi-domicilii viri ipsius.

§ 2: Uxor, a viro perpetuo aut ad tempus indefinitum separata legitime, i. e. per sententiam iudicialem competentis tribunalis ecclesiastici, vel etiam civilis a S. Sede, vi concordati, recognitam, aut per Ordinarii decretum, non sequitur domicilium viri, ideoque conveniri debet vel coram Ordinario loci in quo nuptiae initae sunt, vel coram Ordinario sui domicilii vel quasi-domicilii.

§ 3: Uxor catholica, etsi a viro non legitime separata, virum acatholicum convenire potest vel coram Ordinario proprii ac distincti quasi-domicilii, vel coram Ordinario domicilii viri (Comm. Pont., 14 iulii 1922 ad canon 93 et 1964).—*AAS*, XXVIII (1936), 313-370 (hereafter referred to as *Instructio*).

[17] Canons 1129; 1130; 1131; Vermeersch-Creusen, *Epitome Iuris Canonici* (3 vols., Vol. I, 7. ed., 1949; Vol. II, 6. ed., 1940; Vol. III, 6. ed., 1946, Mechliniae-Romae: H. Dessain), I, 181; Wernz-Vidal, *Ius Canonicim,* II, n. 12; Cappello, *De Sacramentis,* V, n. 827-828; Coronata, *Institutiones Iuris Canonici* (2. ed., 5 vols., Taurini: Marietti, 1939-1947), I, n. 126, ftn. 7: Ojetti, *Commentarium in Codicem Iuris Canonici* (4 vols., Romae: apud Aedes Universitatis Gregorianae, 1927-1931), II, 53.

The matter constitutes a moot point with many divergent opinions, all of considerable merit.

The Code of Canon Law envisages two distinct classes of cases wherein an innocent consort may separate from his guilty partner on his or her own initiative. It states that adultery on the part of one consort grants to the innocent spouse the right to dissolve the community of life, even perpetually, although the bond of marriage remains intact.[18] A temporary separation is the subject of Canon 1131. Here again the same term, *"propria auctoritate,"* is found, but with a qualification. The law permits a temporary separation at the behest of the innocent consort, provided that the grounds outlined in this canon are certainly present, but a condition is added. There must be a state of emergency or some danger in delay, whether physical or moral.

Surely this permission at first sight is to be considered a concession of a remarkable order. Having seen the importance of the common life of the consorts in the Church's exalted doctrine of marriage, all must admit that a great freedom is bestowed here. Because it is an exception to the usual norm, it demands study, and fortunately it has been given much by many esteemed authors.

In this matter there are three outstanding opinions, each supported by authors of merit. Each has been argued well by its proponents and given much attention. However, inasmuch as the law is not absolutely clear, until such time that the Holy See promulgates further authoritative information, each opinion enjoys, so it seems, a parity of probability and may be followed in practice.

Forbes, in his well executed work, presents as the common opinion the view that accords an aggrieved consort who separates according to the law on his or her own authority[19] the capacity of acquiring the canonical effects deriving from a legitimate separation. Most important of these is an independent domicile for the separated wife.[20] This may operate whether the separation is a permanent one

18 Canons 1129; 1130. A fuller study of the necessary qualifications for a canonically recognized sin of unfaithfulness will be treated in the article on judicial exceptions (cf. infra, p. 92).

19 Canon 1129; 1130; 1131.

20 *The Canonical Separation of Consorts,* p. 233.

because of the other spouse's certain and manifest adultery, or a temporary separation based on the causes treated in Canon 1131.[21] In this latter case it is also necessary that the cause be certain and that there be a danger in delay to the innocent spouse. The intervention of the ordinary according to this view is not necessary for the party's attaining of the canonical effects of a legitimate separation. Therefore a wife who is so separated from her husband may acquire her own independent domicile.[22] Although Forbes concludes that this is still the common interpretation of Canon 93, § 2 and Canons 1129, 1130 and 1131, he does so with a certain reserve. In practice, despite the statement of this opinion, he would recommend a decree of the ordinary to obviate any doubt regarding competency in judicial acts.[23]

A more rigid opinion is well presented by Gibbons, who expressly treated the subject of the domicile of the unlawfully separated wife. Viewing the matter in the light of the opinion as proposed by Ragatillo,[24] he distinguishes a legitimate separation from a legitimate

21 Vermeersch-Creusen, *Epitome Iuris Canonici,* I, 181; Ojetti, *Commentarium in Codicem Iuris Canonici,* II, 54; Oesterle, *Praelectiones Iuris Canonici,* Vol. I (Romae: Collegium S. Anselmi, 1931), p. 55; Berutti, *Institutiones Iuris Canonici* (5 vols., Vol. II, Taurini-Romae: Marietti, 1943), II, 13; Wernz-Vidal, *Ius Canonicum,* II, n. 12, ftn. 9; Cocchi, *Commentarium in Codicem Iuris Canonici* (8 vols., in 5, Vol. II, 4. ed., Taurinorum Augustae: Marietti, 1937), II, 23; Cappello, *Summa Iuris Canonici,* I, p. 160, n. 194; Costello, *Domicile and Quasi-Domicile,* The Catholic University of America Canon Law Studies, n. 60 (Washington, D. C.: The Catholic University of America, 1930), pp. 163, 164; Toso, *Ad Codicem Iuris Canonici . . . Commentaria Minora* (5 vols. in 2, Vol. II, *De Personis,* Tom. I, Taurini-Romae, 1922), II, 20; Doheny, *Canonical Procedure in Matrimonial Cases* (2 vols., Vol. I, *Formal Judicial Procedure,* 2. ed., 1947, Vol. II, Informal Procedure, 1943, Milwaukee: Bruce Publishing Co.), II, 649, 650; Beste, *Introductio in Codicem* (Collegeville, Minn.: St. John's Abbey Press, 1938), p. 139.

22 Forbes, *op. cit.,* p. 234.

23 *Op. cit.,* p. 237. This is a general recommendation of authors who favor this opinion.

24 "Effectus separationis propria auctoritate factae—Haec habet effectum *mere moralem,* in ordine ad quietem conscientiae. Scilicet in casibus supra indicatis coniux innocens *licite* discedit. At valore iuridico caret, nempe quoad effectus iuris. [. . .]. Separatio legitima, qua iuxta c. 93 § 2, potest uxor acquirere domicilium proprium, definitur a C. Sacram, loc. cit. art. 6 § 2

departure. The former is a juridical separation with its accompanying canonical effects, permanent or temporary as the case may be, having been decreed in an antecedent canonical procedure before the ecclesiastical authority.[25] The legitimate departure, on the other hand, connotes a juridical state, but devoid of the canonical or juridical effects of the above mentioned authoritatively adjudicated separation. This is the separation *propria auctoritate* of Canons 1129-1131. In this instance, provided that the conditions of a certain cause and a certain urgency in delay are present, should it not be a case of adultery,[26] the aggrieved consort may depart from his or her guilty partner and licitly continue this state of separation. However, until the time that the Church has juridically sanctioned this departure by means of an authoritative sentence or decree, it is not a legitimate separation. The wife in such a case is considered *"legitime non separata"* in the sense of Canon 93, § 2. As a consequence, she retains the domicile of her husband. She can do no more than establish a quasi-domicile of her own.[27]

Kelly and Hines, in treating the separation that is effected *propria auctoritate,* grant it canonical recognition, but demand exactly the same conditions whether it be a permanent separation because of adultery or a temporary separation. In such cases, they demand a certainty of cause, which all would concede, but place the

quae fit *per sententiam iudicis aut per Ordinarii decretum in perpetuum vel ad tempus indefinitum."—Ius Sacramentarium,* II, 398.

25 *Domicile of Wife Unlawfully Separated from Her Husband,* p. 45.

26 Canon 1131.

27 Gibbons, *op. cit.*, p. 90, Gibbons is supported in this view by Regatillo (*Ius Sacramentarium,* II, n. 588), Bouscaren-Ellis (*Canon Law* [Milwaukee: Bruce, 1947], pp. 81, 82), Sartori (*Enchiridion Canonicum,* p. 13, ad Canon 93), Benedetti (*Ordo Iudicialis super Nullitate Matrimonii Instruendi* [ed. nov. Taurini: Marietti, 1938], p. 15), Torre (*Processus Matrimonialis,* p. 14), Toso, "Commentarium ad resp.P.C.I. 14 iulii 1922 ad Canon 93, § 2," *Ius Pontificum* [Romae 1921 - 1940], II [1922], 84) and Doheny (*Canonical Procedure in Matrimonial Cases,* I, p. 31). It is noteworthy that Toso and Doheny in earlier works favored the more lenient opinion stated above, while Regatillo in his earlier *Institutiones Iuris Canonici* (2 vols., Santander: Sal Terrae, 1941-1942), I, 112, although permitting separation *propria auctoritate* in cases of adultery, allowed it only as a provisional measure in cases of a temporary separation.

further requirement of danger in delay in all instances. This last condition, therefore, would even be necessary in cases of certain adultery. They substantiate this position by comparing Canons 1130 and 1131. They note that since Canon 1131 demands the condition of danger in delay in addition to a certain cause, this element must also be present in separations effected *propria auctoritate* for adultery. The reason: if this condition of emergency is necessary for temporary separations, it must also be demanded in perpetual separations, which by comparison are of much greater significance.[28] In treating the canonical effects of separation, both authors favor denying to the separated wife her own domicile prior to an ecclesiastical hearing. They do not, however, espouse this opinion as heartily and forceably as Gibbons.[29]

Another opinion distinguishes the two types of separation effected *propria auctoritate*. It allows the canonical effects immediately to a separation effected because of certain adultery, but in the case of temporary separation it demands an authoritative review of the case if the effects are to follow. This is the correct interpretation of this institute in the opinion of the writer. This preference is not based on an endeavor to reach an arbitrary norm between the two opinions as stated above, but it is stated as the position which retains the spirit of the law most faithfully.

The common opinion of the authors in the period before the promulgation of the Code of Canon Law, as has been noted in the brief historical synopsis presented earlier, embraced this interpretation. For a spouse to separate on his or her own initiative because of a certain sin of marital infidelity perpetrated by the other consort was considered entirely legitimate. No further authoritative decree was needed inasmuch as the right was already granted in the evangelical law.[30] Any sentence by the ecclesiastical authority was considered unnecessary and superfluous.[31]

28 Hines, *De Coniugum Separatione*, p. 19; Kelly, "Separation and Civil Divorce," *The Jurist*, VI (1946), 203; idem, "Divorce—Some Practical Canonical Considerations," *The Jurist*, IX (1949), 196.

29 Hines, *op. cit.*, p. 47; Kelly, *op. cit.*, p. 204; idem, *loc. cit.*

30 Matt., V:32.

31 Sanchez, Lib. X, disp. XII, n. 12; Pirhing *Ius Canonicum*, Lib. IV, tit. XIX, n. 16; Reiffenstuel, Lib. IV, tit. XIX, n. 89; Schmalzgrueber, Lib. IV,

In the matter of temporary separations, the earlier writers postulated as today a just cause and danger in delay. As long as these conditions were present they did not compel an aggrieved consort to risk physical and moral danger in awaiting an authoritative judgment. Rather, such a consort was permitted to depart on his or her own authority to escape any possible harm. This separation was considered an emergency measure, and necessitated subsequent action in the ecclesiastical forum to be legitimate. Consequently, it is termed a *discessus* rather than a *separatio*. Once it had been adjudicated before the Church, the separation was legal and final.[82]

In examining the recent legislation on the institute of separation effected *propria auctoritate,* as contained in canons 1129-1131, it is difficult to find any real departure or developments in this institute from the interpretation of the pre-Code authors. Moreover, it does not seem presumptuous to assert that the incorporation of this institute in the present legislation is actually an acceptance of the common opinion of the earlier authors. As a consequence of this it seems that this interpretation should be preferred today. Inasmuch as the responses of the Holy See on the matter of independent domicile of the wife use the terms perpetually or for an indeterminate period of time, this view is quite reasonable. Since a separation for adultery is perpetual, there is no problem of the intention to remain perpetually in some place to obtain a domicile. In the matter of a temporary separation resulting *propria auctoritate,* the temporal element never clearly relates to a definite or an indefinite period of time. Therefore, the only sensible solution for the avoidance of arbitrary decisions by separated spouses is to demand an ecclesiastical review in every case of temporary separation for the obtaining of the canonical effects.

Although in comparison with the above mentioned common opinion this view might be called that of the minority, nevertheless, there are not lacking authors of merit who favor this view. Although in

tit. IX, n. 11; Feije, *De Impedimentis,* p. 465; Gasparri, *De Matrimonio,* 3. ed., II, n. 1368.

[82] Sanchez, Lib. X, disp. XII, n. 7; Schmalzgrueber, Lib. IV, tit. XIX, n. 112; Feije, *De Impedimentis,* p. 465; Gasparri, *De Matrimonio,* 3. ed., II, n. 1368; Wernz, *Ius Decretalium,* IV, n. 711.

number these do not constitute a formidable array of authors, yet they are not to be summarily dismissed.[33]

By way of summary, then, it is the opinion of the writer that a separation instituted *propria auctoritate* by an aggrieved consort because of a certain and manifest sin of adultery perpetrated by the other spouse obtains legal recognition. As a result, he or she benefits from all the canonical effects of a canonical separation. In this instance the wife would be legitimately separated and therefore capable of acquiring her own domicile. The element of danger in delay is not necessary in this case, since the very nature of such a separation is not that of an emergency measure, but essentially is of a peremptory and decisive character.

In the matter of temporary separations, i. e., such as are undertaken not on the grounds of adultery, the distressed spouse may lawfully depart provided there is present a certain just cause and the exigency of danger in delay, but is not to be considered as legitimately separated. To achieve a canonical sanction for such a state of separation, it is necessary that the case be presented to the ecclesiastical authority for review. Antecedent to this authoritative recognition, the innocent consort is to be considered as having legitimately departed, and subsequent to it, the status becomes one of legitimate separation. In the latter instance the juridical effects would be obtained and a wife so separated could acquire a legal status that permits her to establish a voluntary domicile.

Article 3. The Nature of the Process

The Code of Canon Law in the canons which refer to separation is merely demonstrative of the type of procedure to be observed in

[33] Coronata, *Institutiones Iuris Canonici,* I, n. 126, ftn. 7; Noldin-Schmitt, *Summa Theologiae Moralis* (3 vols., Vol. III, 26. ed., Oeniponte-Lipsiae: Rauch, 1940), III, nn. 666, 667; Merkelbach, *Summa Theologiae Moralis* (3 vols., Vol. III, 5. ed., De Brouwer: Desclée, 1947), III, n. 969; Manucci, "Annotazioni ad alcune ultime risposte della Commissione per la interpretazione autentica del Codice, Canon 93," *Il Monitore Ecclesiastico* (Romae: Desclée, 1876—), Vol. XXXIV (1922), 339, 340; Kinane, "Regarding the Acquisition of Domicile," *Irish Ecclesiastical Record* (Dublin: Browne and Nolan, 1864—), 5. series, XX (1922), 408, 409; Chelodi-Ciprotti, *Ius Canonicum de Matrimonio* (5. ed., Vicenza: Società Anonima, 1947), n. 162 (hereafter referred to as *De Matrimonio*).

invoking the public authority of the Church for the settlement of separation cases. The law is concerned primarily with an exposition of the nature and a description of the causes for separation, it mentions the procedure in merely an incidental fashion. In the legislation for permanent separations on the grounds of adultery, there is found the following brief phrase: "*iudicis sententia,*" [34] when there is question of a temporary separation pleaded on grounds other than adultery, this phrase is used: "*auctoritate ordinarii loci*" and "*ex decreto Ordinarii.*" [35]

At first reading the canons give the impression that a sentence of an ecclesiastical judge subsequent to a full judicial procedure is the norm in cases of separation pleaded on the grounds of adultery. Cases tried on the grounds mentioned in Canon 1131 are to be settled in the administrative fashion by a decree of the ordinary.

However, considered in the light of the law as it was before the present Code of Canon Law, when the judicial process was the ordinary form in all cases of separation, with the administrative process not much more than tolerated,[36] one may readily conclude that this norm still exists.[37] The latter method is of course received with a greater degree of acceptance today than in the earlier law, as a result of the response in 1932 of the Pontifical Commission for the Authentic Interpretation of the Code of Canon Law, which prescribed the use of the administrative process in the cases of temporary separation contemplated in canon 1131, § 1, unless the ordinary, either "*ex officio*" or at the instance of the parties, decided otherwise.[38]

[34] Canon 1130: Coniux innocens sive *iudicis sententia* sive propria auctoritate legitime discesserit, nulla unquam obligatione tenetur coniugem adulterum rursus admittendi ad vitae consortium; potest autem eundem admittere aut revocare, nisi ex ipsius consensu ille statum matrimonio contrarium susceperit.

[35] Canon 1131. *Instructio,* Art. 6, § 2.

[36] Wernz, *Ius Decretalium,* IV, n. 714; Roberti, "De Separatione Coniugis," *Apollinaris* (Romae, 1928—), V (1932), 295.

[37] Wernz-Vidal, *Ius Canonicum,* V, p. 848.

[38] P.C.I. 25 iun. 1932—"D. An separatio coniugum ob causas, de quibus in Canone 1131, § 1, forma administrative decernenda sit. R. Affirmative, nisi ab ordinario aliter statuatur ex officio vel ad instantiam partium.—*AAS,* XXIV (1932), 284.

There are those who in this same response find a basis for holding that the administrative method is now the ordinary form for hearing all separation cases. This is the conclusion of Cappello. He reasons that if the consorts may separate on their own authority,[39] *a fortiori*, the ordinary may regularly decide such cases in the administrative fashion, omitting as a rule the formal judicial process. His argument is based on the fact that canon 1131 omits all mention of an ecclesiastical judge. Furthermore note must be taken of the loss of time and of the greater expense involved in the formal process. He does concede, however, that this is not a necessary rule for at the instance of the parties or even on his own initiative, in keeping with the above mentioned reply, the ordinary may employ the formal process and thus may depart from the ordinary norm.[40]

Both of these opinions seem to be too comprehensive and general. It is true, as Wernz-Vidal state, that the judicial process was the ordinary method before the Code of Canon Law, but at the same time the administrative method had developed more by common usage than through positive legislation and was therefore merely tolerated. The present law, as found especially in Canon 1131, is much too positive to confine this latter method to such a quasi-recognized state today. Rather, it seems that in conjunction with the above mentioned authoritative interpretation, Canon 1131 has raised the administrative method to a much higher level of acceptance. It is now a valid, legal method, equal in status with the judicial form.

The proper conclusion from Canons 1130 and 1131 and the authentic interpretation of the latter is that the two methods share in a parity of legal recognition, and each may be called an ordinary method for the type of case being treated; the judicial process for a permanent suit of separation pleaded on the ground of adultery and the administrative method for cases based on other causes.[41]

39 Canons 1130; 1131.

40 Cappello, *De Sacramentis*, V, 827; Sartori, *Enchiridion Canonicum*, p. 233 ad Canon 1131, § 1.

41 Forbes, *The Canonical Separation of the Consorts*, p. 193; Chrétien, *De Matrimonio* (Metis: Hocquard, 1937), n. 278; Chelodi-Ciprotti, *De Matrimonio*, nn. 161, 162; Jemolo, *Il Matrimonio nel Diritto Canonico* (Milano: Vollardi.

It is to be noted that the response of the Pontifical Commission for the Authentic Interpretation of the Code of Canon Law was concerned with Canon 1131, with no mention having been made of Canon 1130. Keeping in mind the provisions of Canon 1130 a treatment of separation because of adultery, and of Canon 1131, which deals with temporary separation for other causes, the acceptable conclusion seems to be that the administrative method could serve as the ordinary process in the cases contemplated in Canon 1131, and the judicial process as the ordinary procedure for the cases of permanent separation on the grounds of adultery.

This view seems confirmed by even a cursory study of the decisions rendered by the Sacred Roman Rota. There it is seen how difficult the proof of adultery is in the ordinary case, and in consequence there arises the necessity of employing presumptions in order to arrive at a moral certitude. Although comparatively few cases of separation have been heard before this august tribunal since its reconstitution in 1908, nevertheless those that have come before it reflect a good directive norm for judges. Of the thirteen separation suits reviewed from 1908 to 1940, eight were concerned with permanent separations because of adultery. In each case the separation was denied because of insufficient proof. Needless to say, this is ample testimony of the usual difficulty anyone encounters in seeking to prove the fact of adultery and therefore points to the need of detailed consideration.[42]

Moreover, adultery is the only ground for perpetual separation,

1947), n. 178; Roberti, "De Separatione Coniugum," *Apollinaris,* V (1932), 295; Regatillo, *Ius Sacramentarium,* II, nn. 586, 587.

[42] S.R.R., *Separationis,* 3 ian. 1929, coram R.P.D. Henrico Quattrocolo, dec. I—*Decisiones,* XXI (1929), 1; S.R.R., *Separationis,* 6 dec. 1929, coram R.P.D. Francisco Morano, dec. LXIII—*Decisiones,* XXI (1929), 524; S.R.R. *Separationis,* 6 aug. 1930, coram R.P.D. Andrea Jullien, dec. XLVII—*Decisiones,* XXII (1930), 523; S.R.R., *Separationis,* 8 ian. 1937, coram R.P.D. Ioanne Teodori, dec. I—*Decisiones,* XXIX (1937), 1; S.R.R., *Separationis,* 30 maii 1938, coram R.P.D. Arcturo Wynen, dec. XXXIII—*Decisiones,* XXX (1938), 310; S.R.R., *Separationis,* 5 aug. 1938, coram R.P.D. Ioanne Teodori, dec. LVII—*Decisiones,* XXX (1938), 518; S.R.R., *Separationis,* 16 febr. 1940, coram R.P.D. Arcturo Wynen, dec. XII—*Decisiones,* XXXII (1940), 114; S.R.R., *Separationis,* 2 mart. 1940, coram R.P.D. Alberto Canestri, dec. XIX—*Decisiones,* XXXII (1940), 196.

and such a complete cessation of the common life postulates a prolonged and complete deliberation and judgment as a rule. It is such a violent rupture of the integrity of marriage that the common good demands mature consideration, the latter being more readily attained as a general rule through the use of the formal judicial process.[43]

The cases of temporary separation pleaded on the grounds mentioned in Canon 1131 do not generally have this quality of finality and difficulty in proof. They are only causes of separation if they make the common life too difficult. Here the ordinary can issue a decree allowing a temporary separation, and by means of a subsequent decree can demand a resumption of the marital life upon the cessation of the motive cause. Arguing from the possible proofs afforded in these grounds, and keeping in mind the temporary nature of the separation, one can easily discern why the administrative process is the ordinary procedure for these cases.[44]

To accept this view does not necessarily imply that the two processes are so mutually exclusive that they may not be utilized in both permanent and temporary separations. The authentic interpretation of canon 1131, § 1, provides for the use of the judicial process in cases of temporary separation either at the personal initiative of the ordinary or at the instance of the parties. Similarly there seems to be no objection in practice to using the informal administrative process for cases of permanent separation pleaded on the grounds of adultery. In the latter case, of course, the sin should be obvious or provable with great ease. Here the argument of the obvious advantages of the shorter process in the matter of time and expense shows merit.[45]

There is good legal basis for not restricting the use of either process exclusively to its own particular type of case. To confine the scope of the phrase *"auctoritate Ordinarii"* solely to the administrative process is not tenable. The ordinary's authority is both administrative and judicial; this phrase, then, includes both types of

[43] Forbes, *The Canonical Separation of Consorts*, p. 193; Doheny, *Canonical Procedure in Matrimonial Cases*, II, 646.

[44] Doheny, *loc. cit.*

[45] Canons 1747, § 1, 1°; 2197; 1750.

jurisdiction. Because of this the judicial process can readily be employed in cases of temporary separation.[46]

Article 4. The Determination of the Process

It is quite clear from the response of the Pontifical Commission for the Authentic Interpretation of the Code of Canon Law that the ordinary is the authority to determine what process is to be utilized in the adjudication of separation suits. It allows the administrative process to be used in the cases of temporary separation delineated in canon 1131, § 1 unless the ordinary either *ex officio* or at the instance of the parties determines otherwise.[47]

There is no problem involved when the question concerns a permanent separation because of adultery. The ordinary process for these cases is judicial. The question does arise, however, with regard to the ordinary's position in determining the employment of the judicial process in cases of temporary separation. Surely, if the public good demands it or a just cause warrants it, such as the social or even the political prominence of the parties, or the welfare of the offspring or even the advantage of the parties themselves, the ordinary may order the judicial process *ex officio*. This would merely be a fulfillment of his official solicitude for the souls under his care.[48]

If either party requests a judicial hearing of the case, the above mentioned authoritative response directs the ordinary to acquiesce. Can the ordinary deny such a request? It seems that he cannot.[49] The basis for this statement lies in the concession granted in the law that every right may be enforced by means of a corresponding

[46] S.R.R. *Separationis*, 4 febr. 1925, coram R.P.D. Iosepho Florczak, dec. VII—*Decisiones*, XVII (1925), 41.

[47] P.C.I., 25 iun. 1932—*AAS*, XXIV (1932), 284.

[48] Roberti, "De Separatione Coniugum," *Apollinaris*, V (1932), 295; Regatillo, *Ius Sacramentarium*, II, n. 587.

[49] Roberti, ibid., p. 296; Cappello, "De Separatione Coniugum," *Periodica de Religiosis et Missionariis*, Brugis, 1905 - 1919; from 1920: *Periodica de Re Canonica et Morali utilia praesertim Religiosis et Missionariis*, Brugis, 1920-1927: *Periodica de Re Morali, Canonica, Liturgica*, Brugis (1927 - 1936) et Romae (1937—), XXI (1932), 286 (hereafter referred to as *Periodica*); idem, *De Sacramentis*, V, 827; Regatillo, *loc. cit.*; Hines, *De Separatione Coniugum*, p. 40.

action in Court, unless the contrary is explicitly stated.[50] As far as the innocent party is concerned, the right he may petition to vindicate is expressed in Canons 1129, § 1, and 1131. Moreover, even the defendant may request the employment of the judicial process. This is quite clear from the phrase *"ad instantium partium"* in the authoritative interpretation of Canon 1131, § 1. In this case, however the legal institute utilized would be of the nature of a judicial exception: the means by which a defendant is legally qualified to retard or elide an action instituted against him.[51] He has a right to the common life from the marital contract, and a consequent right therefore to defend himself by whatever judicial weapons are at hand in opposition to a separation action brought against him.[52]

It is of interest to note here that the delegate of the ordinary may fulfill this office of determining the proper procedure in hearing separation suits. It is nothing more than the exercise of ordinary jurisdiction, which may be simply delegated.[53] It is not necessarily a form of judicial jurisdiction, since it is not the exercising of a judicial office. Rather, it is directing the employment of the ordinary's judicial jurisdiction. Moreover, whichever process is used, the objective validity of the process is not endangered nor even involved in the judgment of the ordinary or his delegate to utilize either procedure.[54] In practice, therefore, the delegation of this discretionary office by the ordinary to his delegate who may normally hear the preliminary statement in separation cases, in the light of convenience and economy of curial activity, is perfectly legitimate and juridically sound.

[50] Canon 1667—Quodlibet ius non solum actione munitur, nisi aliud expresse cautum sit, sed etiam exceptione, quae semper competit et est suapte natura perpetua.

[51] Roberti, *De Processibus* (2 vols., Vol. I, 2. ed., Romae: Apud Custodiam Librariam Pontificii Instituti Utriusque Iuris, 1941), I, 728.

[52] Canon 1667; Regatillo, *loc. cit.*

[53] Canon 199, § 1.

[54] Regatillo, *op. cit.*, II, n. 587, ter.

CHAPTER V

THE JUDICIAL PROCESS

THE ordinary canonical procedure observed in diocesan courts for contentious cases is the general norm to be followed in the adjudication of separation suits.[1] Since the usual matrimonial case is one in which there may follow a declaration of nullity, there are naturally to be noted for separation cases certain rules which do not concern the bond. As a consequence, to forestall a needlessly long treatment, the writer proposes here simply to deal with those regulations which are peculiar to separation cases.

ARTICLE 1. ORGANIZATION OF THE COURT

A. Competency

As in all marriage cases, the general rule for competency in separation cases is based on territorial limits. The competent judge is the judge of the place in which the marriage was contracted or in which the defendant maintains a domicile or quasi-domicile. In the event that one party is not a Catholic, then the competent tribunal is that of the place where the Catholic party has a domicile or quasi-domicile.[2]

The determination of competency on the basis of domicile and quasi-domicile is especially important in separation cases as a result of the unfortunate fact that the parties are often actually separated prior to the pleading of the case before the ecclesiastical authority. In such an instance, the discussion of separation effected *propria auctoritate*, as presented in the previous chapter, should be kept in mind. It can very readily happen that either spouse will initiate an action to restore the common life or to have certain canonical effects declared in the ecclesiastical forum. To limit a lawful separation to an authorized declaration of the ecclesiastical tribunal or to

[1] Cappello, *De Sacramentis*, V, 830.

[2] Canon 1964; *Instructio*, Art. 3, § 1.

a decree of the ordinary would seem rather peremptory in view of the disputed nature of this matter. Because of the lack of agreement among authors and in view of the absence of absolute authoritative interpretation, it is the opinion of the writer that a diocesan tribunal may determine its competency in a given case on the grounds of domicile or quasi-domicile, in the light of either opinion as noted in the foregoing chapter. There would certainly be no question of the validity of such a decision,[3] and, so it seems not even of licitness.

In an effort to avoid needless repetition, the writer will at this point deal exclusively with actions presented by spouses who are lawfully or unlawfully separated. Those who favor either view on the institute of separation undertaken *propria auctoritate* may in practice simply reduce their opinion to either one of these two alternatives. Needless to say, in a case wherein there is no question of an antecedent separation effected *propria auctoritate,* the determining rule would be the general norm of canon 1964, with the added note that the wife has as a necessary domicile that of her husband.[4] In such a case, therefore, the domicile of the defendant would always be the domicile of the husband.

In a given instance wherein the spouses are not lawfully separated, the judge determining competency on the basis of domicile or quasi-domicile would utilize the following alternatives. If the husband is the plaintiff, the judge of his domicile or of the wife's quasi-domicile will be competent. If the husband is lacking a domicile, then his wife may be cited before the judge of his quasi-domicile.[5] When the wife is the plaintiff, she has the alternative of citing him before the court either of his domicile or of his quasi-domicile. If she is a Catholic and the husband not a Catholic, then according to canon 1964 she can cite him before the judge of her own quasi-domicile or of his domicile.[6]

[3] Canons 1559, § 2; 1680; 1892; *Instructio,* Art. 207.

[4] Canon 93, § 1.

[5] *Instructio,* Art. 7:—Uxor, a viro non legitime separata quae proprium quasi-domicilium habeat, conveniri potest etiam coram Ordinario domicilii viri, non autem quasi-domicilii eiusdem viri, nisi in casu quo hic domicilio careat.

[6] P.C.I., 14 iul. 1922:—"Utrum actrix catholica, a viro non legitime separata, quae proprium ac distinctum quasi-domicilium habet, virum acatholicum

In a suit pleaded by a consort who is lawfully separated the following holds true. Should the husband present the case, then the competent court is that of the wife's domicile or quasi-domicile.[7] Should the wife bring the suit, then the husband may be cited in the court either of his domicile or also of his quasi-domicile. It is important to note that in the instance of lawful separation the wife may only procure a domicile if the separation is perpetual or has been granted for an indefinite period of time. This is clear from the wording of the *Instructio* which uses the phrase: *"perpetuo aut ad tempus indefinitum separata legitime."* Doubtless the reason for such a distinction is that a legitimate separation given by a decree stating a particular period of time would not allow the wife to have the necessary intention to remain permanently in one place to acquire a domicile.[8]

Since quasi-domicile is so common a determinant of competency in separation cases, and also in view of the nature of these suits, special emphasis is to be placed on the directives of the Sacred Congregation of the Sacraments regarding cases tried in the forum of quasi-domicile.[9] This regulation is mentioned here because of the ordinary probatory nature of a separation suit. Since witnesses are regularly close relatives and intimates, and inasmuch as documentary proof is usually not available, then it is to be expected that parties would attempt to obscure the objective truth by pleading their case before a remote tribunal of quasi-domicile. The court

in causa matrimoniali, ad normam Canon 1964, convenire potest tantum coram Ordinario proprii ac distincti quasi-domicilii; an vero etiam coram Ordinario domicilii viri. Resp. Cum uxor in casu habeat proprium ac distinctum quasi-domicilium, et sequatur domicilium viri, potest virum convenire coram alterutro Ordinario."—*AAS,* XIV (1922), 530; *Instructio,* art. 6, § 3.

[7] Canon 93; *Instructio,* art. 6, § 2: Uxor, a viro perpetuo aut ad tempus indefinitum separata legitime, i.e. per sententiam iudicialem competentis tribunalis ecclesiastici, vel etiam civilis a S. Sede, vi concordati, recognitam, aut per Ordinarii decretum, non sequitur domicilium viri, ideoque conveniri debet vel coram Ordinario loci in quo nuptiae initae sunt, vel coram Ordinario sui domicilii vel quasi-domicilii.

[8] Canon 92, § 1: Doheny, *Canonical Procedure in Matrimonial Cases,* I, 31.

[9] S. C. de Sacramentis, instr. 23 dec. 1929—*AAS,* XXII (1930), 168-171; *Instructio,* art. 5.

in question would then ascertain the truth only by overcoming numerous hindrances and could possibly become the inadvertent cause of the inflicting of injustice.

B. The Judge

Separation suits pleaded in the judicial process would naturally be heard before the *officialis* who, by the nature of his office as the diocesan judge, has the power to adjudicate such cases.[10] This rule, of course, would not apply should the bishop expressly reserve these cases as a class, or one special case, to his personal judgment.[11] The Vicar General, although competent for acting when these cases are treated administratively, would be incompetent here unless he were specially designated by the bishop for such action.[12]

A major departure from the ordinary manner of hearing marriage cases is the fact that separation suits do not require a tribunal of three judges. The provisions of canon 1576, § 1, 1°, demand three judges for matrimonial trials in all instances of "*causae contensiosae de vinculo* [. . .] *matrimonii* [. . .]." In a separation case the bond of marriage is not attacked, and despite the importance of such a case, inasmuch as the common life is in jeopardy, one judge would suffice to constitute the tribunal.[13] Granted that the practice of the Sacred Roman Rota demonstrates that in all cases of separation heard since its revival in 1908 a tribunal of three judges has been constituted, there is no obligation for a diocesan court to imitate this practice. Should a diocese be capable of furnishing competent personnel to constitute such a tribunal with ease, it would be a highly admirable undertaking. The importance of mature judgment and complete consideration in separation cases cannot be too much emphasized. Moved by the significance attaching to such cases, an ordinary, by acting in imitation of the practice of the Sacred

10 Canons 1572; 1573; Roberti, *De Processibus*, p. 257, n. 96.

11 Canon 1573, § 2.

12 Canons 1573, § 1; 1892, § 1; *Instructio*, art. 3, § 2.

13 *Instructio*, art. 13, § 1; Roberti, *De Processibus*, p. 289, n. 11; Torre, *Processus Matrimonialis*, p. 18; Vermeersch-Creusen, *Epitome Iuris Canonici*, III, n. 282; Wernz-Vidal, *Ius Canonicum*, V, n. 694.

Roman Rota would find such a procedure entirely within the law, as is clear from canon 1576, § 2.[14]

The Code of Canon Law also provides another method of hearing these cases before an individual judge. It allows a single judge who is conducting a trial to employ two *assessores* or consultors. These are to be selected from among the synodal judges.[15] Although they do not exercise any jurisdiction and the judge remains free to pass judgment as he sees fit, nevertheless their presence might well provide a great assistance to the jurist when he adjudicates separation suits.[16]

To employ well qualified laymen as aides in an effort to stem the present tide of broken marriages, although apparently helpful, would not be in keeping with the proper conduct of an ecclesiastical tribunal. According to specific regulation from the Holy See, the consultors may not be lay people.[17]

Worthy of mention here is the ever increasing practice in this country of constituting a board of experienced priests and canonists for the exclusive hearing of separation cases. In consequence of the unfortunate frequency of divorce in American society, Catholics, despite their training in matters relating to the sanctity of marriage, are greatly influenced by the extant usage. This factor as well as the concomitant problem of the requisite ecclesiastical permission for a civil separation or divorce, has naturally been of great concern to ordinaries. The erection of these boards has developed from their solicitude. Although this practice will be treated at greater length

[14] Loci Ordinarius tribunali collegiali trium vel quinque iudicum cognitionem committere potest etiam aliarum causarum, idque praesertim faciat quando de causis agitur quae, attentis temporis, loci et personarum adiunctis et materia iudicii, difficilioris et maioris momenti videantur; Wernz-Vidal, *op. cit.*, VI, n. 89. If such a practice is followed, it is to be noted that a tribunal of three or five judges must also be employed in the court of second instance. —Canon 1596; Roberti, *De Processibus*, p. 290.

[15] Canon 1575.

[16] Roberti, *op. cit.*, p. 274; Wernz-Vidal, *op. cit.*, VI, n. 90; Noval, *De Iudiciis*, p. 64; Vaughan, *Constitutions for Diocesan Courts*, The Catholic University of America Canon Law Studies, n. 210 (Washington, D. C.: The Catholic University of America Press, 1944), pp. 36, 37.

[17] S.C.C., 14 dec. 1918—*AAS*, XI (1919), 128.

when the administrative process is considered, a few points have suitable place here.

The employment of the judicial process is not to be considered a rarity in the adjudication of separation cases. This has been demonstrated in the foregoing chapter. Accordingly there arises a question concerning the position of such a board of experts when the judicial process is used. The solution lies in the observance of certain canonical formalities as necessary for correct legal action. It is possible for the members of this board to judge separation cases as a tribunal or for the individual members to act as single judges, but not to render a judicial decision as mere administrative delegates. An endowment of judicial jurisdiction is necessary.

The very nature of the office of the *officialis* demonstrates that he is to be considered the judge of the diocese.[18] When a tribunal of three or more judges is constituted, he is the presiding judge.[19] Should the number of cases cause him to be overburdened, the law provides for the appointment of *vice-officiales* who can aid him in his work.[20] Therefore, in the event that a particular expert or board of experts be delegated by the bishop for the administrative hearing of separation cases,[21] such an expert or board of experts are not empowered to judge in the judicial process apart from being duly deputed. The individual judge who hears the case, or the one presiding over the tribunal, must be appointed as a *vice-officialis* by the bishop.[22] The remaining judges of the tribunal, or *assessores,* as the case may be, should be constituted synodal or pro-synodal judges according to the prescriptions of the law.[23] The *officialis* cannot be said to have the power to depute members of such an administrative board to handle all or even one case in the judicial fashion. Admittedly by virtue of his office he enjoys ordinary power,[24] but it is

18 Canon 1573.

19 Canon 1577, § 2; *Instructio,* art. 14, §.

20 Canon 1573, § 3.

21 Canon 199, § 1.

22 Canons 1573; 1577, § 2.

23 Canons 1574, § 1; 1575.

24 Canon 1573, § 1; Capello, *Summa Iuris Canonici,* III, n. 93; Vermeersch-Creusen, *Epitome Iuris Canonici,* III, 16; Wernz-Vidal, *Ius Canonicum,* VI, n. 86; Roberti, *De Processibus,* p. 267; Coronata, *Institutiones Iuris Canonici,*

also quite clear that he is not an ordinary.[25] Any delegation of his power, therefore, although not expressly prohibited in the law, is highly questionable.[26]

C. The Promoter of Justice

In all marriage cases wherein the sacred bond is endangered, the law requires the intervention of the *defensor vinculi*. This demand holds whether it is a case concerned with the validity of the bond,[27] or a question of a papal dispensation dissolving a *ratum non consummatum* union.[28] Separation suits, however, since they concern the unity of conjugal life or the integrity of marriage, are not of a vincular nature. They do not require, therefore, the intervention of this official. In comparing the nature of these cases and the essential character of his office, one cannot conclude that there is any legal prescription to summon him; in fact, his presence would be superfluous.[29] Should a judge make his presence obligatory, the citation would seem to have no canonical basis and its juridic strength would seem reduced to the level of a mere request.[30] This statement gains special recognition in view of the canonical provision, although not expressly stated in the law for separation cases, that the promoter of justice intervene in these suits.

III, n. 1116; Dugan, *The Judiciary Department of the Diocesan Curia,* The Catholic University of America Canon Law Studies, n. 26 (Washington, D. C.: The Catholic University of America, 1925), p. 38.

[25] Canons 198, § 1; 1946, § 2; Coronata, *loc. cit.*; Tobin, *De Officiali Curiae Dioecesanae* (Romae: Apud Aedes Pontificae Universitatis Gregorianae, 1936), p. 159.

[26] "At, quamvis in codice non habeatur expressa prohibitio, officium non potest aliis delegari, quia datur industria personae (c. 199, § 2), nisi agatur de articulo non iurisdictionali (c. 199, § 4)."—Roberti, *op. cit.*, p. 268; Tobin, *op. cit.*, p. 175.

[27] Canon 1588.

[28] S. C. de Sacramentis, *Regulae servandae in processibus super matrimonio rato et non consummato,* 7 maii 1923, n. 27—*AAS,* XV (1923), 396.

[29] Roberti, *op. cit.*, p. 335; Gasparri, *De Matrimonio,* II, n. 1251, Cappello, *Summa Iuris Canonici,* III, n. 90; Wernz-Vidal, *Ius Canonicum,* V, n. 694; Glynn, *The Promoter of Justice,* The Catholic University of America Canon Law Studies, n. 101 (Washington, D. C.: The Catholic University of America, 1936) p. 198.

[30] Roberti, *op. cit.*, p. 336, Cappello, *loc. cit.*

All marriage cases pertain to the public good. This is especially true of separation cases. This is apparent from the intimate connection of conjugal cohabitation with the welfare of society. The Church has ever insisted upon the importance of this aspect of marriage as necessary for the public weal.[31] Moreover, right reason even unaided by any authoritative direction must necessarily conclude that the unity of conjugal life is indispensable for a healthy society. Furthermore, it is a historically evident fact that general marital instability has been a common companion if not efficacious cause for a decadent social economy.

The natural representative of the public good in the diocesan curia is the promoter of justice. It is his duty to see to it that the interests of justice are served, that the common good is safeguarded and that the souls committed to the care of the ordinary are protected from any immediate or possible danger of scandal.[32] It is only a practical and reasonable conclusion, therefore, that his presence be required in suits wherein cohabitation, an obligation founded in public order, is endangered and jeopardized.[33]

One might argue that the absence of any express provision in the common procedural law for the summoning of the promoter of justice in separation cases might permit a judge to dispense with him at will. This position is hardly tenable in view of the increasing ecclesiastical jurisprudence demanding his intervention in separation proceedings. The *Normae* of the Sacred Roman Rota expressly require his presence in causes of separation. These suits are specifically included in the generic list of causes in which the public good is necessarily concerned. This matter is not simply one of recommendation; rather, the promoter of justice has an official duty to

[31] S.R.R., *Separationis quoad Thorum et Mensam,* 5 iul. 1910, coram R.mo.P.D. Michaeli Lega, Decano, dec. XXIV, n. 11—*Decisiones,* II (1910), 243.

[32] Canon 1586; Glynn, *op. cit.,* p. 85; Stitt, *De Promotore Iustitiae eiusque Munere in Curia Dioecesana* (Romae: Apud Ed. Scientifica Internazionale, 1939), n. 97 (hereafter cited as *De Promotore Iustitiae*) Wernz-Vidal, *op. cit.,* VI, n. 116.

[33] Glynn, *op. cit.,* p. 87; Stitt, *op. cit.,* p. 125; Le Picard, *La Communauté de la Vie Conjugale* (Paris: Recueil Sirey, 1930), pp. 45, 243; Roberti, *De Processibus,* p. 329.

intervene in these cases and his intervention is to be considered necessary by the judge.[34]

It is quite difficult to list completely all the various phases of the activity of this official in exercising his office in a separation suit. The circumstances in any particular case will determine the governing norm to be followed. It will suffice to say that he should prepare interrogatories and offer exceptions after the manner of the *defensor vinculi* in the ordinary marriage case. Inasmuch as the promoter of justice is the guardian and defender of the public weal, it is his obligation to make certain that a separation is granted only according to the norms of canons 1128-1132. He must be alert to any attempted fraud or deceit perpetrated by the parties, and in general he must strive to oppose, as much as possible, the separation of the spouses, always however in line with the objective truth. In this endeavor he should be present at the examination of the parties and the witnesses, should object to witnesses if it is in order, should prepare his briefs and opinions, as well as strive to prevent any harm to the public good which might result from a cursory and arbitrary decree of separation.[35]

Article 2. Introductory Stage of the Trial

A. The Parties

Today, as in the earlier law, the innocent party has the exclusive

[34] Normae S.R.R. Tribunalis, art. 27, § 1:—In causis contensiosis Ponentis est ferre iudicium de eo utrum bonum publicum in discrimen vocari possit necne, nisi interventus Promotoris iustitiae ex natura rei evidenter necessarius dicendus sit, ut in causis impedimenti ad matrimonium contrahendum, separationis inter coniuges [. . .] etc.

§ 2:—Si in praecedentibus instantiis intervenerit Promotor iustitiae, huius interventus praesumitur necessarius.—*AAS*, XXVI (1934), 457. This norm was not a new departure in 1934; but it bespeaks simply the jurisprudence of the Rota to cite the promoter of justice in separation cases. An example may be found in the list of Rotal decisions published in 1926. In the cause, *Alexandrina Armenorum*, the name of the promoter of justice in the case is expressly mentioned.—*AAS*, XVIII (1926), 97.

[35] Glynn, *op. cit.*, pp. 200, 201; De Guise, *Le Promoteur de la Justice dans les Causes Matrimoniales*, Universitas Catholica Ottaviensis, Series Canonica, n. 8 (Ottawa, Ontario: Les Editions de l'Universitate D'Ottawa, 1944), pp. 142, 246; Stitt, *loc. cit.*

right to initiate against the guilty consort an action for separation.[36] The present law, however, is more distinct in expressing the essential parity of the spouses in their right to act as plaintiff in a separation suit. In the pre-Code law, it was noted, this concession was merely implied, and a clearer statement had to be sought in the glossators and the Decretalists. It is no longer possible to hold that the husband alone to the exclusion of a like right for the wife, may dismiss an unfaithful or otherwise guilty partner in marital life. The statements in the present law using such terms as, *"coniux innocens"* and *"alter coniux"* are clearly demonstrative of an equal right for both partners in married life to plead a case before the ecclesiastical tribunal.[37]

The law does not oblige the aggrieved consort to separate or to remain separated. There is no legal compulsion for the injured spouse to dismiss or to leave the guilty one unless an obligation arise from some other title.[38] In this category would be the obligation to safeguard one's physical or moral well-being, to secure the welfare of the children, to forestall the emergence of scandal and to achieve the fulfillment of fraternal correction.[39] These obligations would naturally be apparent from each particular case wherein the danger might be present. The moral force of such obligations again depends upon the relative gravity of the existing evils, and is solved through the application of the principles of moral theology concerned with each type of obligation.

Although the aggrieved party alone has the right to petition a suit of separation on the grounds mentioned in Canons 1129-1131,[40]

[36] Canons 1130; 1131; Canon 1971, § 1:—Habiles ad accusandum sunt: 1°—Coniuges, in omnibus causis separationis et nullitatis, nisi ipsi fuerint impedimenti causa; Wernz-Vidal, *Ius Canonicum,* V, n. 698.

[37] Canons 1129, 1130, 1131; Cappello, *De Sacramentis,* V, n. 826, ftn. 9.

[38] The optional nature of separation can be seen from the words *"ius habet solvendi"* of Canon 1129, *"potest autem eundem admittere aut revocare"* of Canon 1130, and *"legitimae causae discedendi"* of Canon 1131.

[39] S.R.R. *Separationis,* 4 febr. 1925, coram R.P.D. Iosepho Florczak, dec. VII, n. 6—*Decisiones,* XVII (1925), 44, 45; Cappello, *op. cit.,* V, n. 827; Forbes, *The Canonical Separation of Consorts,* p. 167; Iorio, *Theologia Moralis* (3 vols., Vol. II, 3. ed., Neapoli: D'Auria, 1947), n. 993.

[40] Canon 1971, § 1, 1°.

as will be pointed out in the subsequent section, this does not forbid the other consort from initiating every action whatsoever. His action, however, would not be for a separation but he could, at a later date, plead a suit for the restoration of the common life when the cause has ceased or the duration of time as decreed by the ecclesiastical authority has elapsed.[41] He may also enter suits that have a relation to a separation cause but do not grant him the benefits which are exclusively the right of the innocent consort. This is apparent from an examination of the available judicial actions recognized in the law and delineated in Canons 1667-1705.

B. *Actions and Exceptions*

In view of the fact that a separation suit is not concerned with dissolving the bond of marriage but with the enforcement of the right stated in the law, namely to live apart because of a canonically just cause, there is opportunity to employ more and varied actions and exceptions than in the ordinary matrimonial cause. One may initiate a judicial action not only for a decree of separation but also for the determination of the individual canonical effects. There is also place for court actions that seek to re-establish the unity of conjugal life, or to declare unlawful a separation already instituted. Corresponding to these actions there are many exceptions which the defendant may employ to protect his own rights.

The common action in this matter is a petition for canonical recognition of the right to separation from an errant consort for a just cause. This action may look to a permanent or a temporary separation, and in the latter case for a determinate or an indeterminate period of time.

In the matter of a just cause, it is noteworthy that although adultery is the only cause for a permanent separation,[42] the causes for a temporary separation as enumerated in Canon 1131, § 1, are not to be considered an exhaustive list. This is apparent from the phrase *"haec aliaque id genus,"* which follows the demonstrative enumerations of causes in the canon. The law is here emphasizing

[41] Cappello, *op. cit.*, V, n. 829, 4.

[42] Canons 1129, 1130.

types of causes rather than offering a particular description of every possible reason. It is considered helpful, therefore, to consider causes for temporary separation under the general classification of: (a) spiritual unfaithfulness; (b) grave moral danger, and (c) grave physical harm.[43]

The innocent consort is bound to re-establish the common life when the cause for the separation has ceased. If the ordinary has decreed the separation, then the resumption of cohabitation is to take place upon the lapse of time stated in that decree, or when the ordinary, by a later decree, directs it.[44] Should the innocent party not co-operate, the former defendant may institute an *actio de spolio* to vindicate his right to cohabitation.[45] At this point he is the aggrieved party since the lapse of time or the decree of the ordinary enjoining the resumption of common life returns the right lost through a previous delinquency. Similarly, the adulterous partner who has lost his right to cohabitation may institute judicial action to restore the common life when the formerly innocent spouse has committed the same sin. If the originally innocent partner separated *propria auctoritate,* this action is especially applicable. It also has place if the decree was issued by the ecclesiastical authority, for by compensating the crime of his consort, the former plaintiff although not bound to return on his own initiative, invites the duty to return upon favorable recognition of his consort's action.[46]

There even seems to be a possibility in these cases to employ an

[43] S.R.R., *Separationis,* 30 iun. 1928, coram R.P.D. Iosepho Florczak, dec. XXIX, n. 2—*Decisiones,* XX (1928), 268; S.R.R., *Separationis,* 6 dec. 1929, coram R.P.D. Francisco Morano, dec. LXIII, n. 4—*Decisiones,* XXI (1929), 526; S.R.R., *Separationis,* 6 aug. 1930, coram R.P.D. Andrea Jullien, dec. XLVII, n. 2—*Decisiones,* XXII (1930), 524; Forbes, *The Canonical Separation of Consorts,* p. 166; Cappello, *De Sacramentis,* V, n. 828; Wernz-Vidal, *Ius Canonicum,* V, n. 645; Gasparri, *De Matrimonio,* II, n. 1177.

[44] Canon 1131, § 2.

[45] Canons 1560, 1°; 1698, § 1; Doheny, *Canonical Procedure in Matrimonial Cases,* II, p. 629.

[46] Gasparri, *op. cit.,* n. 1173; Payen, *De Matrimonio in Missionibus ac Potissimum in Sinis Tractatus Practicus et Casus* (2. ed., 3 vols., Zi - ka-wei; Typographia T'ou - Sé Wé, 1935 - 1936), II, n. 2476 (hereafter referred to as *De Matrimonio*); Doheny, *op. cit.,* p. 651 This against Regatillo, *Ius Sacramentarium,* II, n. 586; (cf. infra, p. 142).

action *ex novi operis nuntiatione.*[47] This could be applied in the case where the alleged consort, antecedent to an ecclesiastical decree, undertakes a civil action for a separation, separate maintenance or even divorce and alimony. The other spouse might initiate this action to halt the new enterprise to protect his own rights and property until the case has been settled in the ecclesiastical forum. In this case the *actio ex novi operis nuntiatione* is preferable to a *suspensio exercitii iuris.*[48] The latter action contains the notion of suspending the exercise of a right, but no Catholic has a right to plead a marriage case in the civil courts since Christian marriage for whatever judgment needs to be rendered must look exclusively to the ecclesiastical authority.[49] Although authors for the most part limit the action *ex novi operis nuntiatione* to the halting of a new physical enterprise,[50] pre-Code authors gave it a broader scope [51] and Noval granted its use with reference even to moral works.[52] Arguing from Canon 6, 4°, namely that in the event of a doubt the older law is to be preferred, one cannot discern any prohibition against its employment in this circumstance.

Since the married persons have a right to mutual cohabitation, one might argue that a *suspensio exercitii iuris* would have usefulness in the case where the separation suit is pending, and the plaintiff desires to reside apart to avoid exposure to physical or moral harm. There is provision for such a case in the ordinary marriage process concerning the bond.[53] In separation suits this need not be utilized. The law has already made provision for such an emergency measure to protect the innocent consort in the institute of separation *propria auctoritate.*[54]

The exceptions applicable in separation cases again are more numerous than in other marriage cases. This is especially notable in

[47] Canon 1676.

[48] Canon 1672, § 2.

[49] Canons 1960, 1961; Gasparri, *op. cit.*, n. 1305.

[50] Roberti, *De Processibus,* p. 668; Coronata, *Institutiones Iuris Canonici,* III, n. 1207; Wernz-Vidal, *Ius Canonicum,* VI, n. 287.

[51] Cf. Lega, *De Iudiciis Ecclesiasticis,* I, n. 239.

[52] *De Iudiciis,* n. 322.

[53] *Instructio,* art. 63.

[54] Canons 1130; 1131, § 1.

regard to cases pleaded on adultery, since the law determines the necessary conditions of this sin quite completely. The absence of some essential property or condition can be employed by the defendant as an exception in the suit. Without entering upon an exhaustive analysis of the conditions postulated before this sin can be canonically recognized as such, it is sufficient to point out here the following possible exceptions.[55]

The exception that the alleged sin of unfaithfulness was not an *adulterium in sensu stricto* is perhaps the most common and so the mere intention of sin, or immodest or indiscreet conduct, although most dangerous and unbecoming, does not constitute this particular delict.[56] Similarly, the absence of culpability may be proposed as an exception by the defendant. If internal consent was lacking and the act occurred as the result of ignorance, error, deceit or force, no formal guilt would be present.[57] Marital separation is a penalty inflicted upon the errant consort,[58] and therefore as any penalty it presupposes moral guilt.[59]

Another exception is the express or tacit consent of the aggrieved party to the sin of adultery perpetrated by the other spouse.[60] Because of the former's consent to the unfaithfulness, the right to separate is forfeited.[61]

If the plaintiff caused the defendant to be unfaithful, the right to separate is lost and this fact may be used as an exception.[62] For

[55] Informative treatments on adultery as a cause for permanent separation may be found in Cappello, *De Sacramentis,* V, n. 826, 827; Wernz-Vidal, *Ius Canonicum,* V, n. 639; Doheny, *Canonical Procedure in Matrimonial Cases,* II, 620; Forbes, *The Canonical Separation of Consorts,* pp. 151-165; Hines, *De Coniugum Separatione,* pp. 22-27; Gasparri, *De Matrimonio,* II, nn. 1172-1174.

[56] Gasparri, *op. cit.,* II, n. 1172; Cappello presents a full treatment of *adulterium perfectum and consummatum*. cf., *op. cit.,* V, n. 826.

[57] S.R.R., *Separationis,* 6 dec. 1929, coram R.P.D. Francisco Morano, dec. LXIII, n. 3—*Decisiones,* XXI (1929), 526.

[58] *Dictum Gratiani* ad c. 4, C. XXXIII, q. 2.

[59] Cappello, *loc. cit.*

[60] Canon 1129, § 1.

[61] "Scienti et consentienti non fit iniuria"—Reg. 27, R.J. in VI°.

[62] Canon 1129, § 1.

this exception to be valid, the cause must be efficacious and proximate, not merely a remote influence or an occasion of sinning.[63]

Somewhat similar to the exception deriving from the plaintiff's consent for the defendant's act of adultery is that which derives from an act of condonation. This exception would hold when the plaintiff had surrendered the right to separate by expressly or tacitly condoning the unfaithfulness of the other consort.[64] Inasmuch as the aggrieved spouse is not obligated to separate, he may freely forfeit the right by condoning the other's act of adultery. Canon 1129, § 1, distinguishes express and tacit condonation. Naturally, express condonation, if clearly stated in words or similar signs, is of unmistakable import. The law, however, explains the meaning of tacit condonation and describes the presumption of law granted to it. If the innocent party, cognizant of the other's unfaithfulness, continued to live with the erring consort with *affectio maritalis,* tacit condonation exists. If the innocent spouse has not dismissed, left or instituted a separation suit against the guilty one within a period of six months, the law grants the presumption of tacit condonation.[65] It is clear from the words: *"postquam de crimine adulterii certior factus est,"* that the lapse of time is to be computed as a *tempus utile* and as beginning from the time that the aggrieved consort became aware of the breach of marital faith.[66] There would be an additional presumption against the innocent party should the adultery be notorious.[67]

Canon 1129, § 1, also leaves room for the defendant's employment of an exception based on the fact of a reciprocal compensation deriving from the plaintiff's act of adultery. This has the effect that a sin of adultery perpetrated by one spouse is compensated through

[63] Payen, *De Matrimonio,* II, n. 2459; Chelodi-Ciproti, *De Matrimonio,* n. 161; Doheny, *Canonical Procedure in Matrimonial Cases,* II, 626; Wernz-Vidal, *Ius Canonicum,* V, n. 639.

[64] Canon 1129, § 1.

[65] Canon 1129, § 2.

[66] Canon 35.

[67] Canon 16, § 2:—Ignorantia vel error circa legem aut poenam aut circa factum proprium aut circa factum notorium generatim non presumitur; [. . .]. Both are presumptions of law and therefore admit of contrary proof whether direct or indirect—Canon 1826; Regatillo, *Ius Sacramentarium,* II, n. 586.

a like sin or cancelled out by the same sin of the other. Both parties by their mutual delicts surrender the right to separate.[68] There is no essential difference because of the number of acts. Thus many acts by one spouse would be compensated through one act by the other.[69] If the sin of adultery was committed by the original plaintiff after a sentence of separation was granted, then, according to many, the consideration of reciprocal compensation would not be available as an exception to the defendant. This view is based on the premise that through the unfavorable sentence the original defendant lost his right to cohabitation.[70] Gasparri pointed out that under the aforementioned conditions the fact of reciprocal compensation intervenes if the innocent party has separated *propria auctoritate,* but that the available remedy at law is a suit for the restoration of the common life rather than the raising of an exception against the plaintiff.[71] The latter view seems more acceptable in the light of the recent authentic interpretation that separation cases are to be considered never irrevocably judged according to Canons 1903 and 1989.[72]

[68] "Paria delicta mutua compensatione tolluntur" - c. 6, X, *de adulteriis et stupris,* V, 16. Canon 2218, § 3:—Mutua iniuria compensatur, nisi una pars propter maiorem iniuriae ab eadem illatae gravitatem damnari debeat, deminuta, si casus ferat, poena. It is commonly held that other external sins against marital fidelity may be considered as the equivalent of adultery and therefore be the basis of a compensation. Thus the Roman Rota has stated: *"Ex communi autem interpretatione sunt causa separationis perpetuae etiam sodomia et bestialitas."*—S.R.R. *Separationis,* 6 dec. 1929, coram R.P.D. Francisco Morano, dec. LXIII, n. 3—*Decisiones,* XXI (1929), 525, 526; Wernz-Vidal, *op. cit.,* V, n. 629; De Smet, *Tractatus Theologico - canonicus de Sponsalibus et Matrimonio* (4. ed., Brugis: Car. Beyaert, 1927), n. 225; Payen, *De Matrimonio,* II, n. 2464; this against Cappello, *De Sacramentis,* V, n. 826.

[69] Doheny, *Canonical Procedure in Matrimonial Cases,* II, 628; Forbes, *The Canonical Separation of Consorts,* p. 163; Gasparri, *De Matrimonio,* II, n. 1173.

[70] Regatillo, *Ius Sacramentarium,* II, n. 586; Forbes, *op. cit.,* p. 163.

[71] *Op. cit.,* II, n. 1173; Payen, *De Matrimonio,* II, n. 2476. The earlier authors favored this view—Reiffenstuel, Lib. IV, tit. XIX, n. 81; Schmalzgrueber, Lib. IV, tit. XIX, n. 135; Santi, *Praelectiones Iuris Canonici,* Lib. IV, tit. XIX, n. 55.

[72] P.C.I., 8 apr. 1941:—"An causae separationis coniugum recensendae sint inter causas nunquam transeuntes in rem iudicatam de quibus in canonibus 1903 et 1989." R. "Affirmative."—*AAS,* XXXIII (1941), 173.

Applicable in separation cases pleaded on the ground of adultery as well as for other causes is the *exceptio spolii.* Since spoliation would be present when one is unlawfully deprived of the quasi-possession of a right,[73] the defendant may raise the exception, and claim he is not bound to answer in the suit until the right to cohabitation is restored. To use this exception, the defendant must, of course, prove that the other partner has unlawfully separated *propria auctoritate* either before or during the pending suit.[74]

In the matter of temporary separations, the exceptions that can be employed are not as clearly evident. Since the causes may be multiple, only a general statement of exceptions is possible. A good suggestion to be kept in mind is the fact that separation actually deprives a partner of a right, the right to cohabitation; the causes outlined in Canon 1131, § 1, therefore, are subject to strict interpretation.[75] As an example, the mere failure to practice one's faith is not the equivalent of affiliation with a non-Catholic sect, and one so accused might use this as an exception.[76] The same holds true with reference to serious moral or physical dangers. These considerations are subject to a strict interpretation for the same reason, and the dangers must in addition be continuous in character. One or two isolated incidents would not be sufficient, nor would mere imaginings of cruelty as a result of normal conjugal disputes and arguments. The whole tenor of Canon 1131, § 1 emphasizes habitual and repeated delinquencies. A well founded and substantial denial of these is, therefore, a useful exception for the defendant.[77]

C. The *Libellus* and *Litis Contestatio*

The *supplex libellus* in separation suits will be for the most part the same as that in the ordinary matrimonial case. It will be drawn up therefore in conformity with Canons 1706-1710 and articles 55-60

73 Roberti, *De Processibus,* p. 721.

74 Canon 1699, § 2; Coyle, *Judicial Exceptions,* p. 110.

75 Canon 19:—Leges quae [. . .] aut liberum iurium exercitium coarctant, [. . .], strictae subsunt interpretationi.

76 Canon 1325, § 2; Doheny, *Canonical Procedure in Matrimonial Cases,* II, 631.

77 S.R.R., *Separationis,* 30 iun. 1928, coram R.P.D Iosepho Florczak, dec. XXIX, n. 2—*Decisiones,* XX (1928), 268.

of the *Instructio*. Without treating these legal enactments as such, one may opportunely emphasize at this point as peculiar to separation cases the following considerations.

The plaintiff should clearly state the precise nature of the cause or causes upon which the separation is pleaded.[78] Long narrations of conjugal disputes and vicissitudes are not to be included. These complaints are irrelevant here and should be reduced to a statement of some certain cause. If at all, they should have place in the subsequent probatory stage.[79] Since parties are not necessarily separated in fact when the *libellus* is presented, special note should be taken of the actual residence of the parties. Furthermore, if the plaintiff has separated *propria auctoritate,* the reason and the exact time should be stated since this factor may affect the determination of competency [80] and be of instrumental aid for the decision regarding the presence or the absence of condonation in adultery cases.

In petitioning the separation, the party should also specify the period of time for which the separation is desired. Since adultery alone suffices to allow a perpetual separation, the judge will be faced with the problem of determining the warrant in the length of time asked for in each case. When such causes as apostasy and insanity are proffered it is not excessive to request a separation for an indefinite period of time. The period to be set is not so apparent in other cases. To make the judge's office somewhat less burdensome, a statement in the *libellus* describing the intention of the petitioning party, will aid him to adjust this request to the merits of the case as the cause proceeds.

Moreover, since *praesumptiones hominis* are applicable in separation cases, especially in the matter of infidelity, the general facts and indications upon which the presumptions rest should be indicated. Any proofs by documents and witnesses will follow the ordinary matrimonial procedural norms.[81]

Mention of the effects of the separation such as the custody of children, the support of the separated wife, etc., should also be in-

78 Canon 1708, § 2°; *Instructio,* art. 57, 2°

79 *Instructio,* art. 57, 3°.

80 *Instructio,* art. 57, 4°.

81 *Instructio,* art. 59.

cluded. In view of the present lack of civil recognition in the United States of ecclesiastical decrees, civil action normally follows the sentence of the court. It is feasible, therefore, that a petition to initiate civil action be incorporated in the *libellus*. Important also is a specific designation of the type of action required. Circumstances are not standard in this matter and the petitioner should explicitly mention whether a separation, separate maintenance, divorce and alimony or merely support is desired. Cognizant of this request, the judge may better be able to decide in favor or against the necessary permission by studiously weighing this request throughout the subsequent stages of the trial.

Noteworthy also is the fact that the rejection of the *libellus* does not mean that the separation was refused. In such a case the plaintiff could resort to the tribunal of second instance to define the question of rejection.[82] If the Court sustains the plaintiff's plea the tribunal of first instance must hear the case and pass a sentence of permitting or forbidding the separation.[83]

Particular emphasis should be placed on the provisions of the *Instructio* for the reconciliation of the spouses. The estrangement already extant between the consorts will only be aggravated by the bitterness or by the antipathy which usually accompanies the probatory stage of a separation suit. It is indicated then, for the judge to make every attempt at reconciliation before the trial gets underway. There does not seem to be any special time for this, although it should be done before or during the *litis contestatio*. Nor is this a light recommendation to the judge; it is apparent from the instructions of the Sacred Congregation of the Sacraments that, whenever a valid marriage or one easily validated is being treated, attempts at reconciliation are to be made whenever possible.[84] In keeping with this notion of reconciliation, every effort should be made to acquaint the defendant with the cause in the citation [85] and

[82] Canon 1703, § 3; *Instructio*, art. 66.

[83] Regatillo, *Ius Sacramentarium*, II, n. 587.

[84] S. C. de Sacramentis, *Regulae servandae in processibus super matrimonio rato et non consummato*, 7 maii 1923, n. 10—*AAS*, XIV (1923), 394; *Instructio*, art. 65.

[85] Canon 1711, § 1; *Instructio*, art. 74, 76.

to have the defendant make a personal appearance in court. This is not only necessary if reconciliation is to be possible at all, but it would obviate any danger of an attempted alienation of affection suit against the ecclesiastical authority by the party defendant.

Article 3. Probatory Stage of the Trial

A. *Proofs*

In view of the evident danger of collusion between the parties in cases concerning the bond of marriage, the general sources for the obtaining of legal proof are of a more limited character than in the ordinary trial.[86] Although separation suits are marriage cases, nevertheless because of their singular nature the ordinary rules governing the probatory stage of a trial may be employed with less restraint. As a consequence of this, the provisions of Canon 1747 [87] may be employed more freely than in the ordinary marriage trial which permits of only the first two sections of this canon.[88] Facts which are *notoria notorietate facti* are common proofs in these suits. Newspaper accounts and otherwise publicly known evidence of a spouse's infidelity, cruelty, apostasy or other delict may be accepted at times as so well substantiated that further legal proof is not necessary. Similarly, there is the possibility of accepting in these cases the judicial confession of the defendant, made in court according to Canon 1750, with less restriction than in a trial concerning the bond of marriage. Such a confession could not be accepted as *notoria notorietate iuris* in the sense of Canon 2197, 2°, as is evident from Canon 1751,[89] and from the omission of this institute in the provision

[86] Canons 1974 - 1975.

[87] Non indigent probatione:

1° Facta notoria ad normam Canon 2197, nn. 2, 3;

2° Quae ipsa lege praesumuntur;

3° Facta ab uno ex contendentibus asserta et ab altero admissa, nisi a iure vel a iudice probatio nihilominus exigatur.

[88] Instructio, art. 93.

[89] Si agatur de negotio aliquo privato *et in causa non sit bonum publicum*, confessio iudicialis unius partis, dummodo libere, et considerate facta, relevat alteram ab onere probandi.

of the *Instructio* that repeats all but the third section of Canon 1747 containing the law on judicial confessions.[90]

It is senseless to deny that separation cases pertain to the public good as do other marriage cases, and are therefore unaffected by the conditions set in Canon 1751. One cannot argue that a separation suit partakes of the nature of a penalty that further distinguishes it from other marriage cases, and that in consequence there accrue to separation suits all the advantages that can derive from a judicial confession. Despite the truth of the penal aspect of separation, one must keep in mind that criminal cases likewise pertain to the public good,[91] and the ecclesiastical law, as distinguished from modern civil practice, does not regularly permit a judicial confession of the defendant to free the plaintiff from the burden of proof.

It does not seem, however, that judicial confessions are to be accorded no credibility whatsoever in separation suits. Separation does partake of the nature of a penalty and is inflicted upon a delinquent spouse as a consequence of his misbehavior. Because of this, it is to be expected that the danger of collusion and perjury, which is so common in other matrimonial cases in which the parties may seek to be relieved of the bond of marriage, is not normally present. Moreover, the moral stigma that attaches to such assertions, when one considers the grave nature of the causes for separation, usually favors the confessing party's credibility. Naturally there is ever the danger of perjured assertions, but the law invokes due provisions and safeguards against these through its demand of further proof whenever either the law itself or the judge orders it.[92] In marriage trials as such further proof is demanded,[93] but the nature of a separation suit appears to mitigate this condition somewhat. Since admissions or confessions are to the detriment of the confessing party in other similar or comparable circumstances, this view gains certain strength. Canon 1947 allows the ordinary in some criminal trials, upon the confession of the delinquent, to dismiss him with a rebuke or penance instead of instituting criminal proceedings.

[90] Art. 93.

[91] Coronata, *Institutiones Iuris Canonici,* III, n. 1277.

[92] Canon 1747, 3°.

[93] *Instructio,* art. 117.

Wherefore, a judge in a separation suit, if he be presented with a canonically recognized confession of the defendant, might accord it a greater degree of acceptance than in the ordinary marriage case. It remains his office of course, as well as that of the promoter of justice, to weigh such a confession so that the judge may exact whatever additional proof he may feel to be serviceable and helpful.

Despite the importance of the defendant's confession or admission of his delinquency which the plaintiff pleads as the cause of separation, he is not obliged to answer incriminating questions. His acknowledgment of transgressions before the court must be voluntary, for he is justified in refusing to answer interrogations that would incriminate him.[94] This does not mean the promoter of justice must omit all questions pertaining to the defendant's admission of his delict as leading and offensive questions. This does not seem to be the meaning of Canon 1775.[95] Rather, such questions are most relevant to these cases and are permissible at the discretion of the judge. If the party refuses to answer questions of this nature, it is the office of the judge to estimate whether the refusal is justified or can be considered as an admission of guilt.[96]

B. Presumptions

Of special import in separation cases is the invoking of presumptions for the ascertainment of the alleged facts. The law distinguishes two chief types of presumption. The first is the legal presumption (*praesumptio iuris*) the other a personal presumption (*praesumptio hominis*).[97] Legal presumptions are further divided into *praesumptiones iuris simpliciter* and *praesumptiones iuris et de iure*.[98] The latter may not be impugned directly while the *prae-*

[94] Canon 1743, § 1; *Instructio,* art. 111.

[95] Interrogationes breves sunto, non plura simul complectentes, non captiosae, non subdolae, non suggerentes responsionem, remotae a cuiusvis offensione et pertinentes ad causam quae agitur.

[96] Canon 1743, § 2; *Instructio,* art. 112. The matter of extra-judicial confessions is accorded the same consideration as in other marriage cases.—*Instructio,* art. 113.

[97] Canon 1825, § 1.

[98] Canon 1825, § 2.

sumptio iuris simpliciter admits of direct contrary proof. A personal presumption or *praesumptio hominis* is deduced by the judge himself and varies in force with the circumstances.

The outstanding presumptions employed in separation suits are the following. The innocent party in a separation case is presumed by law to be cognizant of the notorious acts of the other spouse.[99] There is an additional *praesumptio iuris* stated in Canon 1129, § 2, to the effect that a tacit condonation is present when the innocent party, aware of the other's infidelity, continues cohabitation with "*affectio maritalis*" for a period of six months. Since both are *praesumptiones iuris simpliciter,* although they relieve from the burden of proof the party offering them, nevertheless they yield to contrary evidence.[100] Substantial evidence that the innocent spouse lived with the errant consort for a period of six months in order to procure definite testimony in anticipation of the present suit would serve to directly impugn the presumption of condonation.

The judge too may deduce a presumption, although not of the law, since it has its origin not in the law but in the mind of the judge in consequence of some certain or determinate fact in the case.[101] Presumptions enjoy more or less value in proportion to their nature as temerarious, probable or violent presumptions.[102] Light presumptions should be dismissed, probable presumptions offer partial proof, and violent presumptions full proof.[103] In conflict, presumptions of law prevail over personal presumptions and the latter regarding special facts supersede presumptions concerning generalities.[104]

Personal presumptions of the judge are particularly pertinent to

[99] Canon 16, § 2.

[100] Regatillo, *Ius Sacramentarium,* II, n. 586.

[101] Canon 1828.

[102] Coronata, *Institutiones Iuris Canonici,* III, n. 1356; Wernz-Vidal, *Ius Canonicum,* VI, n. 517.

[103] Reiffenstuel, Lib. II, tit. XXIII, n. 29-31; Coronata, *op. cit.* III, n. 1358; Wernz-Vidal, *op. cit.,* VI, n. 520; Vermeersch-Creusen, *Epitome Iuris Canonici,* III, 206.

[104] Reiffenstuel, Lib. II, tit. XXIII, nn. 80, 92; Wernz-Vidal, *loc. cit.,* Coronata, *loc. cit.*

separation cases pleaded because of adultery. A study of the jurisprudence of the Sacred Roman Rota in judging these cases clearly establishes them as suitable evidence. Most cases of this nature reviewed before this Roman Tribunal contain references to the difficulty in establishing strict proof of this sin in consequence of the rarity of witnesses *de visu.*[105] Even if eye witnesses are proposed, then because of the extraordinary and unexpected nature of their testimony, they should be rejected as incredible or at least suspect. Such testimony would be so rarely true that one might almost call the attitude of a court a jurisprudential presumption against it. As a consequence, in the absence of testimonial proof, the court must refer to conjectures and violent presumptions from which a moral certitude of the fact may be induced.[106]

The classic norm for the use of presumptions in these cases is taken from a separation suit settled by Pope Alexander III. The testimony that the delinquents were seen: *"solus cum sola, nudus cum nuda, in eodem loco iacentes* [. . .] *in multis secretis locis, et latebris ad hoc commodis, et horis electis,"* moved the Pontiff to regard this testimony as a sufficient presumption for the fact of infidelity.[107] The decisions of the Sacred Roman Rota continue to use this papal example as a norm today, but also present some general norms. This august Tribunal has often demonstrated the use of presumptions as suitable evidence. The presumptions should arise from particular acts and circumstances that have a peculiar

[105] S.R.R., *Separationis,* 4 febr. 1925, coram R.P.D. Iosepho Florczak, dec. VI, n. 4: "Ast crimen adulterii in foro externo non potest facile evinci, quia, in genere, clam perpetratur et directe fere nunquam probari potest."—*Decisiones,* XVII (1925), 42; S.R.R., *Separationis,* 3 ian. 1929, coram R.P.D. Henrico Quattrocolo, dec. I, n. 5—*Decisiones,* XXI (1929), 4; S.R.R., *Separationis,* 8 ian. 1937 coram R.P.D. Ioanne Teodori, dec. I, n. 6—*Decisiones,* XIX (1937), 4; S.R.R., *Separationis,* 2 mart. 1940, coram R.P.D. Alberto Canestri, dec. XIX, n. 4—*Decisiones,* XXXII (1940), 198.

[106] S.R.R., *Separationis,* 4 febr. 1925, coram R.P.D. Iosepho Florczak, dec. VII, n. 1: "Si testis deponeret, directe de visu copulae, esset falsus, seu de falso suspectus, [. . .]. Hince res demonstranda est per coniecturas et praesumptiones violentas ex quibus saltem moralis certitudo de adulterio commisso inducatur."—*Decisiones,* XVII (1925), 42.

[107] C. 12, X, *de praesumptionibus,* II, 23.

relationship to the fact of infidelity. Mere suspicions, whether they be probable or not, although not peremptorily dismissed, are insufficient. The facts and circumstances brought forward as testimony must be so naturally connected with marital unfaithfulness that the court must accept them as violent presumptions and as sufficient to give rise in the mind of the judge to a moral certitude. The damage and injustice that results from an unlawful separation demand a proportionate uncontestable proof. Violent presumptions furnish that proof.[108]

In formulating presumptions, then, the judge must seriously weigh all the circumstantial evidence offered, the character and probity of the witness who supplies the information, as well as the circumstances of the alleged delinquents, since all are essential in ascertaining the fact of infidelity. His personal views, opinions and suspicions are not the equivalent of presumptions. He must substantiate certain and specific facts which are so directly related to the alleged delict that they are undeniably a basis for a violent presumption.[109]

108 S.R.R., *Separationis,* 4 febr. 1925, coram R.P.D. Iosepho Florczak, dec. VI, n. 4: "Hinc, quoad adulterium, etsi non levia habeantur indicia, certitudo tamen partrati criminis non habetur; sed constat procul dubio graves haberi in casu causas quae separationem quoad habitationem, mensam et thorum, ad tempus indeterminatum postulant, ut damna et mala et familia removentur."—*Decisiones,* XVII (1925), 42; S.R.R. *Separationis,* 6 dec. 1929, coram R.P.D. Francisco Morano, dec. I, n. 3: "Cum vero adulterium sit crimen quod generatim patratur in occulto, eius probatio fieri solet per praesumptiones violentas, nempe per coniecturas ex factis quae non nisi in casu adulterii contingere solent."—*Decisiones,* XXI (1929), 525; S.R.R., *Separationis,* 30 maii 1938, coram R.P.D. Arcturo Wynen, dec. XXXIII, n. 2: ". . . tamen adulterium probari potest per testes, qui referunt de actis adulterio proximis vel de circumstantiis quae violentam praesumptionem de patrato crimine gignunt, v.g. de facto quod maritus cum alia muliere in eodem lecto inventus sit. Non vero sufficiunt suspiciones plus minusve probabiles. Quoniam culpa non moraliter certa, sed dumtaxat probabilis, non sufficit ad privandum aliquem hominem certo iure ad vitae coniugalis communionem."—*Decisiones,* XXXIII (1938), 310; Gasparri, *De Matrimonio,* II, n. 1172; Cappello, *De Sacramentis,* V, n. 826.

109 Canon 1828; *Instructio,* art. 173.

Article 4. Concluding Stages of the Trial

A. The Sentence

Upon the presentation of all the testimony and proofs, the examination of the advocate's briefs and the animadversions of the promoter of justice, the judge must strive to procure a moral certitude about the existence of the alleged cause for a canonical separation.[110] His prudent conscience is to be his guide in the evaluating of these proofs unless the law explicitly grants some special efficacy to some particular proof. Witnesses recognized in the law as *"omni exceptione maiores"* are included in this category.[111] Often in separation suits, relatives or intimates of the parties, armed with incontestable character references, testify as eye witnesses to the alleged cause. This is especially applicable in cases of grave physical or spiritual harm. Their testimony is given a special preference by the law and the judge may accept it as beyond challenge. Similarly, the presumptions treated in the foregoing article are considered as most efficacious.[112]

As in all cases of doubt, the judge who cannot arrive at a moral certitude necessary for a sentence is obliged to pronounce that the plaintiff's right has not been established and the defendant retains the right to cohabitation.[113] This is clear enough in a suit for canonical separation. Another problem arises when the situation is reversed. The case may very well be pleaded for the restoring of cohabitation after a separation has been pronounced but the cause is alleged to have ceased. In a similar fashion a suit may be presented as an *"actio de spolio,"* wherein the plaintiff wishes the already instituted separation to be declared unlawful and cohabitation to be restored. Does the same rule apply here, and is the doubtful judge obliged to declare the right to cohabitation not established, thus permitting the separation to continue? It seems not. Canon 1014 states that marriage enjoys the favor of the law and in doubt the marriage is to be considered valid until the contrary is proved. In a suit attacking the marriage bond, therefore, the validity of the

110 Canon 1869, §§ 1, 2.

111 Canon 1791.

112 Canon 1826.

113 Canon 1869, § 4.

bond is a *causa favorabilis* and in doubt it is favored.[114] One might argue that Canon 1014 is limited to the bond of marriage and that on the contrary the right to conjugal unity is treated as the subject of any contentious case. This position is unwarranted. Despite the law's lack of explicit mention of cohabitation as a *causa favorabilis,* the whole ecclesiastical legal history on this institute favors its inclusion. There is no exhaustive list of favored causes in the law; [115] as a consequence, the community of conjugal life cannot be denied this privilege by such elimination. On the other hand as proof for its legal preference, there is a scholarly sentence by Cardinal Lega (+ 1935), then Dean of the Sacred Roman Rota, in which he clearly demonstrates that conjugal unity must be considered a favored cause. The sentence stated: *"omnia iura clamant ut coniugale consortium non disiungatur, nisi invicte comprobatur, adesse causam canonicam separationis."* [116] Although not in the sense of a law, it is clear from this statement studied in the light of Canon 1128 [117] that the community of conjugal life is to be considered a *causa favorabilis* whenever a judge is faced with a positive doubt and unable to arrive at the necessary moral certitude.

Since separation cases require only a single judge, he alone frames the sentence.[118] Should a tribunal of three or even five judges try the case, the drafting of the sentence will follow the norms set in Canons 1871-1872 and article 198 of the *Instructio.* It is quite possible that a judge in his paternal desire to attempt a reconciliation might procrastinate in rendering the decision and thus hope for a restoration of the common life in the intervening period. This would be unlawful and the aggrieved party who has the right to separate

[114] Canon 1869, § 4.

[115] Wernz-Vidal, *Ius Canonicum,* VI, n. 589.

[116] S.R.R., *Separationis quoad Thorum et Mensam,* 5 iul. 1910, coram R.mo P.D. Michaeli Lega, Decano, dec. XXIV, n. 11—*Decisiones* II (1910), 244.

[117] Coniuges servare debent vitae coniugalis communicationem, nisi iusta causa eos excuset.

[118] Canon 1872.

according to Canons 1129-1131, once the presence of a just cause is proved, could have recourse to the bishop or to the Sacred Congregation of the Sacraments, as the case may direct, for the protection of this right.[119]

From the several cases of separation reviewed before the Sacred Roman Rota between the years 1908 and 1940, suitable norms for framing sentences may be found. According to the practice of the Rota the sentence is to be rendered with the invocation of the Divine Name at the beginning. Then there is a list of the court personnel, a mention of the parties and a statement of the specific facts in the case. The decisions of the Rota especially in adultery cases present a general outline of the delicts alleged as committed by the respondent in a more or less narrative form. At the conclusion of this narration the doubt as formulated by the Tribunal is stated, usually: *"An locus sit separationi coniugum a toro, mensa et cohabitatione, in casu."* This is followed by a statement of the law on canonical separation, as a rule it is Canons 1129 and 1130 for perpetual separations, and Canon 1131 for those of a temporary nature, with a commentary on the more salient legal aspects of the case at hand. Next there is an exposition of the relation between the law and the facts of the case simply entitled: *In facto.*[120] Here are expressed not only the accusations of the plaintiff accompanied with a summary of the testimonial proof, but also the exceptions of the defendant; likewise the judicial or extra-judicial confessions and legal as well as personal presumptions are duly delineated and accordingly valuated. The deductions of the Tribunal are then set down with a clear presentation of the reasons why the plea has been accepted or rejected. A good example is the following, taken from a case pleaded by a husband on the grounds of his wife's infidelity:—

"1° adulterium uxoris certo probatum non esse;

[119] Canon 1625, § 1.

[120] Canons 1605, § 1; 1871; § 2; 1873, § 1, 3°, indicate that the motives *in facto* are to precede those *in iure*. The Sacred Roman Rota, however, in common practice uses the reverse form. Either order may be used, although the long experience of the Rota has doubtless proved its own method as the most practical.

2° probatum esse, etsi non plenissime, huius adulterii condonationem ex parte viri;

3° graves et violentas presumptiones adesso de mariti adulterio." [121]

Any other statements necessary to complete the case in addition to an analysis and appraisal of the advocate's and promoter of justice's brief are given. The sentence is then concluded with a response to the earlier stated *dubium*, e. g. *"Negative, seu non esse locum separationi coniugum a toro, mensa et cohabitatione, in casu."* [122] Should the facts warrant a favorable decision then the sentence would read: *"Affirmative, seu constare de legitima separationis causa ad tempus indefinitum iuxta uxoris instantiam."* [123] A decision must be given for each *dubium*, if more than one has been considered.[124] This is demonstrated in a decision of the Rota where two *dubia* were proposed; the one concerned a permanent separation because of adultery, and the other a temporary separation because of mutual physical harm to the parties. It reads: *"Locum non esse separationi perpetuae ex causa adulterii, utpote compensati; locum esse separationi ad tempus indeterminatum ob iniurias, et quidem culpa utriusque coniugis, in casu.*[125]

The length of time of the granted separation is always noted in the sentence and should be clearly stated. When the sentence grants a separation perpetually or for an indefinite time there is no difficulty, but other temporary separations require accurate terminology to preclude all misunderstanding. If the time is not definitely stated or the period ends upon the cessation of the cause, a clear enunciation of each should be made. The two sentences are not synonymous, and any lack of clarity may lead to ambiguity. Similarly, temporary separations given for a definite period of time

[121] S.R.R., *Separationis,* 8 ian. 1937, coram R.P.D. Ioanne Teodori, dec. I, n. 7—*Decisiones* XXIX (1937), 4.

[122] *Loc. cit.*

[123] S.R.R., *Separationis,* 17 martii 1913, coram R.P.D. Antonio Parathoner, dec. XIX, n. 18—*Decisiones,* V (1913), 225.

[124] Canon 1873, § 1, 1°.

[125] S.R.R., *Separationis,* 2 martii 1940, coram R.P.D. Alberti Canestri, dec. XIX, n. 10—*Decisiones,* XXXII (1940), 202.

should state accurately just how long the right of separation may last. If a positive statement of months, or years, as the case may call for, is issued, there will be no danger of subsequent harm to either of the parties at the hand of the judge.[126]

In these cases the judge has a certain discretionary authority which he lacks in cases of perpetual separation. The latter leave room for but one sentence but temporary separations are ruled by circumstances. The judge should issue a sentence, then, according to a due proportion between the established just cause and the gravity of the obligation of maintaining conjugal unity. The period of time stated in the sentence should be an expression of this suitable adjustment arrived at upon prudent deliberation and judgment.

Since permission for civil action is usually petitioned with a separation action; mention of this should be made in the sentence or at least in a corollary thereto. Such permission is usually necessary in view of the complete absence of civil recognition of ecclesiastical sentences. One cannot deny that the ecclesiastical judge may decide matters relating to the so-called civil effects of marriage such as property settlements and payments of alimony. Although these matters may not be explicitly *res spirituales* as are the separation suits themselves, nevertheless, they pertain to it most intimately *ex connexione causarum,* and the ecclesiastical judge is canonically competent to adjudicate them.[127] Be this as it may, the diocesan judge is still faced with the problem of civil recognition of his sentence as requisite for the protection of the parties. This necessitates a grant of permission to the parties to seek it. The types of civil action and the conditions requisite for a grant of permission will be treated in a later chapter. It will suffice here to say that whatever permission the judge issues in this regard is not of his own official

126 Canon 1873, §. 1, 2°:—Sententia debet determinare (saltem quatenus fas sit et materia patiatur), quid pars damnata dare, facere, praestare, aut pati debeat, aut a quo abstinere; itemque quo modo, loco vel tempore obligatio implenda sit.

127 Canon 1553, § 1, 1°:—Ecclesia iure proprio et exclusivo cognoscit de causis quae respiciunt res spirituales et spiritualibus adnexas.

Canon 1961:—Causae de effectibus matrimonii mere civilibus, si principaliter agantur, pertinent ad civilem magistratum ad normam Canon 1016; sed si incidenter et accessorie, possunt etiam a iudice ecclesiastico ex propria potestate cognosci ac definiri.

authority. The Code is silent on this matter and there remain only the directions of the Roman Congregations as guiding norm. A response of the Sacred Congregation of the Holy Office clearly states that the granting of such a permission belongs to the bishop.[128] The judge, therefore, must be delegated to issue any permission for civil action. In the absence of such a commission, a separate decree from the ordinary or his delegate is a necessary requisite.

B. Publication of the Sentence

The best procedure for the publishing of the sentence would seem to be the summoning of the parties to hear it solemnly read by the judge sitting in court.[129] This method is preferable to having them read it at the Curia or receive it by registered mail.[130] These alternate methods would suffice, but the more solemn form would be more appropriate in this type of suit. By solemnly reading the sentence to both parties, if it is at all possible, the judge has an opportunity to advise them of the significance of his decision. Thus he can explain the effects of the separation according to the particular nature of the case and, if it is a temporary separation, point out the conditions for future reconciliation.[131] Moreover, if permission has been granted for civil action, he might use this opportunity to administer the required oath. It is prescribed that the consorts affirm on their oath that any action in the civil courts is a necessary and unavoidable formality. In addition they must swear that they are cognizant of their always intact bond of marriage, and that whatever action they have permission to plead is for the purpose of determining the civil effects of their separation and not for the purpose of dissolving their marriage. This oath should upon its recording be kept in the acts of the case.[132]

[128] S.C.S. Off., 22 maii et 19 dec. 1860, n. 4: ". . . posse tolerari ut catholici in eo foro actoris et advocati partes agant, dummodo adsint iustae separationis causae iudicio Episcopi, . . ."—*Collectanea,* II, n. 2272.

[129] Canon 1877; *Instructio,* art. 204, § 1.

[130] *Loc. cit.*

[131] Canon 1873, § 1, 2°.

[132] S.C.S. Off., 6 aug. 1906: Gasparri, *De Matrimonio,* II, n. 1324. This response directs the oath to be taken before the ordinary or his delegate; the judge, then, should receive additional delegation to administer it.

COROLLARY: Some Salient Points on the Juridical Effects of a Canonical Separation

Although by a canonical sentence of separation the consorts are relieved of their obligation of sharing bed, board and cohabitation, the other rights and duties from their still undissolved bond of marriage remain intact. They are still husband and wife and, should God have blessed their union with children, parents.[133] As a consequence, the matter of support of the separated wife and the custody of children are of paramount importance.

The complete absence in this country of civil recognition of an ecclesiastical judge's sentence has been noted above. His determination of these matters in his sentence might therefore seem futile and especially so with regard to the support of the separated wife. Moreover, in the absence of any canonical regulation on this point of support, authors generally refer the matter to the civil courts according to Canons 1016 and 1961.[134] If no civil action is to take place and the judge should be obliged to determine this question in his sentence, relative norms may be found in the Decretal Law.[135] Since dowry is no longer an important factor in marriage, especially in this country, these regulations may seem obsolete. However, inasmuch as they were prescribed with the justice and equity of ecclesiastical law at the time, their spirit, if not their letter, would be a good criterion for the judge to follow.

The unfortunate yet so important effect of a separation action is the proper determination of the custody of children. Here the law is clear and express; despite the necessity of civil recognition, which may be to the contrary, the ecclesiastical judge must attempt the observance of these provisions as far as possible. Canon 1132 grants the guardianship of the children to the innocent party as a general rule. In most cases there would be little conflict with the civil courts in this instance in view of a similar practice there. However, the universal law of the Church, concerned as always

[133] Wernz-Vidal, *Ius Canonicum,* V, n. 647.

[134] Wernz-Vidal, *loc. cit.*; Hines, *De Coniugum Separatione,* p. 46; Forbes, *The Canonical Separation of Consorts,* p. 240.

[135] C. 1-8, X, *de donationibus inter virum et uxorem, et de dote post divortium restituenda,* IV, 20.

with the preservation of the faith, states an exception to this rule in the case of mixed religion. Here the Catholic party is preferred as the custodian of the children according to the obvious presumption that their Catholic rearing will be better safeguarded. The law is not impractical by stating this as an ironclad rule. It bestows an additional discretionary power upon the ordinary for obvious reasons. Where the circumstances clearly demonstrate that the dubious character of the Catholic party would make such a ruling impractical if not dangerous, the ordinary, according to his own prudent judgment, will grant the children's custody to whichever consort he deems most suitable for the protection of their spiritual and physical welfare.[136]

The civil courts may not always agree with the ordinary's decision, but this conflict cannot always be avoided. However, in most instances, since both authorities are concerned with the children's best interests, although the ordinary must place paramount importance on their Catholic education, a conflict between the two judgments would not ordinarily exist.

Adultery is the one and sole cause for a permanent separation; consequently there is no provision in the law for subsequent reconciliation unless the innocent spouse desires it [137] or, by the commission of the same delict, has given the other spouse occasion for an action to restore the common life.[138]

The general theme of this matter is that the guilty partner has lost the right to the community of marital life, while the innocent party retains it and may demand its resumption at will. Wherefore, even after a sentence of separation, the guilty partner would

[136] Canon 1132: Instituta separatione, filii educandi sunt penes coniugem innocentem, et si alter coniugum sit acatholicus, penes coniugem catholicum, nisi in utroque casu Ordinarius pro ipsorum filiorum bono, salva semper eorundem catholica educatione, aliud decreverit. Cf. Wernz-Vidal, *loc. cit.*; Hines, *op. cit.*, p. 45; Forbes, *op. cit.*, pp. 237 - 241.

[137] Canon 1130: Coniux innocens, sive iudicis sententia sive propria auctoritate legitime discesserit, nulla unquam obligatione tenetur coniugem adulterum rursus admittendi ad vitae consortium; potest autem eundem admittere aut revocare, nisi ex ipsius consensu ille statum matrimonio contrarium susceperit.

[138] Gasparri, *De Matrimonio*, II, n. 1103.

be bound to return upon the summons of the innocent consort. The only circumstance in which this would not be compulsory is the embracing of the clerical or religious state by the guilty one with the other's consent. This life by its nature is contrary to the married state and therefore obviates any reconciliation.

Provision for reconciliation in cases of temporary separation is found in Canon 1131, § 2.[139] Here it is stated that, once the cause which permitted the separation has elapsed the common life is to be restored. This applies immediately if one has departed *propria auctoritate*.[140] However, in the light of the phraseology of the remainder of Canon 1131, § 2, which provides that if the separation was pronounced by the ordinary for a definite or indefinite period of time, the innocent party is not obliged to return unless the ordinary decrees it or the time as specified in the sentence has elapsed, a question can arise here. Perhaps the ordinary has decreed the separation "until the cause ceases." Is the innocent party obliged to return upon the cessation of the motive cause? It definitely seems so. Canon 1131, § 2, permits only a delay in the reconciliation when the ordinary has decreed the separation for a definite or an indefinite period of time. In this case the ordinary has decreed the separation, but although it is for an indefinite period of time since it is until the cause ceases, nevertheless, the express mention of this element earlier in the canon is the legislation for this point and the innocent party therefore is bound to return upon the cessation of the cause. His right to separation has ceased and his continued state of separation has no longer any canonical sanction.[141]

In issuing his decree of reconciliation, the diocesan judge will do well to acquaint himself with the ecclesiastical jurisprudence on this phase of canonical separation. Not only modern authors but even the older authors and decisions of authoritative sources direct caution and thorough consideration of both sides of the question. They

139 In omnibus his casibus, causa separationis cessante, vitae consuetudo restauranda est, sed si separatio ab Ordinario pronuntiata fuerit ad certum incertumve tempus, coniux innocens ad id non obligatur, nisi ex decreto Ordinarii vel exacto tempore.

140 Cappello, *De Sacramentis,* V, n. 829.

141 Cappello, *loc. cit.*; Forbes, *The Canonical Separation of Consorts,* p. 229.

note that in all too many cases the guilty partner may on the surface make extreme promises and even by exemplary conduct unjustifiably procure a restoration of his marital rights. It is pointed out that the innocent party is not to be compelled or forced to accept the guilty spouse back to the common life when there is a very real suspicion of deceitful and hypocritical correction. This is especially true in cases of separation granted on the grounds of cruelty. It is quite possible that a brutal husband especially will seek to delude a judge into becoming convinced that a reform has been effected. At the same time the wife, victim of his past rages, would be equally convinced of his hypocrisy and feigned veneer of virtue. A general conclusion, established as a general criterion, is that the innocent spouse should not be forced to return or receive back an errant partner unless there are obvious signs of conversion and good faith. There should not only be no very profound doubt in the mind of the judge when he seeks to effect this marital reunion but if the case warrants them, then sufficient guarantees should also be demanded as testimony of a corrected life and as security to the hesitating innocent consort.[142]

Article 5. The Appeal and the Court of Second Instance

The heterogeneous nature of a separation suit is perhaps most clearly shown in the appellate stage of the action. Since it is a cause *"de statu personarum,"* it is similar to the ordinary matrimonial case concerning the bond and partakes in the same privilege of never becoming an adjudged case.[143] Marriage cases *de vinculo,* however, require a mandatory appeal by the defender of the bond when the first sentence favors the nullity of the marriage.[144] The nature

[142] S.C.C., *Firmana,* 16 maii 1789—*Thesaurus Resolutionum S.C.C.,* LVII, 100; S.C.C., *Nullius S. Martini,* 28 iul 1804—*Fontes,* n. 3920; *Austrian Instruction,* Sec. 208—*Collectio Lacensis,* V, col. 1311; Sanchez, Lib. X, disp. XVIII, n. 2; Schmalzgrueber, Lib. IV, tit. XIX, nn. 143, 163; Wernz, *Ius Decretalium,* IV, n. 713, III; Gasparri, *De Matrimonio,* 3. ed., n. 1371; Wernz-Vidal, *Ius Canonicum,* V, n. 645, ftn. 130; Forbes, *loc. cit.*

[143] Canon 1903; P.C.I., 8 apr. 1941: "An causae separationis coniugum recensendae sint inter causas nunquam transeuntes in rem iudicatam, de quibus in canonibus 1903 et 1989. R. Affirmative."—*AAS,* XXXIII (1941), 173.

[144] Canon 1986.

of these suits also necessitates two concordant sentences before the parties are considered free to enter upon a new marriage.[145] These requirements are not stated in separation cases. Like any ordinary contentious suit, the sentence of the first instance stands, unless the party aggrieved by it appeals to a higher tribunal.

The court of second instance will be the ordinary tribunal in which an appeal is lodged against the sentence of the lower court unless the party wishes to use his right of appeal to the Sacred Roman Rota.[146] Here, too, a single judge suffices to hear separation suits since the appellate tribunal is constituted in the same manner as the court of the first instance.[147] However, should the ordinary of the lower court constitute a collegiate tribunal of three or even five judges to hear the suit, the same number of jurists are required in the appellate stage. Three judges, although a collegiate tribunal, would not suffice to review the sentence of a court composed of five judges. The higher court must comprise a number of judges not fewer in number than that employed in the lower court.[148]

If only one judge in the appellate court reviews the sentence of a collegiate tribunal of first instance, such a decision would be at least illicit according to Canon 1596, but seemingly valid. This view is supported by a decision of the Sacred Roman Rota in 1930. The case involved property rights and the tribunal of first instance was composed of three judges, but only one judge reviewed the decision in the appellate court. The Rota declared the latter's sentence valid but illicit according to Canon 1596.[149] The reason is that Canon 1576, § 1, although demanding a collegiate tribunal in

145 Canon 1987.

146 Canon 1599.

147 Canon 1595; Noval, *De Iudiciis,* n. 158; Coronata, *Institutiones Iuris Canonici,* III, n. 1131. It is necessary that the judicial process be used in the appellate tribunal if it was followed in the lower court: P.C.I., 2 iunii 1932: "An in causis separationis coniugum de quibus in canone 1131, § 1, in secundo gradu eadem servanda sit forma ac in primo gradu. R. Affirmative."—*AAS,* XXIV (1932), 284.

148 Canon 1596: Si collegialiter causa in prima instantia cognita fuerit, etiam in gradu appellationis collegialiter nec a minore iudicium numero definiri debet.

149 S.R.R., *Proprietatis,* 11 aug. 1930, coram R.P.D. Francisco Parrillo, dec. LII, n. 6—*Decisiones,* XXII (1930), 586.

the first instance for marriage cases *de vinculo,* does not demand it for separation cases and the like which do not concern the bond of marriage or of sacred ordination.[150]

There is no restriction in the law, however, for the converse. Thus a sentence of one judge in the lower court can be heard by a collegiate tribunal in the appellate instance. Canon 1596 makes no restriction in this regard, but is concerned with forbidding action on appeal through fewer judges than the number used in the lower court.[151] Moreover, the practice of the Rota sanctions this assertion. All cases of separation tried before this tribunal have been reviewed by a collegiate tribunal of three judges and there is even one decision given by a tribunal of eleven judges.[152]

Worthy of note among the standard court personnel is the presence of the promoter of justice in the court of second instance.[153] Since his presence was proved to be necessary in the lower court it is also necessary in the appellate stage of the trial in due consequence of the constitution of the latter court in the same manner as the court of first instance.[154] His duties, of course, will be the same.[155]

The right to appeal, as in all cases, falls to the party who feels himself aggrieved by the sentence. Thus the invoking of a legal redress in a separation suit is the right of the party who has lost the suit and of the promoter of justice, should the circumstances warrant it.[156] As has been noted, the promoter of justice plays a very important rôle in these cases. It is somewhat similar to the office

[150] Kay, *Competence in Matrimonial Procedure,* The Catholic University of America Canon Law Studies, n. 53 (Washington, D. C.: The Catholic University of America, 1929), p. 105; Coronata, *Interpretatio Authentica Codicis Iuris Canonici* (2. ed., Torino: Marietti, 1948), p. 267 ad Canon 1596.

[151] Noval, *De Iudiciis,* n. 159.

[152] S.R.R., *Separationis quoad Thorum et Cohabitationem,* 20 apr. 1912, coram R.mo.P.D. Michaeli Lega, Decano, dec. XVI—*Decisiones,* IV (1912), 203.

[153] Canon 1586.

[154] Canon 1595.

[155] Glynn, *The Promoter of Justice,* p. 310.

[156] Canon 1879: Pars quae aliqua sententia se gravatam putat, itemque promotor iustitiae et defensor vinculi in causis in quibus interfuerunt, ius habent a sententia appellandi, idest provocandi ab inferiore iudice qui sententiam tulit, ad superiorem, salvo praescripto Canon 1880.

of the defender of the bond in matrimonial cases *de vinculo*. Although the promoter of justice does not have a rôle that makes it mandatory for him to appeal an unfavorable decision in every case; [157] nevertheless, as guardian of the public weal, he must in virtue of his office seek legal redress against a sentence which in his opinion places the public good in jeopardy. His position is somewhat the same here as that of the defender of the bond after two concordant sentences in favor of the nullity of the marriage.[158] Wherefore, whenever he considers the sentence of the lower court which has allowed the separation to be unwarranted and to endanger the public good, he has not only the right but also the duty to appeal the case.[159]

The filing of the appeal, the transfer of the acts and the other ordinary formalities are observed according to the general law on these matters. Worthy of note is the fact that separation cases only require a *causa gravis* for the admission of new proofs in this instance since they never become adjudged cases.[160]

There is some doubt as to the application of article 219, § 2, of the *Instructio* to separation cases in the appellate stage. According to the prescriptions of this norm, if a new basis for nullity arises during the course of the appellate proceedings and if it is admitted by the tribunal without objection from anyone, the decision on this point may be pronounced, but as related to a case heard in first instance.[161] It may happen in a separation suit that the fact of adultery has not been proved in the first instance, and that accordingly a negative sentence was given. The plaintiff seeks redress and in the appellate stage alleges another sin of infidelity by the defendant in the period intervening between the two suits or com-

[157] Glynn, *op. cit.*, p. 307; Stitt, *De Promotore Iustitiae*, n. 138.

[158] Canon 1987; *Instructio*, art. 221.

[159] Canon 1879; Glynn, *op. cit.*, pp. 304, 305; Augustine, *A Commentary on the New Code of Canon Law* (2. ed., 8 vols., St. Louis - London: Herder, 1918 - 1922), VII, 318; Stitt, *loc. cit.*

[160] Augustine, *op. cit.*, VII, 234; Regatillo, *Ius Sacramentarium*, II, n. 658; Muñiz, *Procédimentos Eclesiasticos*, (3 vols., Vol. III, 2. ed., Sevilla, 1926), III, n. 298.

[161] Si vero novum hoc nullitatis caput afferatur in gradu appellationis, illudque nemine contradicente a collegio admittatur, de eo iudicandum est tanquam in prima instantia.

mitted prior to the initial suit but never presented as evidence in the court of first instance. Can the judge of the appellate court adjudicate this new delict and base his sentence upon it? Regatillo is of the opinion that the above mentioned article 219, § 2, of the *Instructio* may be utilized in this case and the newly alleged infidelity may be judged by the court of appeal but sitting as the court of first instance. He takes note, indeed of Canon 1891, § 1,[162] but excepts such an instance as this by reason of the above cited article as applicable to separation cases.[163]

A further question can arise in the case when the appellate court in judging a suit for permanent separation on the grounds of adultery finds that this action is not sustained, but that there is evidence to allow a temporary separation. Would the same rule apply? It seems not. Here there is not only a new ground for separation but an entirely different judicial action, since permanent and temporary separations are quite distinct.[164]

Although he does not treat this express case, it seems that Regatillo's view does not apply here. He speaks of the same action for a permanent separation on the grounds of adultery but in his hypothesis the fact of infidelity unproven in the first instance is now proven in the appellate stage but because of a different act. The overall action is still the same, while in a temporary separation the very nature of the action is different and not just its specific identity. They are distinct causes and would therefore expressly come under the provision of Canon 1891, § 1. Regatillo's treatment of article 219, § 2, of the *Instructio* later in his work, where he mentions his earlier reference to separation cases as included under this article, also seems to confine the discussion entirely to causes tried on the ground of adultery and not to extend to cases distinguishable on the basis of their permanent and temporary nature.[165]

162 In gradu appellationis non potest admitti nova petendi causa, ne per modum quidem utilis *cumulationis*; ideoque litis contestatio in eo tantum versari potest ut prior sententia vel confirmetur, vel reformetur sive ex toto sive ex parte.

163 *Ius Sacramentarium,* II, n. 587, ter, e.

164 Canon 1891, § 1; Wernz-Vidal, *Ius Canonicum,* VII, n. 613; Coronata, *Institutiones Iuris Canonici,* III, n. 1413.

165 *Op. cit.,* II, n. 657.

CHAPTER VI

THE ADMINISTRATIVE PROCESS

In the brief historical synopsis presented in the earlier section of this work, it was noted that the administrative hearing of separation cases developed by custom rather than by direct authoritative legislation. During the post-Tridentine period especially, doubtless as the result of the increasing development of secularism, Catholics were naturally influenced by the current laxity in regard to the sacredness of marriage. As a result, petitions for separations became more numerous than in the earlier ages of faith. Moreover, this was a period of great missionary activity, and aside from continental Europe most of the countries of the world were still mission territories. Diocesan tribunals were for the most part unequipped to handle separation cases with dispatch in a formal judicial manner; as a consequence, a custom arose by which the bishop or the parish priest reviewed a petition and decreed a separation without any formal process.[1] This was especially true for cases of temporary separation.[2] Although not a designated legal method at the time, such treatment of separation cases was tolerated by the ecclesiastical authority as a substitute for the formal judicial process, the ordinary procedure for these suits.[3]

In this period before the Code of Canon Law, there was not always a clear distinction between what is known today as the administrative method and a summary judicial procedure somewhat comparable to the process now outlined in Canons 1990-1992. In fact, the summary judicial process was accepted then with a greater degree of recognition than the administrative method,[4] but the law of the Code of Canon Law, as expressed in Canon 1131 and its recent authoritative interpretation,[5] has altered this situation. Today,

[1] Smith, *The Marriage Process in the United States*, nn. 79, 80.

[2] *Loc. cit.*

[3] S.C.C., *Monacen*, 23 ian. 1875 - *Thesaurus Resolutionum S.C.C.*, CXXXIV, 103; S.C.C., 31 iul. 1869 - *AAS*, V (1869), 3, 11; Bouix, *De Judiciis*, II, 441; Feije, *De Impedimentis*, p. 491; Wernz, *Ius Decretalium*, IV, n. 714.

[4] Wernz, *loc. cit.*

[5] P.C.I., 24 iul. 1932—*AAS*, XXIV (1932), 284.

the formal judicial procedure and the administrative process are equal in status, with the summary process, in the opinion of the writer, now completely unwarranted for separation suits.

Cappello and Vidal (+ 1938) state that the summary process may still be employed. Cappello described it thus: ". . . *quatenus citentur partes, colligantur probationes iisque mature perpensis legitima feratur pronuntiatio, ceteris omissis iuris sollemnitatibus.*" [6] Vidal merely mentioned the fact of a summary process, but through a comparison of texts, it is obvious that his treatment, both in text and sources cited, is identical with the earlier commentary of Wernz on the decretal law.[7]

There seems to be no reason for including this summary process among the procedures for separation suits today. Surely these cases cannot be said to receive mention in Canon 1990, since the seven diriment impediments stated there as permitting the summary process present an exhaustive list.[8] Moreover, any necessity for another shortened process as a substitute for the longer and more expensive formal trial, the only reason for its existence, is unwarranted today with the authoritative acceptance of the administrative method. To prescribe it would only lead to needless duplication and unnecessary additional formalities. As has been noted above, the formal judicial process is the ordinary method of hearing suits of permanent separation and the administrative process, those involving a temporary separation,[9] although in certain circumstances the two procedures may be interchanged. Should a sin of infidelity be apparent enough not to warrant the full judicial process, a briefer procedure would be most practical in its obvious facility, but separation cases already have a shortened process in the administrative method, which is equal to any of the advantages of a summary judicial process. To make any provision for the latter today is unreasonable and unwarranted.

[6] *De Sacramentis,* V, 826.

[7] *Ius Canonicum,* V, n. 646; Wernz, *Ius Decretalium,* IV, n. 714.

[8] P.C.I., 6 dec. 1943: I. Utrum casus excepti canonis 1990 sint taxative, an demonstrative enunciati. R. Affirmative ad primam partem; Negative ad secundam—*AAS,* XXXVI (1944), 94.

[9] Cf. *supra,* p. 107 ff.

Article 1. Nature and Character of the Administrative Process

In the absence of any prescribed formalities in the Code of Canon Law for the administrative hearing of separation suits, any treatment of this method must depend on an analysis of the requirements for such a case, along with a consideration of acceptable practical norms derived from the customary method of proceeding in diocesan curias. Although the hearing of a case in the administrative manner is quite informal and relatively brief, nevertheless such treatment does not minimize or lessen in any degree the gravity of the case or the caution to be exercised in all separation suits. These cases by their nature are intimately concerned with the public good and therefore all are of equal importance, despite the process employed in their adjudication. The ordinary should exercise no less diligence in these cases than in other administrative procedures such as the pauline privilege and the process for a dispensation from a *ratum non consummatum* union.[10] Cases of this latter type are accorded the most scrupulous care and attention; yet, as a decision of the Sacred Roman Rota testifies, separation cases are of greater import since the validity of the marriage is certain and uncontested and there is no question of a dissolution of the bond.[11] An even greater observance of caution is necessary, therefore, in hearing separation suits than in other processes concerned with dissolving the bond of marriage.

Although the administrative process in separation cases approximates in some aspects other informal hearings, it must be noted that this is a purely non-judicial process and many familiar properties of other informal procedures are not necessary.[12] So the judicial characteristics of summary cases according to Canons 1990-1992 are not prescribed, nor are the judicial formalities as found in other administrative proceedings, as in a ratified and not consummated mar-

[10] Forbes, *The Canonical Separation of Consorts,* p. 195; Hines, *De Coniugum Separatione,* p. 42.

[11] S.R.R., *Separationis quoad Thorum et Mensam,* 5 iul. 1910, coram R.mo.P.D. Michaeli Lega, Decano, dec. XXIV, n. 11—*Decisiones,* II (1910), 243.

[12] Regatillo, *Ius Sacramentarium,* II, n. 587, ter.

riage case. These cases necessitate special procedural formalities as a result of directives issued by the Holy See, formalities not found in purely administrative cases such as separation suits.

The description to be presented here of the administrative process will endeavor to avoid purely arbitrary and unfounded recommendations and suggestions; rather, it will attempt to analyze the nature of the suit, and to submit whatever processual regulations appear most congruous with correct canonical practice and legitimate custom, as far as this last may be determined. Certain characteristics are governed completely by explicit canonical provisions, while other stages of the process may only be inferred or recommendably deduced from similar procedures and common curial methods. Moreover, authoritative sources are lacking for the most part, and recourse must be made to the treatment of canonical writers; even these, since the procedure for separation is merely incidental to their work, treat it in brief fashion.[13]

Despite the absence of the judicial formalities and of the safeguards for truth as found in the formal process, no less moral certitude is necessary in the ecclesiastical authority's mind to decide a separation case in the administrative manner. The shorter process is allowed, not because the subject is unimportant, but because of the convenience it affords when proof is more readily obtainable. Although it is not proper to carry the proportion too far, one may compare this shorter process to the judicial summary procedure of vincular cases. This brief process of Canons 1990-1992 is gratifying to all concerned because it expedites the case so swiftly and without complication. Nevertheless, it demands the same serious and important consideration as the formal process in its quest for truth. The ordinary still acts as a judge in these cases and he cannot render a decision without previously establishing a firm certitude, gleaned from incontestable documentary proof and testimony. Moreover, that important official in marriage litigations, the defender of the

[13] The most complete treatment is given in Forbes, *The Canonical Separation of Consorts,* pp. 194 - 199; briefer accounts may be found in Kelly, "Separation and Civil Divorce," *The Jurist,* VI (1946), 208; Hines, *De Coniugum Separatione,* p. 42; Doheny, *Canonical Procedure in Matrimonial Cases,* II, 643 - 646.

bond, must intervene, and, if he prudently thinks the necessary moral certitude concerning the presence of the asserted diriment impediment is not had, he is obliged to appeal to the court of second instance. The requirements for this process are few, but still very important, for any marriage once celebrated enjoys the favor of the law. It must, then, be considered valid, until its nullity is definitely demonstrated.

A like comparison should be observed in separation suits. The administrative process is brief and uninvolved, yet it is still concerned with the integrity of marriage, and should therefore incorporate the essential properties of the formal case which its gravity warrants. These important requirements may be summarized in the following definition, which seems to the writer to incorporate the necessary elements of the procedure to be observed in separation cases heard in the administrative fashion. Upon the presence of a canonical just cause as stated in Canon 1131, § 1, or upon clear proof of the sin of infidelity as described in Canon 1129, the ordinary or his delegate, having interviewed the parties and examined whatever testimony and documentary proof is available, and omitting the usual formalities of a solemn trial, may decree a temporary or, in the case of adultery, a permanent separation, having first, however, consulted the promoter of justice to learn his view after he examines the case. The reasons for arriving at this description of the process will now be explained.

Article 2. The Proper Authority for the Administrative Hearing of Separation Cases

It is clear from the phraseology of Canon 1131 [14] that the local ordinary is the proper authority for the administrative hearing of separation suits. His jurisdiction is divided into judicial and voluntary power. The basis of this distinction is not the nature or source of his power, but the form in which the jurisdiction is exercised.[15]

[14] § 1: ". . . auctoritate Ordinarii loci,"; § 2: ". . . sed si separatio ab Ordinario pronuntiata fuerit [. . .] ex decreto Ordinarii. . . ."

[15] Coronata, *Institutiones Iuris Canonici,* II, n. 282; Wernz-Vidal, *Ius Canonicum,* II, . 375; Roberti, *De Processibus,* I, n. 43.

Because of this twofold authority special attention must be paid to the ordinary's source of competency in this process. It is clear that the lack of any judicial form in the administrative process for separation cases confines them to the exercise of the ordinary's voluntary jurisdiction. This power may again be divided into legislative administrative and punitive jurisdiction. Its employment in this instance is administrative; it is part of the governing power of the ordinary.[16]

The ordinary's competency then must be determined according to Canon 201,[17] and not Canon 1964. Therefore the ordinary of the place where the marriage was contracted or of the domicile of the respondent is not competent to hear these cases on that basis; he must be the ordinary of domicile or quasi-domicile of either party, or, if either lacks a domicile or a quasi-domicile anywhere, the ordinary of the territory in which they are actually residing.[18] Worthy of mention here also is that the wife not legitimately separated necessarily retains the domicile of her husband, although she may acquire her own quasi-domicile.[19]

[16] Regatillo, *Ius Sacramentarium,* II, n. 587, ter.

[17] § 1: Potestas iurisdictionis potest in solos subditos directe exerceri.

§ 2: Iudicialis potestas tam ordinaria quam delegata exerceri nequit in proprium commodum aut extra territorium, salvis praescriptis Canon 401, § 1, 881, § 2, et 1637.

§ 3: Nisi aliud ex rerum natura aut ex iure constet, potestatem iurisdictionis voluntariam seu non-iudicialem quis exercere potest etiam in proprium commodum, aut extra territorium existens, aut in subditum e territorio absentem.

[18] Canon 94; Most writers on this subject do not distinguish the state of the *vagus* and the *peregrinus.* They merely state that the competent ordinary is the ordinary of the place where either party has a domicile or a quasi-domicile, or the ordinary of the place where either party is actually staying. Thus: Forbes, *The Canonical Separation of Consorts,* p. 194; Kelly, "Separation and Civil Divorce," *The Jurist,* VI (1946), 208; Hines, *De Coniugum Separatione,* p. 42. If both spouses have a domicile or a quasi-domicile and are actually in another place and so referred to as *peregrini,* the ordinary of the place where they are actually staying is not competent to hear their case. They would not be his subjects (Canons 91; 94; 201, § 1). These cases are not exceptions to the general rule which is stated in Canon 14, § 1, 1, and such a case would have to be referred to the ordinary of domicile or quasi-domicile, who can exercise his power over his subjects even when they are outside his territory (Canon 201, § 3).

[19] Canon 93.

Since Canon 1131 mentions the ordinary of the place and not the bishop exclusively, besides the bishop the vicar general may hear these cases in administrative procedure without any express delegation.[20] Should the Bishop reserve their hearing to himself alone, then the vicar general could not act; but these cases do not necessitate any special mandate for the vicar general to be competent.[21]

Although the officialis has ordinary power,[22] he is not an ordinary in the sense of Canon 198 and is therefore not competent by virtue of his office to review these cases in the administrative procedure. His power is judicial, and he is not empowered to exercise non-judicial jurisdiction unless he be duly deputed with this voluntary power by the ordinary of the place. He would then act as any other delegated priest, as a delegate of the ordinary.

The bishop or the vicar general are free to delegate any priest they desire to exercise the administrative process in these cases, since in the law there is no prohibition of this delegation.[23] However, in keeping with the grave nature of separation cases, it would not be prudent for the ordinary to be so excessive with his delegations that the administrative hearing of separation cases becomes a matter of minor moment. It is true that, in this country, a custom existed before the promulgation of the Code of Canon Law for the parish priest to review petitions and to decree a separation in the administrative fashion.[24] In view of the very positive statement of Canon 1131 which demands the permission of the ordinary of the place for intervention, and in the light of the ecclesiastical jurisprudence relative to the gravity of these cases, it is quite clear that this custom no longer has place. Moreover, were the bishop to delegate every priest or pastor to hear these cases, it seems that the whole purpose of the law would be frustrated, and the firm attitude of the Church on the integrity of marriage could in consequence be considered a matter of small importance. The history of this institute demon-

[20] Canon 198.

[21] Canons 368, § 1.

[22] Canon 1573, § 1.

[23] Canon 199, § 1; Canon 1131; Kearney, *The Principles of Delegation*, The Catholic University of America Canon Law Studies, n. 55 (Washington, D. C.: The Catholic University of America, 1929), p. 79.

[24] Smith, *The Marriage Process in the United States*, n. 79, 80.

strates its grave significance. Excessive delegation would only serve to destroy a sacred tradition.

One method of conducting the hearing of these cases administratively is the erection of central boards for the exclusive hearing of separation cases, and of their companion problems, petition for civil action. In some American dioceses, as a result of the overburdening number of separation cases brought about by the current unfavorable influence of secularism upon the sacrament of marriage, bishops have found the erection of these delegated boards quite helpful. Usually they are set up as collegiate boards and sometimes individual members are delegated as single agents to reach a settlement. Where the geographic extent of the diocese makes it possible, these boards may operate from the diocesan curia, or, if the extent of the territory is so large that one central office would be difficult of approach for many of the faithful, similar boards are erected in several or even all of the individual deaneries. These delegated priests are concerned exclusively, as far as marriage cases are considered, with canonical separation. They use the later outlined process in securing testimony and attempt by whatever means are at hand to effect a reconciliation of the parties in their effort to stem the advancing tide of broken marriages. Their principal work is, of course, to act as the delegates of the bishop in awarding or refusing a separation.

The employment of this method is quite canonically feasible. There is no danger of minimizing the gravity of separation cases by excessive delegation, since the members of the boards are chosen for their prudence and canonical erudition. Moreover, this method has rather the opposite effect in stressing the importance of these cases, and potentially serves as a positive influence against the marital abuses which face the Church in the United States of America today.

As far as the matter of delegation is concerned, attention must be paid to the manner in which the jurisdiction is deputed to these boards that their operation may be valid. If the ordinary expressly delegates these groups to act as a collegiate board in reviewing separation petitions, they must proceed as a moral unit in rendering a decision. It is not necessary that their consent be unanimous; it suffices that there be a majority vote of the members.[25] The ordinary may also when constituting such a board distinctly delegate each member. The priests making up the board then enjoy their delegation severally as well as cumulatively (*in solidum facta*) and each delegate is equally competent to decide separation cases.[26] Since the administrative process in separation cases involves an exercise of voluntary jurisdiction, a presumption as stated in the law in cases of doubt concerning the manner of delegation is of interest. Non-judicial jurisdiction is in any case of doubt presumed to be held severally rather than in a collegiate manner.[27] Therefore, in the absence of any proof that points to a contrary intention of the ordinary, members of these boards must be presumed to enjoy their delegated jurisdiction as individuals severally, and not only as a group united together.

Article 3. The Process

Mention has already been made regarding the dearth of canonical literature on the administrative hearing of separation cases. The writer has endeavored therefore to inquire among several curias of the country to ascertain a legitimate and practical method of conducting these cases. What is to follow is an attempt to demonstrate as faithfully as possible the salient features of their practical processual suggestions.[28]

A. *Introductory and Probatory Stages of the Process*

The initial element of the administrative process is the submitting of a petition to separate by the aggrieved party. This should state the name, address, religion and other pertinent facts of the petitioner's personal history. It should also identify the other spouse in such a way as to permit his being interviewed by the ordinary for his own defense. In addition, the petition should state, in a general

[25] Canons 205, § 3; 1577, § 1; Kearney, *op. cit.*, p. 109.

[26] Canon 205, §§ 1, 2; Kearney, *op. cit.*, p. 108.

[27] *Loc. cit.*

[28] Not only the information presented here but also the interrogatories contained in the appendices are the result of this inquiry.

manner at least, the canonical causes alleged as grounds for the separation. The names and the address of at least two witnesses to the asserted delinquency should also be mentioned. It would be proper that there be appended a concluding paragraph in which a declaration of intention would be contained. Therein the petitioner could state his recognition of the sacramental and indissoluble nature of his marriage, that he is cognizant of the impossibility of another marriage and of the actual occasion of sin in any attempted courtship. This declaration could then conclude with an expression of intention to co-operate whenever future reconciliation becomes feasible.

Attached to this petition or on a separate enclosure, a more complete statement of the case should be given. This can be achieved through the use of prepared interrogatories similar to those presented in the appendix to this work. A questionnaire should be so prepared that it will normally serve to determine the following important facts: the length and general character of the conjugal relationship to date; the present marital situation of each spouse, i.e., whether cohabitation has ceased or still continues; whether either has attempted another marriage, and a complete history of all former separations. The number and age of the children should be given as well as any pertinent information regarding their custody and education. Then a clear and detailed exposition of the canonical cause or causes should be presented with reference made to any available documentary proof that would advantageously serve the ordinary in the framing of his decision.

Since the other spouse has a right to defend himself from any accusations made against him, an attempt must always be made to interview him. This can be achieved by a personal interview or through a prepared interrogatory similar to that presented to the petitioner. In addition to containing the ordinary preliminary questions, the respondent's questionnaire should inform him of the canonical cause for separation asserted by the petitioner and whatever other information is deemed necessary to enable him to formulate a defense. The respondent should also be permitted to offer whatever proof he wishes and to suggest the names and addresses of witnesses who might substantiate his claim.

Inasmuch as the intrinsic nature of these cases demands that every attempt be made at a possible reconciliation, attention should be given to the mind of each spouse on this matter. Forearmed with a knowledge of their mutual dispositions, the ordinary would be better prepared to discuss the resumption of common life with a greater assurance of success.

Similarly prepared interrogatories may be presented to the witnesses proposed by each party. Besides questions eliciting the pertinent personal information customarily prefacing these forms to establish identity, this interrogatory should contain questions especially relevant to proving or disproving the alleged cause. The witness should be questioned regarding the source of his knowledge, and his familiarity with the petitioner's request for a separation and his personal reasons why it should be granted or refused. After this preliminary interrogation, he may be informed of the cause the petitioner has proposed and then be requested to give whatever information he possesses that could serve to prove the objective fact. The witness should also be requested to give his opinion on the possibility of reconciliation whether at the present or some later date. Since these people are usually relatives or intimate friends of the parties, their knowledge of the personalities involved may very often be the sole basis afforded the ordinary to attempt a restoration of the common life.

In the procurement of information, not only from the parties but also from the witnesses, the aid and intervention of the parish priest should be employed as much as possible. Besides an allotted space for his signature when he acts as a notary, space should also be provided on the prepared forms for the pastor's opinions both with regard to the credibility of the deponent as well as his opinion of the merits of the case itself. His statements should contain not only an expression of opinion on the advisability of the separation but any pertinent information he may possess regarding the history of the marriage and the possibilities of reconciliation. Many dioceses even have specially prepared forms for the testimony of the priest to aid him in presenting his information as completely as possible.

As a result of the very large number of parishioners in so many parishes in our country today, the personal knowledge of a pastor or of his assistants concerning many members of his flock is unfortunately at a practical minimum. To assume an intimate knowledge on their part of the implications of every separation case presented from their territory would be expecting the physically impossible. As a consequence, the parochial clergy can do no more than act as notaries of the depositions sworn before them. The enlistment of the services of other priests who have a more intimate knowledge of the case at hand is the practical solution of the difficulty. It seems feasible then to request the parties to present the names of any priests who may know them quite well, and who could be of assistance to the ordinary in deciding the existence of a just cause, as well as in serving effectively in attempts to reconcile the parties. There is no violation of parochial rights in the employing of this practice [29] and its obvious advantages are a strong recommendation for its use.

Since the causes mentioned in Canon 1131, § 1, often have a physical or psychological basis, it is the practice of many curias to employ the services of well qualified medical men and psychiatrists in an effort to forestall separations by removing the grounds for them. Although their opinion would be necessary in a case where the cause of insanity was alleged, nevertheless, their important office could very often be useful in other cases in which it would possess a more positive nature in working toward the reconciliation of the parties. It would be at the discretion of the ordinary or of his delegate to request their help and co-operation in any particular case, and it is a practice that would certainly have canonical foundation.[30]

The testimony and proofs offered in the administrative process should be accepted and rejected with no less scruple than evidence in a formal trial. There have already been pointed out the elements which are necessary for a just separation and the means of acceptable proof. These should be the criteria in whatever process the case is reviewed. Moral certitude is necessary for a decision in all cases.[31]

In the matter of evidence in the administrative process, the principal problem appears to be the legality of employing a presumption

[29] Cf. Canon 462.

[30] Cf. Canon 1792.

[31] Forbes, *The Canonical Separation of Consorts*, p. 195.

when the ordinary decides to hear by this method a separation petition pleaded on the grounds of adultery. Although the ordinary process for these cases is the judicial trial, nevertheless, as was noted earlier [32] the shorter administrative process may be employed when it is a question of an easily proved delict of infidelity. Since presumptions are the usual elements of proof in matters of adultery, the question arises concerning their acceptance in the administrative process. May they be considered, or must the case, in the absence of more direct proof, be remanded by the ordinary to a judicial trial? Surely the ordinary would be acting within his competence by demanding the formal procedure, since he would be merely employing the ordinary process for these cases. Such action, however, does not seem absolutely necessary.

The evidence in these cases rarely exceeds the limits of a violent presumption. This is the normal proof.[33] Moreover, as authors demonstrate, violent presumptions offer full proof of what is alleged.[34] It is for this reason that they are acceptable even in the administrative process; otherwise, this method could rarely be employed for permanent separations. Probable presumptions in offering only partial proof are, of course, insufficient in themselves. Should they be the sole evidence proposed and the ordinary be unable to arrive at the necessary moral certitude, then he must place the case on the judicial calendar. These probable presumptions are acceptable as means of proof, but the safeguards of the formal process seem necessary to guarantee a proper appraisal of their merit. Violent presumptions based on acts proximate to the delict of infidelity are the normal proofs; doubts and uncertainties can hardly be firmly founded as contradictions to them. Their use then seems perfectly acceptable in the administrative process.

The employment of presumptions in the administrative hearing of cases of temporary separation is perfectly admissible. They are acceptable canonical methods of proof, and since these cases have the administrative method as their ordinary process, the use of pre-

[32] Cf. *supra*, p. 77.

[33] Cf. *supra*, pp. 101-104.

[34] Coronata, *Institutiones Iuris Canonici*, III, n. 1356; Wernz-Vidal, *Ius Canonicum*, VI, n. 520; Vermeersch-Creusen, *Epitome Iuris Canonici*, III, 206.

sumptions is entirely legitimate. Their employment here would observe the ordinary canonical practice in the matter.[35]

B. *The Promoter of Justice*

Although the administrative process is brief and informal, the intrinsic gravity of the case is by no means diminished by its use. Whether a separation is granted after the observance of full judicial formalities or upon briefer consideration, cases in which it is granted are always cases of separation and must be accorded equally thorough consideration. It is only reasonable, then, since conjugal integrity concerns the public good,[36] that the office of the promoter of justice must find application even in the administrative hearing of a separation case. In placing the requirement for his presence in these suits, authors do not distinguish the method of procedure; they simply demand his intervention whenever marital cohabitation, a matter of the public good, is endangered and jeopardized.[37]

To require his presence only in a formal trial and not in administrative hearings is hardly congruous with the intrinsic nature of the case when one considers similar canonical institutes. In the summary process of Canons 1990-1992 and the procedure investigating a *ratum non consummatum* marriage petition, the full processual formalities are omitted; nevertheless, the defender of the bond must always intervene.[38] The administrative treatment of separation cases is similar in its absence of formality. However, just as informal cases concerning the bond remain suits *de vinculo* and require the intervention of the defender of the bond, so this brief separation hearing is a matter of the public good equally with a formal trial, and requires the office of the promoter of justice.[39]

[35] Canons 1825 - 1828.

[36] Normae S.R.R. Tribunalis, art. 27, § 1, 2—*AAS,* XXVI (1934), 457.

[37] Glynn, *The Promoter of Justice,* p. 87; Stitt, *De Promotore Iustitiae,* p. 125; Le Picard, *Le Communaute de la Vie Conjugale,* pp. 45, 243.

[38] Canons 1990 - 1992; S.C. de Sacramentis, *Regulae servandae in processibus super matrimonio rato et non consummato,* 7 maii 1923, n. 27—*AAS,* XV (1923), 398.

[39] Forbes, *The Canonical Separation of Consorts,* p. 196; Doheny, *The Canonical Procedure in Matrimonial Cases,* II, 645.

His office will naturally concern itself with guarding the public welfare from injury caused by groundless separations. Not that his presence is necessary at every stage of the process, but he should serve as the consultant to the ordinary before the decree permitting or rejecting the separation is issued. To fulfill this charge, it would be sufficient for him to review the evidence obtained from the parties and witnesses and give an expression of his opinion on the merits of the case.

If there is any element of doubt in the entire process, it appears imperative for the promoter of justice to demand more evidence. If this is not forthcoming and he feels a formal trial is necessary because of the circumstances, it seems that he has the right and even the obligation to present his opinion and petition a judicial trial from the ordinary. Although in the response issued by the Holy See regarding the process to be used in separation cases, he is not mentioned as one who can petition a formal trial,[40] it appears quite congruous with the nature of his office that he should do so whenever he feels a judicial procedure will better safeguard the public good.

C. *The Decree of Separation*

Since the administrative hearing of separation cases is an exercise of the governing jurisdiction of the ordinary,[41] his decision in the case should be incorporated in a formal decree.[42] Besides the usual formalities specifying the title and the number of the case, the date of the precept and the identification of the litigants, elements necessary for any such document, the decree of the ordinary should clearly grant or refuse the petition of separation. If the separation is allowed, the decree must state explicitly whether it is to be permanent

[40] P.C.I., 24 iun. 1932—*AAS,* XXIV (1932), 284.

[41] Regatillo, *Ius Sacramentarium,* II, n. 587, ter.

[42] Canon 1868, § 2; "Decretum [. . .] diverso sensu adhibetur. Hoc nomine designantur [. . .] acta gubernationis Episcoporum et aliorum qui auctoritate publica gaudent in Ecclesia. Hoc ultimo sensu intellecta, decreta sunt decisiones latae in casu particulari, vi potestatis, non legislativae vel iudiciariae, sed gubernativae et executivae, et possunt vocari praecepta data communitati vel singulis quibus vel lex executioni mandatur, vel quid novi et specialis iniungitur." —Van Hove, *Commentarium Lovaniense in Codicem Iuris Canonici,* Vol. II, *de Legibus Ecclesiasticis* (Mechlinae: H. Dessain, 1930), n. 371, 2°.

or temporary and, if the latter, whether it is for an indeterminate or a determinate period of time.[43]

If the separation is temporary, some provision should be made for future reconciliation. The time for this may be given as a future date, as that coinciding with the lapse of the cause or as specified in some similar statement; that method is to be adopted which, in the discretion of the ordinary, the circumstances warrant. Some brief statement regarding the indissolubility of marriage, to call attention to the fact that this decree does not provide opportunity for any future marriage, seems appropriate.

By attaching it to this decree, the ordinary may express whatever permission he wishes to allow in the matter of civil action. If this method is followed, special emphasis must be placed on the impossibility of the contracting of a future marriage and even of the indiscretion of any courtship in view of its nature as a very real occasion of sin. Moreover, the oath of the petitioner attesting to a sincere intention to be freed sofely of the obligations arising from the marriage contract in the civil forum is required.[44] The oath should be appended to the decree of separation if both the decree and the permission for civil action are contained in the one document.

The decree should be signed by the ordinary or by his delegate and notarized in the usual manner. Moreover, the oath of the party mentioned above should also contain not only the signature of the deponent but also the signature of two witnesses.[45]

Since the decree of separation and the provisions for civil action are essentially distinct matters, the ordinary may use separate documents to express his will regarding them. After granting a canonical separation he may wish to consider at greater length the causes presented for civil action. To do this would be most appropriate when one considers the gravity of his decision; for this reason at least, a separate decree permitting or refusing the petition for civil action may be executed. If this procedure is observed, for the avoidance of needless confusion, then the decree of permission should be incorporated in the file of the separation proceedings.

[43] Doheny, *op. cit.*, II, 645; Forbes, *op. cit.*, p. 197.

[44] Forbes, *op. cit.*, p. 251.

[45] S.C.S. Off., 6 aug. 1906—Gasparri, *De Matrimonio,* II, n. 1324.

Article 4. Legal Redress Against the Decree of the Ordinary

Since the appellate stage of a separation case must be conducted according to the same method as that used in the first instance, the legal remedy employed as redress against the decree of the ordinary must also be administrative.[46] In the place of appeal which is judicial, the form of redress allowed in these cases is its extra-judicial counterpart, administrative recourse. This may be described as a plea made to a competent superior against the extra-judicial acts of a lesser superior with the view of obtaining a more favorable decision.[47] Unlike judicial appeal, which proceeds under many legal limitations,[48] administrative recourse is much more informal and not strictly regulated by similar requirements of time, form and place. It need not be interposed before the ordinary against whom the redress is sought nor is there required any special format. A simple appeal to the Holy See in letter form suffices. This letter should state the names and the addresses of the parties, the name of the ordinary who issued the decree in the case, and, most important, the reasons why the party regards the decree of the ordinary unjust and injurious.[49]

Although competent to receive judicial appeals from the tribunals of suffragan dioceses or other designated courts of first instance, the Metropolitan is not the higher superior to receive an administrative recourse against the decree of a suffragan bishop.[50] A cursory reading of the authoritative interpretation mentioned above might lead one to conclude erroneously that the ordinary of the court of second

[46] P.C.I., 2 iun. 1922: An in causis separationis coniugum de quibus in Canone 1131, § 1, in secundo gradu eadem servanda sit forma ac in primo gradu. R. Affirmative.—*AAS,* XXIV (1932), 284.

[47] "Recursus dicitur provocatio a Superiore inferioris gradus ad Superiorem gradus altioris. Recursus datur ab actibus positis in ordine administrativo"—Roberti, *De Delictis et Poenis,* Vol. I—pars 1, *De Delictis in Genere* (2. ed., Romae: Libraria Pontificii Instituti Utriusque Iuris, 1938), n. 288; Beste, *Introductio in Codicem,* p. 773.

[48] Canons 1879; 1880; 1881; 1882, § 1; 1889, § 2.

[49] McClunn, *Administrative Recourse,* The Catholic University of America Canon Law Studies, n. 240 (Washington, D. C.: The Catholic University of America Press, 1946), pp. 37, 38.

[50] Canons 274, 7°; 1594, § 1; 1601.

instance should receive this redress but consider it in an administrative manner. This is the interpretation presented by Doheny [51] and he refers to Cappello as an authority in agreement. Actually there is no basis for concord in the two treatments. Cappello's article is a commentary on the authoritative interpretation that Doheny refers to. He does state, and correctly, that appeal from a sentence of a separation case heard judicially would be to the tribunal of the Metropolitan, but he clearly demonstrates that recourse would follow the rules for that particular remedy and be directed to the Sacred Congregation of the Sacraments.[52] This is the correct procedure in matters of administrative redress.

The reply of the Pontifical Commission for the Authentic Interpretation of the Code of Canon Law was not demonstrating an exception to the general law on administrative recourse. It merely pointed out that whatever process is used in the first instance must also be employed in the appellate stage. Whether this latter instance should be the court of the Metropolitan, if the process is judicial, or the Holy See, if the administrative method is used, is not directly mentioned, since there is no necessity of mentioning this distinction in view of the law's clarity on the subject.

The Roman Pontiff alone, not the Metropolitan, has jurisdiction over the extra-judicial acts of ordinaries.[53] It is only when the law explicitly grants certain rights to Metropolitans that they can

[51] "A consort has the right of recourse against the decision granted in the administrative process. In the second instance the case would be reviewed and decided in the administrative manner, as indicated in the reply of the Pontifical Code Commission of June 25, 1932. If the consorts seek recourse from the decree of the Ordinary of second instance, the case would be remanded to the Sacred Congregation of the Sacraments."—*Canonical Procedure in Matrimonial Cases*, II, 645.

[52] "Itaque si causa separationis in primo gradu ordine *iudiciali* cognita ac definita fuerit, verae appellationi locus erit, de qua videre debebit iudex ad quem, normis processualibus adamussim servatis. Si causa separationis in primo gradu disceptata ac soluta fuerit forma *administrativa*, locus non erit appellationi proprie dictae, sed recursui, et sequendae erunt leges propriae recursus (cfr. Canon 1601, 1880, 6°). Igitur appellatio fiet ad iudicem superiorem (Metropolitam, S.R. Rotam, etc.), recursus ad S. Congregationem de Sacramentis."—"De Separatione Coniugum," *Periodica*, XXI (1932), 288.

[53] Canons 218, § 1; 327, § 1.

exercise jurisdiction over other ordinaries.[54] There is no mention of any exception in the matter of administrative recourse; in fact, the law clearly states that such recourse must be made to the Sacred Congregations,[55] which in turn act in the name and by the authority of the Roman Pontiff. In separation cases the Sacred Congregation of the Sacraments is competent, since these are matters that are linked with the Sacrament of Marriage.[56] If one of the parties is a non-Catholic, the recourse is made to the Sacred Congregation of the Holy Office.[57]

Since most curias handle the administrative hearing of separation cases through delegates of the bishop, mention should be made of another possibility of recourse against the delegate's decree. Forbes would have such recourse directed to the Sacred Congregations as a general rule in accordance with Canon 1601; however, if the ordinary should delegate his power in such wise as to reserve the right to review a negative decision before it becomes final, and even in the instance when this limitation is not mentioned, Forbes is of the opinion that the ordinary could receive a petition to review the acts of his delegate in those cases, and even reverse his decision. This author argues well that such a step does not strictly constitute the making of recourse. It is more a plea for the rehearsing of the facts in the case by the same judicial authority in the person of the ordinary. If the ordinary should reverse the decision of his delegate, then his decree has full judicial effect. If the ordinary confirms his delegate's act, the way for recourse to the Holy See is still open.[58]

[54] Canons 274, 1°, 5°; 432, § 2; 1610, § 3; 1709, § 3; 1710.

[55] Canon 1601: Contra Ordinariorum decreta non datur appellatio seu recursus ad Sacram Rotam; sed de eiusmodi recursibus exclusive cognoscunt Sacrae Congregationes; P.C.I., 22 maii 1923: Utrum ad normam Canon 1552-1601 institui possit actio iudicialis contra Ordinariorum decreta, acta, dispositiones, quae ad regimen seu administrationem dioecesis spectent, ex. gr. provisionem beneficiorum, officiorum, etc., aut recusationem seu denegationem collationis beneficii, officii, etc. R. Negative.—*AAS,* XVI (1924), 251.

[56] Canon 249, § 3.

[57] Canon 247, § 3.

[58] *The Canonical Separation of Consorts,* p. 198. This view is supported by McClunn, *Administrative Recourse,* p. 30; Cappello, *Praxis Processualis* (Tourini-Romae: Marietti, 1940), n. 4.

CHAPTER VII

CANONICAL SEPARATION AND CIVIL ACTION

Article 1. The Problem

It is common knowledge that ordinaries in most countries of the world find themselves in an anomalous and oftentimes embarrassing position after rendering a decree of canonical separation. What they have directed to be binding in the ecclesiastical forum has no force whatever before the civil law. In fact decrees of canonical separation are there considered as matters of a purely private religious counsel, which, as far as the civil law is concerned, are enforceable or not at the will of the parties. This unfortunate state of affairs gives rise to a very real and difficult problem, namely: when and under what condition may petitions for civil action in the matter of marital separation, or even of absolute divorce, be countenanced by the ordinary?

Although there are a few exceptions,[1] the general state of the question is a universal problem throughout the world,[2] a problem becoming increasingly complex as one examines the various civil statues, in view of the formidable array of divergent legal provisions and

[1] Spain is the only country wherein a separation, when decreed by the ecclesiastical authority, is recognized as endowed with full civil effects.—Regatillo, *Ius Sacramentarium,* II, n. 590. By virtue of a concordat with other nations, the Holy See has shared its power over the separation of consorts with the civil tribunals, and Catholic spouses in those countries may present themselves before the civil courts, the latter acting validly and licitly as long as they do not contradict the divine or eccelesiastical law. Noteworthy are those in Italy: *Concordato fra la Santa Sede e l'Italia,* Art. 34: "Quanto alle cause di separazione personale, la Santa Sede consente che siano giudicate dall'autorità giudiziaria civile."—*AAS,* XXI (1929), 291, and in Austria: *Konkordat Zwischen dem Heiligen Stuhle und der Republik Oesterreich, Zusatsprotokoll,* zu Artikel VII, n. 2: "Der Heilige Stuhl willigt ein, dass das Verfahren bezüglich der Trennung der Ehe von Tisch und Bett den staatlichen Gerichten zusteht."—*AAS,* XXVI (1934), 277; Cappello, De Sacramentis, V, n. 831.

[2] Ottaviani, *Institutiones Iuris Publici Ecclesiastici* (2 vols., Vol. II, 2. ed., *Ius Publicum Externum,* Romae: Typis Polyglottis Vaticanis, 1936), II, 203.

their consequent difficult inconsistencies. There is a complete absence of uniformity among nations of the world and the states of our own country when the nature and causes for the different types of civil marital action are treated. In some instances, absolute divorce is the sole legal action recognized, while other civil authorities provide for a less objectionable action, which is somewhat comparable to the institute of canonical separation. Provision is also made in some states for other actions which do not directly affect the integrity of the union. They have reference primarily to the financial and material aspects or what might be termed the civil effects of the marriage and are known by the terms: "separate maintenance," "alimony without divorce," or under other similar designations.

In addition to this lack of uniformity, other difficulties arise from a consideration of the grounds recognized in civil law as permitting these actions. These are almost as many and varied as the different legislators and, what is even more troublesome, they run counter, in very many instances, to the causes given as sufficient for marital separation in the ecclesiastical law.

To illustrate this problem in more detail one may submit the following brief summary of the civil law as now existing in the United States relative to separation actions.[3]

The legal institute of "separate maintenance," sometimes called "alimony without divorce," is an action which seeks independent subsidy for a wife separated from her husband without a petition for divorce or even separation. In no wise does it have any effect upon the bond of marriage nor does it alter in any way the marital status of the spouses. Its basis lies in the obligations of the husband

[3] The writer has taken this summary from the complete treatment of the subject by Hines, *De Coniugum Separatione*, pp. 55-172. This author has expressly studied the subject of separation and divorce in canon law and civil law of the various states in this country. After a consideration of canonical separation, the work is concerned with the problem of ecclesiastical tolerance allowed a Catholic pleading a case of separation or of divorce before a civil tribunal, with the present law regarding these actions among the various states, and in conclusion with a suggestion of remedies to combat this pernicious evil in this country. Similar information on the comparison between the eccelsiastical and civil law in the United States is also found in Alford, *Ius Matrimoniale Comparatum* (Romae: Anonima Libraria Cattolica Italiana, 1938), pp. 351-527.

deriving from the fact that while the marriage lasts the wife must be supported. It is usually joined with a decree of separation from board, and although it exists generally in favor of the wife, it may happen that a wife will be compelled to support an infirm husband. This institute exists in all states but New Hampshire. Although only ten states have special laws referring to this legal provision, the other states wherein it exists without special laws recognize it through actions in the court of equity.[4]

Legal separation, an action somewhat comparable to canonical separation, exists in thirty-three states. Those states which lack this particular institute and in which it is impossible for a spouse to obtain any redress except by way of an absolute divorce are the following: Connecticut, Idaho, Illinois, Kansas, Iowa, Mississippi, Minnesota, Nevada, Ohio, South Carolina, Texas, Washington, West Virginia and Wyoming. Of those states which allow the action of legal separation, Arizona, Colorado, Pennsylvania and South Dakota concede it only in favor of the wife. In only one state, Florida, is judicial separation expressly prohibited by law.[5]

Although until quite recently South Carolina was the only state not to allow absolute divorce, now, upon the results of the elections of 1948, that state permits divorce. Today, therefore, absolute divorce is recognized in every state.[6]

In addition to these discrepancies, as affecting the type of action available the causes for the varied actions are also variant and thus increase the difficulty of establishing definite suggestions for ecclesiastical authorities. So divergent are the laws for an action of separate maintenance, that only individual study of the particular laws for each state would be a practical course to follow.[7]

Legal separations, too, may be conceded solely for the causes expressly enumerated in the laws of each state. Here also great discrepancy is found among the states. The most common causes are malicious desertion (in thirty-three states) and cruelty (in thirty states). Even here the duration of the desertion postulated for the

[4] Hines, *op. cit.*, p. 125.
[5] *Op. cit.*, p. 119.
[6] *Op. cit.*, p. 94.
[7] *Op. cit.*, p. 126.

instituting of an action varies among the various states involved. Adultery is cause for separation in twenty-three states, but in two states, viz. Arizona and Pennsylvania, this action is allowed only to the wife, while in Kentucky a husband may seek this remedy because of his wife's immoral conduct, but it is open only to the wife, if it is proved that her spouse is living in a continuous state of adultery. Habitual drunkenness is a ground for this action in twenty states, again with variant terms of the duration of the habit postulated for the action to be accepted. In Arizona, only the wife may plead this case, and not the husband. To add to this variety, there are thirty-two other causes which permit of legal separation among the various states, the majority of which are not canonical grounds for separation.[8]

The causes for absolute divorce are too numerous to mention. It will suffice to say that the universal cause is adultery, and generally one act is sufficient, but Kentucky and Texas demand a continuance of the delict or a living in adultery on the part of the man.[9]

In view of so many inconsistencies and variations, and these even in a single country, it is no wonder that the compilers of the Code of Canon Law have omitted inclusion of any universal law that would serve as a guiding norm for bishops when they are faced with requests by parties to institute civil action after a separation has been granted by the Church. The universal law of the Church does, however, recognize the competency of the State over the civil effects of the marriage contract,[10] but at the same time adamantly declares the Church's exclusive competence over the marriages of baptized persons.[11] These unions are not subject to the state whether it is a matter of separation or of dissolution, for these aspects of marriage are by no means limited to the mere civil effects of the sacrament.[12] Yes, despite these assertions in the ecclesiastical law, the problem remains and its practical solution necessitates some authoritative directions. With no directive norms presented in the universal

[8] *Op. cit.*, p. 121.

[9] *Op. cit.*, p. 94.

[10] Canons 1016; 1961.

[11] Canons 1016; 1038; 1960.

[12] *Loc. cit.*

law, one must have recourse to particular responses of the Roman Curia to establish any acceptable rule of operation for those faced with requests to approach the civil courts with marriage problems. All of these replies were given prior to the promulgation of the Code. A fair treatment then would best consider them in their temporal circumstances through a brief historical review rather than confine the discussion merely to the period after the Code.

Article 2. Historical Synopsis of the Question

The period from the Council of Trent to the Code of Canon Law was an era of constantly increasing recognition by the civil authority of divorce with provision for entering a new marriage. The Council of Trent, confronted with the new doctrines of the reformers which allowed divorce, saw fit to issue a decree in opposition to their errors; since adultery was the ground accepted by the latter as the basis for these absolute divorces, the Council decreed that absolute divorce and remarriage based on this crime was contrary to faith.[13]

Although the great wave of divorce practices did not begin until the revolutionary period of the late eighteenth century, nevertheless, in the intervening time there were ample incidents of the exceptions taken by the Popes to this evil, especially among the Greeks in communion with the Holy See. These had hitherto admitted divorce, at least for adultery; now, in the light of the Tridentine provisions, it became imperative that the ecclesiastical discipline be enforced. The Popes were most firm in enforcing the prohibitions against any divorce *a vinculo* and any attempt at remarriage.[14]

With the wide advocacy of divorce in intellectual circles in France during the eighteenth century, it is no wonder that writers fostered the introduction of legalized divorce as demanded by the times. In line with this trend, both the French Revolution and subsequent Napoleonic legislation promoted the gradual adoption of civil marriage in Europe and America. Concomitant with this concept of

[13] Conc. Trident., sess. XXIV, *de matrimonio*, Canon 7.

[14] Clemens VIII, instr. *Sanctissimum*, 31 aug. 1595—*Fontes*, n. 179; Urban VIII, const. *Magnum in Christo*, 20 iun. 1637—*Fontes*, n. 217; Benedictus XIV, const. *Etsi pastoralis*, 26 maii 1742—*Fontes*, n. 328; *idem*, ep. *Nuper ad Nos*, 16 mart. 1743, *Professio fidei Maronitis praescr.*—*Fontes*, n. 335.

marriage as a civil contract, the recognition of divorce was a natural conclusion. The power that supported the contract was considered also competent to allow its dissolution.[15]

The great Pope Pius IX (1846-1878), on two memorable occasions, denounced the practice of regarding marriage as a mere civil contract with its companion complete divorce.[16] His admonitions were reiterated by his eminent successor Leo XIII (1878-1903), in his encyclical on Christian Marriage, wherein he described the evil results of such practices.[17]

The basis of the erroneous ideas on marriage and divorce then so prevalent, is found in the purely secular concept of the state; no longer was the ecclesiastical law an independent authority with the state, but the nineteenth century saw the gradual usurpation of the rights of the Church over marriage by the secular power. Religion was considered a personal matter, not a concern of the state which was supreme in every department.[18]

As a result of this claim of exclusive jurisdiction of the state, a very real problem was present in the determination of the civil status of those Catholics who had been granted decrees of separation by the Church. Since the sentence of the ecclesiastical court was not recognized in the civil forum, a definite difficulty faced all concerned. With the long history of opposition to civil divorce as such a great evil before them, canonists at the time did not consider the situation easy of solution. All based their opinions on identical responses of the Holy See in answer to particular questions regarding civil action for separation, but their opinions differed widely. These responses and the comments of the authors were concerned with the position of Catholic judges, lawyers and parties in these suits. Historical material for discussion regarding the first two offices is, needless to say, of the utmost importance. However, in keeping with the nature of the present treatment, the remarks to be made here will be confined to the conditions that will permit a Catholic to institute a civil action for separation or divorce.

[15] Joyce, *Christian Marriage,* pp. 401, 403.

[16] Pius IX, alloc. *Acerbissimum,* 27 sept. 1852—*Fontes,* n. 515; *idem, Syllabus Errorum* (a. 1864), n. 67—*Fontes,* n. 543.

[17] Leo XIII, encycl. *Arcanum,* 10 febr. 1880—*ASS,* XII (1880), 385.

[18] Joyce, *Christian Marriage,* p. 260.

An appeal to the civil authority to settle property claims and other purely civil effects of marriage was deemed permissible at that time, for this action did not include any interference with the bond of marriage. This action was considered entirely different in kind from divorce or even separation. Whenever the civil effects could be achieved without the issuance of any decree of separation or of divorce, no canonical problem was present.[19] However, when there was question of civil action for separation or for divorce in the case of a marriage which was valid in the eyes of the Church, the solution was uncertain. There was no doubt that the permission of the ordinary was necessary for the entering of this action, for the III Plenary Council of Baltimore had decreed that Catholics who sought a divorce in the civil courts were guilty of grave sin and that those who committed this delict and attempted another union incurred an excommunication *ipso facto,* which was reserved to the ordinary.[20] The same assembly of the American hierarchy also prohibited Catholics from seeking even a separation *a thoro et mensa* in the civil forum without ecclesiastical permission. This prohibition was fortified with the threat of a *ferendae sententiae* penalty to be inflicted at the discretion of the ordinary.[21]

The problem facing the bishops of the time was resolved into the question of whether a divorce or a separation was ever allowed and, if so, under what conditions. Many of them sought a solution from the Holy See and to their inquiries the Sacred Congregation of the Holy Office as well as the Sacred Penitentiary responded. It is these

[19] S. C. C., *Basileen.,* 31 iul. 1869—*Fontes,* n. 4215.

[20] ". . . manifeste apparet gravissimae culpae illos esse reos, qui a Magistratu civili matrimonium dissolvi postulant, vel, quod gravius est, divortio civili obtento, novum matrimonium inire attentant legitimo vinculo posthabito, quod coram Deo et Ecclesia adhuc manet. Ad haec crimina compescenda poenam excommunicationis statuimus, Ordinario reservatam, *ipso facto,* incurrendam ab eis, qui postquam divortium civile obtinuerint, matrimonium ausi fuerint attentare."—*Acta et Decreta Concilii Plenarii Baltimorensis Tertii, A. D. MDCCCLXXXIV,* n. 124.

[21] Praeterea, . . . iis omnibus, qui matrimonio conjuncti sunt, praecipimus, ne inconsulta auctoritate ecclesiastica, tribunalia civilia adeant ad obtinendam separationem a thoro et mensa. Quod si quis attentaverit, sciat se gravem reatum incurrere et pro judicio Episcopi puniendum esse."—*op. cit.,* n. 126.

replies that first of all will be reviewed here, and then a consideration of the authors' views on the subject will be presented.

A. *Responses of the Roman Curia*

The earliest response in this matter came in answer to a case presented to the Holy Office by the Bishop of Southwark. It was asked:

> Utrum licet advocati, iudicis vel actoris partes agere, quando finis litis est simplex separatio absque ulla sententia nullitatem matrimonii secum ipsa trahente.

The reply:

> Dummodo pars catholica nullum aliud tribunal adire possit, a quo sententiam obtineat separationis quoad thorum et mensam, et dummodo sententia huius tribunalis nullum alium habeat effectum quam separationem praedictam, posse tolerari ut catholici in eo foro actoris et advocati partes agant, dummodo adsint iustae separationis causae iudicio Episcopi, et si quid habeat praeterea dubii, recurrat, plenius exponens omnes circumstantias et legis dispositiones.[22]

Eighteen years later, the same Congregation replied to the Bishops of France. The content of this response was identical with the above mentioned communication to the Bishop of Southwark.[23] In 1885 and 1886 this Congregation issued replies to questions on the matter of civil divorce. While in these instances the question involved the action of a judge pronouncing a sentence of civil divorce and then officiating at a marriage bigamously attempted by Catholics, the reply to whether the judge could so proceed was: *Negative*.[24]

In addition to the responses issued by the Holy Office, several similar documents were issued by the Sacred Penitentiary. These are especially important since they greatly influenced the authors of the period. An early case considered by this Tribunal was that

[22] S. C. S. Off., 22 maii et 19 dec. 1860, n. 4—*Collectanea*, II, n. 2272.

[23] S. C. S. Off., *S. Galli*, 3 apr. 1878—*Collectanea*, II, n. 1491.

[24] S. C. S. Off., 25 iun. 1885, 27 maii 1886—*Collectanea*, II, n. 1636 et *loc. cit.*, nota 1.

which concerned a woman who had received a decree of legal separation; in order to support herself she sought a position with the government, a position she could not fill as long as she was not civilly divorced from her husband. The petition stated:

> . . . ipsa petere vellet, sed, in sua intentione, semper salvo ligamine. Parochus qui est illius Confessarius petit num admitti possit ad Sacramenta, et lumen seu consilium circa reliqua, ut infra.

The Sacred Penitentiary responded:

> Mulieri poenitenti, in casu, nihil aliud esse consulendum, nisi ut a petendo divortio sub gravi se abstineat.[25]

Again a woman sought permission for a civil divorce, *"ad damna gravissima avertenda,"* as a result of desertion by her husband. She needed the civil divorce to preserve and administer legally what remained of the family funds after his squanderings. The Roman tribunal replied: *Negative.*[26] In response to the petition of another woman who required a civil divorce to fulfill the legal qualifications of guardianship for her orphaned granddaughter, the same Tribunal again replied: *"Negative."*[27] At the beginning of the following year, a similar petition was refused by the Sacred Penitentiary; this was the request of a man wishing to protect his family and fortune from an adulterous wife.[28] The last case referred to by authors is that of a man separated from his wife by means of an ecclesiastical decree because of her adultery. To protect himself from his wife's illegitimate offspring, he requested permission to sue for a civil divorce. The answer differed from the usual in this case and contained the recommendation: *"Orator consulat probatos auctores."*[29]

[25] S. Poenit., 5 ian. 1887—The writer has been unable to procure a primary source for this and the following responses of the Sacred Penitentiary. They have, therefore, been incorporated from *Nouvelle Revue Theologique* (Paris, 1869—), XIX (1887), 74, 75 (hereafter referred to as *NRT*).

[26] S. Poenit., 14 ian. 1891—*NRT*, XXIII (1891), 671.

[27] S. Poenit., 3 iun. 1891—*NRT*, XXIII (1891), 678.

[28] S. Poenit., 7 ian. 1892—*NRT*, XXIV (1892), 528.

[29] S. Poenit., 3 iun. 1892—*NRT*, XXIV (1892), 530.

B. *The Opinions of the Older Authors*

From the foregoing responses, especially from those of the Sacred Penitentiary and that of the Holy Office given on June 25, 1885, and May 27, 1886, many authors argued that Catholic consorts joined in a valid union before God could never seek an absolute divorce in the civil courts. The basis for this strict opinion was that divorce is intrinsically evil and contrary to the divine law protecting the indissolubility of marriage. They contended that a civil dissolution of the marriage gave the couple in the civil law absolute freedom from the marriage bond. Since the law no longer considered them husband and wife, they were deprived of the right to live together as consorts, and the road was open for them to contract marriage again, and to do that validly in the eyes of the civil law. This, these authors reasoned, was intrinsically evil when the marriage was actually valid before God. So firm in their stand were the proponents of this extremely severe opinion, that they in no way mitigated their views even when a divorce was clearly intended for the civil effects only and for very grave reasons. Divorce, they held, was so intrinsically evil that under no conditions could it be petitioned by a Catholic, and they asserted this as the reason for the numerous refusals of permission by the Sacred Penitentiary.[30]

In answer to the foregoing statements made by very reputable authors, there existed before the advent of the Code a contrary opinion which, by comparison, was considered quite lenient. It was supported by authors of considerable repute. These writers, while not minimizing the grave evils of divorce, nevertheless opposed the assertions that it was intrinsically evil and, therefore, never to be permitted. Their treatment considered this matter as never licit unless very grave and proportionate causes were present, as measured by a consideration of the evils and the insecurity afflicting an innocent spouse when there was no civil protection available and by a balancing of the good and evil which would result from the divorce.[31]

[30] Bucceroni, *Institutiones Theologicae Moralis* (4. ed., 2 vols., Romae, 1900), II, n. 983; Ballerini, *Opus Theologicum Morale* (absolvit et editit Dominicus Palmieri, 7 vols., Prati, 1889-1893), VI, 397; Planchard, "Divorce Civil," *NRT*, XXIII (1891), 664; Gasparri, *De Matrimonio*, 3. ed., II, n. 1554.

[31] Feije, *De Impedimentis*, p. 467; Kenrick, *Theologia Moralis* (2. ed., 2

In general, their argument was resolved into disproving the alleged intrinsic malice of divorce. They pointed out that no decree of the Holy See made this statement and that the authoritative answers in these responses in stating that a civil divorce was not licit even for very grave reasons, did not necessarily mean that such action was evil in itself. They further alleged that the replies of the Holy See were answers to particular cases and that as a consequence it would be quite bold to resolve them into a general prohibitory rule for all occasions.[32] They found further support for their view in the contention that the civil law did not intend to interfere with conscience in the matter of dissolving a marriage which is valid before God. The law was impersonal in this regard and considered only the civil effects of the marriage, abstracting from any decision on what is valid before God and the Church.[33]

It is noteworthy that this opinion, although quite benign in comparison with the rigid view of the day, was not an all-embracing endorsement of a permission for Catholics to plead for a divocre in the secular courts; rather, it allowed such action only in those cases in which it was necessary to establish civil effects for an ecclesiastically granted separation. Moreover, it insisted on a very grave and proportionate cause and the permission of the ordinary in every instance.

In resolving the question of preferring a legal separation to an absolute divorce, the proponents of this view were naturally in favor of an action for separation. In a separation, they saw that the improbability of a reconciliation and the normal evils following upon the cessation of the common life were less pronounced, inasmuch as the damage to marital integrity was not so complete as in a divorce.[34]

vols., Mechliniae-Baltimorae, 1866), II, n. 112; Konings, *Theologia Moralis* (Boston, 1874), n. 1053; Waffelaert, "Question du Divorce," *NRT,* XVII (1885), 231; Smith, *Marriage Process in the United States,* nn. 47, 48; De Becker, *De Sponsalibus et Matrimonio,* p. 435; Lehmkuhl, *Theologia Moralis* (12. ed., 2 vols., Friburgi, 1914), II, 530; Sabetti, *Compendium Theologiae Moralis* (concinnatum a Timotheo Barrett, 19. ed., Ratisbonae, 1906), n. 559; Genicot, *Institutiones Theologiae Moralis* (6. ed., 2 vols., Bruxellis, 1909), II, 582; De Smet, *De Sponsalibus et Matrimonio* (Brugis, 1909), p. 254.

32 De Becker, *op. cit.*, p. 433; De Smet, *loc. cit.*

33 Smith, *loc. cit.*

34 Feije, *De Impedimentis,* p. 470; Kenrick, *Theologia Moralis,* II, n. 112;

When the petition of the party was limited to a separation suit, there was little difficulty in reaching a practical solution. They Holy Office in its reply to the Bishop of Southwark had presented the norms to be observed in such a case (cf. *supra*, p. 145) and authors used it as a guiding norm. If any further doubts should arise, no matter, pastors, confessors and bishops were always advised to have recourse to the Holy See.

ARTICLE 3. SUGGESTED NORMS OF ACTION TODAY

Since the extent of ecclesiastical directives on the subject of petitions of Catholics for separation and divorce in civil tribunals was limited in the period before the Code to the aforementioned responses of the Holy Office and the Sacred Penitentiary, it is difficult to state with certainty just what the Church's policy was on this matter or to conclude from them any absolute norms of action for the present. The reticence of the Holy See in not establishing common rules of procedure, evidenced in the absence of any provisions in the Code of Canon Law, seems to be demonstrative of the relative nature of the question. The Church legislates for the whole world and it seems to have preferred silence to the providing of norms that might be acceptable in one country and, perhaps, be almost impossible to observe in others.

Authors today, as their predecessors before the Code, in considering the question of civil action, treat the obligations of Catholic judges, attorneys and spouses. The consideration presented here, however, as in the foregoing historical review, will be confined to the particular problems of the ordinary or his delegate in ascertaining the conditions necessary for permitting an action in the civil courts to a party engaged in an ecclesiastical suit of separation.

The least objectionable civil action is that which seeks a separate maintenance or alimony without divorce. Since it is not an action concerned with dissolving the bond or even concerned with the integrity of marriage, as would be an action for separation, it is the preferable course to follow when legal action is found to be necessary.

Konings, *Theologia Moralis*, n. 1053; Genicot, *Institutiones Theologiae Moralis*, II, 582; De Smet, *De Sponsalibus et Matrimonio*, p. 256.

This is especially applicable in cases of temporary separation. Moreover, since it relates exclusively to the canonically termed "civil effects" of the marriage, there seems to be no real objection to its employment.[35] In actual practice, however, it may not be sufficient or, because of the circumstances depending on the force given it in the particular states, it may be impractical. It is for this reason that this action, although most often recommended in curial practices, is rejected by the party seeking legal protection in favor of the more secure guarantees of legal separation or even divorce. It remains for the individual ordinary to determine the value of this legal remedy in his jurisdiction and to adopt that norm which, in his prudent judgment, is the most appropriate according to the circumstances of the case presented.

Although many of the earlier authors held that the Church could never permit Catholic consorts to plead a suit of separation before the civil tribunals, the basis for this reasoning being the contention that such action was essentially evil because of the implied usurpation of ecclesiastical jurisdiction, today it is the common opinion of canonists and theologians that a petition of this kind may be presented for a grave reason.[36]

The principal basis for this opinion is the reply of the Holy Office to the Bishop of Southwark in 1860. (Cf. *supra,* p. 145). If this type of separation were intrinsically evil, the Holy See would never have permitted it even in a particular instance. This legal remedy, although in no wise implying any recognition of ecclesiastical jurisdiction by the civil power, nevertheless does retain and protect, at least implicitly, the exalted doctrine of the Church on the indissolubility of marriage. This statement is not meant to imply that a general permission has been given Catholics to plead this action, but it does mean that, provided the conditions indicated by the Holy

[35] S. C. C., *Basileen.,* 31 iul. 1869—*Fontes,* n. 4215; Wernz-Vidal, *Ius Canonicum,* V, n. 647; Cappello, *De Sacramentis,* V, n. 830.

[36] De Smet, *De Sponsalibus et Matrimonio* (4. ed.), n. 401; Prümmer, *Manuale Theologiae Moralis* (3 vols., 4. et 5. ed., Friburgi Brisgoviae, 1928), III, n. 892; Genicot, *Institutiones Theologiae Moralis* (10. ed., 2 vols., quam recognovit I. Salsmans, Bruxellis, 1922), II, 528; Vlaming, *Praelectiones Iuris Matrimonii* (2 vols., Vol. II, 3. ed., Bussum, 1921), n. 697.

Office are observed, it seems to be an acceptable action and may be tolerated by the ordinary.

The Holy Office enumerated the following conditions as essential for the toleration of this legal remedy. These stated conditions in view of their clarity, necessitate no further comment. (1) Just causes must be present in the judgment of the ordinary; (2) the Catholic party must lack any other tribunal to which he could go to obtain a separation recognized in civil law; and (3) the sentence of the tribunal must have no other effect than that of separation of bed, board and cohabitation.

In view of the fact that the same Congregation, in reply to a petition from France, used the very same words, the use of these norms as practical rules of action gains special merit.[37] To the contrary, however, there are some authors who hold that the use of this norm in countries other than England and France would be illicit. They point out that these responses were given in answer to petitions from these two nations, and as special permission conceded in particular cases by the Holy See they pertained only to the countries to which they were directed. Gasparri among others accepted this position; he held that Catholics in nations other than England and France explicitly had to petition and obtain the same favor of tolerance from the Holy See, since what has been conceded *gratiose* to one person cannot be extended to others even in the same circumstances.[38] Today, most of the authors do not accept Gasparri's view. They base their stand on what might be called an opposition to the Cardinal's unproved assertions that these responses were granted *gratiose*. They also demonstrate the absence of any good reason for limiting the tolerance of this practice to two nations when this very same tolerance, since it is founded in the prescription of the divine law to avoid greater evils when possible, should be applicable anywhere under the same circumstances. They concur in permitting this action in other nations when the above outlined

[37] S. C. S. Off., *S. Galli*, 3 apr. 1878—*Collectanea*, II, n. 1491.

[38] "Hae declarationes ad alias nationes, quae in iisdem circumstantiis reperiuntur, extendi per se non possunt, quia 'quod alicui gratiose conceditur trahi non debet aliis in exemplum'; Reg. 74, R. J., in VI°; proinde necesse est eiusdem tolerantiae gratiam petere et obtinere."—*De Matrimonio*, II, n. 1237.

conditions are present on the ground that, despite the particular nature of the replies, it can be considered to have at least the tacit tolerance of the Holy See, until express provisions are made to the contrary.[39]

The direct statements of the Holy See on legal separation are most helpful for practical solutions in the case of requests of this nature today, and it would be indeed gratifying if the problems connected with petitions to initiate an action of civil divorce were as easily resolved. The division of opinions among authors dealing with the latter subject in the period before the Code has been shown, and it must be admitted that there is very little change today. Although no new source of information has been issued since 1918, Gasparri has helped the situation somewhat by including in his latest work (1932), a response to the Holy Office, a document hitherto unknown to canonical writers. This rescript was given in reply to a question on divorce. According to Gasparri, the Holy Office was asked whether a Catholic woman could be permitted to petition for a civil divorce *"ob gravissimas causas."* The reply was the following:

> Attentis peculiaribus circumstantiis in casu concurrentibus, permitti posse, dummodo mulier oratrix coram Ordinario vel eius delegato ac duobus testibus etiam iureiurando declaret se matrimoniale vinculum nullatenus abrumpere, sed tantummodo a civilis ritus oneribus exsolvi velle; remoto scandalo quo meliori modi iudicio Episcopi fieri poterit.[40]

The nature of the *"causae gravissimae"* for which the permission was granted is not contained in Gasparri's treatment. Hines, however, received privately a decree from the Holy Office permitting him to publish the explicit reasons and they have become public for the first time in his work. The causes for this concession are there described as:

> Mulier in casu, iam a duodeviginti annis nupta, volebat divortium civile ob rationes, quae sequuntur:

[39] Cappello, *De Sacramentis,* V, n. 831; Wernz-Vidal, *Ius Canonicum,* V, n. 711, ftn. 11; De Smet, De Sponsalibus et Matrimonio (4. ed.), n. 398; Noldin-Schmidt, *Summa Theologiae Moralis,* III, n. 671; Merkelbach, *Summa Theologiae Moralis,* III, n. 978.

[40] S. C. S. Off., 6 aug. 1906—Gasparri, *op. cit.,* II, n. 1324.

> 1.—ut bona a parentibus sibi suisque relicta melius et in proprium commodum servaret; dum maritus, quod nisi ita esset, statim ac plene ea perderet;
> 2.—ut filios liberaret a patria potestate, quae eisdem fieret perniciosa. Ad quem necesse erat ut mulier, cui data esset curatio suorum filiorum, divortium obtineret ob viri culpam;
> 3.—ut satisfacere valeat continuis iurgiis, vexationibus et repetitis nimis patris matrisque seu amborum parentum, qui, quantocumque pretio ac summa ope, sedulo optant civile divortium pro filia.[41]

According to Gasparri, this reply of the Holy Office has been adopted as a general practical norm by the Sacred Penitentiary when questions of this nature arise.[42] Kelly lends further credence to this statement by professing knowledge of a similar petition in 1945, which was answered by the Holy Office in the self-same words.[43]

From the replies of the Roman Curia, most of the authors today are of the opinion that the petitioning and obtaining of a civil divorce cannot be proved to be intrinsically evil.[44] If this action were intrinsically evil, then, even when there is no intention of remarriage, the Holy See could not have permitted it even in a single case. Moreover, even if one argue from the nature of the Catholic party's petition to initiate action for a divorce, granted that the necessary conditions are fulfilled, the rigid view is not tenable. In the case under consideration here it does not seem merely pragmatic to assert that the very object of the act is not evil. In seeking a divorce the petitioner is concerned merely with a dissolution of the civil rights and duties arising from the marriage contract, and not with a dissolution of the sacramental bond.[45] Similarly, the argument that would presume a general intention on the part of Catholic spouses to dissolve the marriage and thereby to enjoy freedom to enter an-

[41] *De Coniugum Separatione,* pp. 72, 73.

[42] *Loc. cit.*

[43] "Separation and Civil Divorce,"—*The Jurist,* VI (1946), 222.

[44] Gasparri, *op. cit.,* II, n. 1324; Cappello, *op. cit.,* V, n. 837; De Smet, *loc. cit.*; Vermeersch-Creusen, *Epitome Iuris Canonici,* III, n. 278; Prümer, *Manuale Theologiae Moralis,* III, n. 892; Genicot, *Institutiones Theologiae Moralis* (10. ed.), II, 528; Merkelbach, *op. cit.,* III, n. 977; Iorio, *Theologia Moralis,* III, 998; Noldin-Schmitt, *loc. cit.*; Wernz-Vidal, *loc. cit.*

[45] Cappello, *loc. cit.*; Iorio, *op. cit.,* III, 996; Merkelbach, *loc. cit.*

other invalid union is hardly acceptable. For the circumstance of such a position, inasmuch as the party has demonstrated his good faith by observing the ecclesiastical law on separation, gives rise, rather to the opposite presumption namely that of the absence of any such evil intent toward a later bigamous union.[46]

Any arguments in opposition to the very strict opinion on this matter need not necessarily signify that these Roman documents afford arguments from authority and therefore include general permissions to be used as a matter of course. These replies were answers to specific cases and they do not present a general norm of action; rather, since no universal prescription has been promulgated by the Holy See, these responses, although helpful directives for an ordinary faced with such problems, are not to be made general rules of practice.[47] However, in the absence of a general decree of the Holy See forbidding any divorce action by a Catholic, it seems to be a reasonable conclusion that such action may be tolerated exclusively under certain important conditions. In the United States, especially, the civil law is not directly concerned with impugning or denying the rights and the laws of the Church,[48] therefore, the replies of the Holy See in forbidding this action in certain countries because of the grave harm caused by laws aimed intentionally at the rights and authority of the Church are hardly applicable,[49] and since the action cannot be certainly rejected on the grounds of intrinsic evil, it is tolerable.

If this action is allowed, however, it must under careful guard be permitted only under the following conditions, which seem appropriate for forestalling the many evils which any abuses in this matter would create and, at the same time, for preserving as much as possible the exalted attitude of the Church on the indissolubility of marriage.

Of paramount importance is the observation that there is absolutely no necessity to permit a Catholic to petition for an absolute divorce when the civil legislation in that particular region accords

[46] Hines, *De Coniugum Separatione,* p. 75.

[47] Gasparri, *De Matrimonio,* II, n. 1323; Cappello, *loc. cit.*

[48] Forbes, *The Canonical Separation of Consorts,* p. 218.

[49] Cappello, *loc. cit.*

equal effects to a separation action. The fact that this latter remedy is so much less objectionable than a divorce action warrants its preference in every instance. The same norm should be applied to other legal institutes by which similar legal guarantees and safeguards may be attained. The actions for separate maintenance and alimony without a separation or divorce would be embraced in this category, since they usually afford sufficient civil protection.[50]

Lest there be any mistake in interpretation, special emphasis should be placed on the fact that a Catholic can never licitly seek a divorce to dissolve a valid marriage and to enter a new union, even if this is merely a civil attempt at marriage. This is clear from the penalty stated in Canon 2356. There the Church's law inflicts the *ipso facto* incurred penalty of infamy of law on such a person and also provides that, if the parties refuse to discontinue their illicit concubinage after being admonished by the ordinary, they should be punished with excommunication or personal interdict.[51] Moreover, the penalty of the *ipso facto* incurred excommunication as stated in the III Plenary Council of Baltimore (1884) for the same delict is, according to accepted principle still in force in this country, since it supplements the Code rather than contravenes the law as therein enacted.[52]

Although there is no penalty in the Code or in the particular conciliar law for this country against those who seek a civil divorce, nevertheless the same decree of the Council of Baltimore calls attention to the grave sin involved in seeking such action.[53] Therefore, the permission of the local ordinary is a necessary requisite for licit

[50] Cappello, *op. cit.*, V, n. 838; Merkelbach, *loc. cit.*; Genicot, *op. cit.*, II, n. 562; Hines, *op. cit.*, p. 74.

[51] Bigami, idest qui, obstante coniugali vinculo, aliud matrimonium, etsi tantum civile, ut aiunt, attentaverint, sunt ipso facto infames; et si, spreta Ordinarii monitione, in illicito contubernio persistant, pro diversa reatus gravitate excommunicentur vel personali interdicto plectantur.

[52] *Acta et Decreta Concilii Plenarii Baltimorensis Tertii, A. D. MDCCCLXXXIV*, n. 124; Barrett, *A Comparative Study of the Plenary Councils of Baltimore and the Code of Canon Law*, The Catholic University of America Canon Law Studies, n. 83 (Washington, D. C.: The Catholic University of America, 1932), p. 134; Hannan, "Marriage after Civil Divorce," *The Jurist*, VII (1947), 311.

[53] Cf. *supra*, p. 144, ftn. 21.

action in every instance. It is his office to judge the gravity of the reasons for seeking this legal remedy, and it is but reasonable, as a means of preventing the abuses arising from private judgment in this matter, that he, the guardian of faith and morals in his territory, thoroughly familiar with the local civil statutes, should be the authority to issue this permission in worthy cases.[54]

The causes alleged for seeking the divorce must be very grave and proportionate to the evils which result from such actions. There can be no doubt that divorce does leave the party free to marry again in the civil forum if he should be of the mind to do so. There are many other bad effects which such action may have in influencing others. As a consequence, whereas a grave reason was recommended as sufficient for the action of legal separation, most grave reasons would be necessary for the more absolute remedy of divorce.[55]

That the Church may have some guarantee of good faith and cooperation from the petitioner, the Catholic seeking this legal remedy of divorce should declare, under oath, his right intention in the matter. He should, therefore, swear before the ordinary or his delegate and two witnesses that he does not intend to dissolve his marriage which he believes to be valid before God and therefore indissoluble, but that he is seeking this civil action simply to procure the protection of the civil law which will follow upon it.[56]

There is an added obligation for the ordinary in these matters as in all such cases wherein there is danger of misunderstanding. It is the office of the ordinary to make every endeavor to remove whatever scandal might arise from this action of a Catholic,[57] for there is no doubt that people, aware of the Church's centuries old and

[54] S. C. S. Off., 6 aug. 1906—Gasparri, *op. cit.*, II, n. 1324; Cappello, *loc. cit.*; Noldin-Schmitt, *Summa Theologiae Moralis*, III, n. 671.

[55] Cappello, *loc. cit.* Kelly demands a cause to be one of the public order as well as the private order before he is ready to deem it proportionate to the evils involved.—"Separation and Civil Divorce," *The Jurist*, VI (1946), 232; Forbes agrees with this view.—*op. cit.*, p. 219; but Hines dissents in this fashion: "Difficile tamen est intelligere quid sit causa gravissima ordinis publici, quae sollicitationem divortii iustificet. Quapropter mihi videtur, praesertim post considerationem responsorum S. Sedis, quod sufficit causa gravissima etiam ordinis privati."—*De Coniugum Separatione*, p. 76.

[56] S. C. S. Off., 6 aug. 1906—Gasparri, *op. cit.*, II, n. 1324.

[57] *Loc. cit.*

adamant stand against this spreading evil, would be scandalized at the knowledge of such action when the details of the situation are not fully explained. However, in the case envisaged here, the scandal that might be attendant upon ecclesiastical permission for a Catholic to plead a civil divorce action, may be considered as being somewhat less in the light of the extant circumstances than many would claim. Since the party has shown good faith in securing a canonical separation and has sought previous permission before initiating any civil action, it seems safe to presume that those associates and intimates who are aware of the civil divorce are also cognizant of the facts of the case and of the party's intention to procure only the civil effects. Since only very grave reasons are acceptable for such a permission, those who know of the conditions for which the permission has been granted are less likely scandalized than someone who has no other knowledge than the fact that a Catholic is a plaintiff in a divorce suit.[58]

Although, as a general rule, permission for civil divorce should be granted only after an ecclesiastical decree of permanent separation, this is by no means an ironclad rule. Adultery is the sole cause for permanent separations, yet decrees of temporary separation which are granted for an indeterminate period of time very often approximate a permanent separation in their actual duration. It should be left to the prudent discretion of the ordinary, therefore, to determine whether a temporary separation wherein future reconciliation can hardly be termed probable, e. g. in cases involving apostasy, moral depravity, etc., would sufficiently warrant the issuance of this permission. The grave causes necessary to permit any divorce action would of course be necessary in this instance also.[59]

[58] The probability or, in some cases, certainty that the other consort will attempt a bigamous union after the plaintiff has succeeded in winning a divorce is not a determining factor here. Authors agree that the innocent consort is not responsible for the possible or probable sins of his errant spouse.—Noldin-Schmitt, *op. cit.*, III, n. 670; Kelly, "Separation and Civil Divorce," *The Jurist*, VI (1946), 229; Hines, *op. cit.*, p. 77.

[59] Hines, *op. cit.*, p. 76; Forbes, *op. cit.*, p. 220; This against Kelly, who considers an ecclesiastical decree of permanent separation a *conditio sine qua non* for the granting of permission to plead a divorce action.—*op. cit.*, p. 231 and Hannan, "Marriage after Civil Divorce," *The Jurist*, VII (1947), 311.

A recommended condition in this case is an additional sworn statement, on the side of the party seeking the permission, to resume cohabitation if a reconciliation should become possible at a later date. There is little difficulty from the civil law in arranging such a reconciliation, since remarriage is quite a common occurrence in this country. However, in witnessing a renewal of consent by the parties to fulfill the prescriptions of the civil law, the priest in question should take pains to advise the parties of the nature of this action. Since the matter and form of the sacrament consist in the exchange of consent,[60] there is no danger of a *simulatio sacramenti,* for in reality the exchange of consent stands as something permanent and perpetual and therefore cannot be repeated except materially. Accordingly the parties should be informed that they are married and that the ceremony now being held is no more than an endeavor to satisfy the requirements of the civil law, which before God has no significance as far as their marriage is concerned.

It is only reasonable to mention in passing that persons involved in cases of temporary separation wherein a definite period of time is specified could never use the remedy of civil divorce. It is difficult to conceive of a case involving a temporary separation in which it would ever be necessary, since the decree is made binding for but a brief and definite period of time, and always is issued with a well-founded hope of an early reconciliation.

The fulfillment of the above outlined conditions, then, seems to be necessary as a prerequisite for any civil divorce action by a Catholic. Even with these safeguards the matter is one to be treated with grave caution and deliberation. Especially is this so today with the number of permanent marriages so fast diminishing as to be scarcely equal to the number of marriages dissolved. These are cases to be admitted as a last resort, and the practice of diocesan curias demonstrates a recognition of this fact. Therein it is the usual practice, so far as the writer has been able to ascertain, to utilize the lesser legal remedies whenever possible. Legal separations are the usual last resort, and divorces are permitted only when the circumstances, relative both to the needs of the parties and to the difficulties in the civil law, force this extreme remedy as the sole solution.

[60] Canon 1081, §§ 1, 2.

CONCLUSIONS

1. The proper canonical procedure for separation cases in the pre-Code period was the formal judicial process. Although there are indications that a shorter process was utilized in practice as early as the fourteenth century, such procedure was not clearly evident until the post-Tridentine era. Even at that time there was not always a clear distinction between the summary judicial process and the administrative method, as it is known today. Since these briefer processes arose more by common usage, in consequence of the need that was felt for a shorter process in mission territories, inasmuch as they were never legally prescribed methods, they were at the least tolerated by the ecclesiastical authority.

2. Although separation suits are, as a general rule, subject to a hearing before the Church to be legitimate, the institute of separation undertaken *propria auctoritate* as stated in Canons 1130-1131 must be given consideration. Not all canonists are in agreement in their interpretations of this matter, but it is the opinion of the writer that an innocent consort, if he has separated because of a certain and manifest sin of adultery, is legitimately separated. One who leaves in view of the grounds given as sufficient for a temporary separation in Canon 1131, provided there is a danger in delay, could indeed be considered as having legitimately departed, but would need a decree of the ordinary before the separation can be considered legitimate. (Pp. 66-73.)

3. Under the present discipline the ordinary procedure for cases of permanent separation because of adultery is the formal judicial process. The cases of temporary separation as stated in Canon 1131, have as their ordinary process the administrative method. The two processes are not so mutually exclusive, however, that they cannot be used for either type of separation case provided that certain conditions are present. (Pp. 73-78.)

4. The ordinary may, at the instance of the parties or even *ex officio,* employ the judicial process for temporary separations and, so it seems, even hear a case of permanent separation in the admin-

istrative method, when it is an easily provable sin of marital infidelity that is presented as the alleged cause. (Pp. 76-78.)

5. The formal process follows generally the ordinary matrimonial procedure with the following notable exceptions. Only one judge is prescribed, since this is not a case *de vinculo matrimonii.* The ordinary is not prohibited, however, from constituting a collegiate tribunal for the hearing of these cases. The office of the *defensor vinculi,* so necessary in litigations concerning the bond of marriage, is not required in separation suits; this rôle is taken by the promoter of justice whose presence, although not explicitly enjoined in the Code law, is considered necessary in separation cases in view of the eccesiastical jurisprudence which prescribes his intervention. (Pp. 80-110.)

6. Although there is no general requirement for the lodging of an appeal after the sentence of the lower court, separation suits never become adjudged cases according to a recent authentic interpretation. (Pp. 114-115.)

7. In the appellate stage, the tribunal must be constituted as in the first instance. Thus, if a collegiate tribunal was employed in the lower court, it is also necessary in the appellate tribunal. This is not an invalidating requirement. Similarly, the promoter of justice must intervene in the suit in every instance. (Pp. 115-116.)

8. A newly alleged sin of adultery not submitted as evidence in the lower court but presented in the appellate stage may be judged therein; the latter court would consider it, however, as a court of first instance. When the case is not one of proved adultery, but another cause is presented that only permits a temporary separation, the aforementioned conclusion would not apply, since the two are distinct actions. (Pp. 117-118.)

9. No explicit norms are stated in the Code law for the administrative hearing of separation cases. From the nature of the case, however, this process should consist of an interview of both parties, as also of clear proof of the alleged cause, in consultation with the promoter of justice, and the separation should be granted or denied through a decree of the ordinary or his delegate. (Pp. 119-123.)

10. In view of the gravity of these cases, even though the ordinary is not prohibited from granting to whomsoever he desires the

authority of hearing these cases, he should not be so general with his delegations that these cases are resolved into matters of minor have as their ordinary process the administrative method. The two istrativemethod, when it is an easily provable sin of marital infidelity moment. Since this is a non-judicial process, only the bishop and the vicar general are radically competent to review these cases. The *officialis* is not empowered to act in these cases by virtue of his office and would therefore need an express delegation to issue any decree of separation in the administrative process. (Pp. 123-127.)

11. The legal remedy against a decree of the ordinary in the administrative process is administrative recourse. This recourse must be taken before the competent Roman Congregation. Recourse against a decree of the ordinary's delegate may be made to the ordinary without any loss of right to make further recourse to the Holy See. (Pp. 135-137.)

12. In the absence of any prohibitive or permissive legislation on civil action, it seems under the present law a Catholic consort may under very special conditions plead for a legal separation, or even an absolute divorce, in the civil courts. (Pp. 138-158.)

APPENDIX

SOME SUGGESTED INTERROGATORIES FOR THE ADMINISTRATIVE HEARING OF SEPARATION CASES

I. Request and Interrogatory of Petitioner for Ecclesiastical Separation

CHANCERY OF THE DIOCESE

Num. Prot. ....
PETITIONER .... Subject: REQUEST OF PETITIONER FOR ECCLESIASTICAL SEPARATION
RESPONDENT ....

I, the undersigned, ..., a baptized Catholic, do hereby request permission of the Most Reverend Ordinary of the Diocese, to institute a canonical separation as to bed, board and dwelling place in accordance with the prescriptions of Canons 1129-1132, from .... with whom I contracted marriage in (City, County) of .... in the State of .... on .... 19.......

I respectfully submit herewith the following documents:

1. Record of my Catholic Baptism
2. Record of my marriage from the Church Register.

Date: ....
Priest Notary: .... Petitioner

The Priest Notary will administer the following oath:

> "I, the undersigned, recognizing the sacred character of an oath as a calling upon God to witness the truth of what I say, do solemnly swear that in answer to your questions I shall tell the truth, the whole truth and nothing but the truth. So help me God and these His Holy Gospels which I touch with my hand."

A. Information Concerning Petitioner

1. What is your name (maiden name if wife)?
2. What is your present address?
3. Have you some identification?
4. What is your religion?
   - (a) Date and place of birth?
   - (b) Date and place of baptism?
5. What are the names and addresses of your parents?

....	....
Father's Name	Address
....	....
Mother's Name	Address

6. Have you always been a practical Catholic? Describe.

B. Information Concerning Respondent

1. What is the name of your spouse?
2. What religion does your spouse profess?
3. Is (he) (she) a practical member?
4. What is the present address of your spouse?

C. Information Concerning Marriage

1. When and where did your marriage with the respondent take place?
   - (a) Before whom?
   - (b) Did a civil marriage precede your marriage before a priest?
2. How long did you live together before difficulties arose?
3. What was the cause of your first difficulty?
   Explain in detail:

D. History of Any Previous Separations

1. How often did you and the respondent separate?
2. When did the first separation take place?
3. What was the cause?

4. After the first separation did you resume marital life?
    (a) What persons were instrumental in effecting this reconciliation?
    (b) Explain their rôle.
    (c) Give their names and addresses.
5. How long after this first separation did reconciliation take place?
6. How long did you remain together after this first reconciliation?
7. Were there any other separations in the intervening period until the present?
8. If so, give the causes, length of time, date of reconciliation and names and addresses of persons instrumental in the reconciliation.
9. When did the final separation take place?
    (a) What was its cause?
    (b) How long for the present have you been separated from your (husband) (wife)?

E. Children of the Marriage

1. How many children have been born of your marriage?
2. What are their names and ages?
3. Did your spouse treat and care for the children as a true parent?
4. Were your children educated as Catholics?
5. Were they sent to a Catholic school?
6. Who has their custody at present?
7. Who will have their custody in the event of a separation?

F. Grounds for Separation

According to Canon 1129, § 1, formal adultery, i. e. adultery not caused, permitted, condoned or compensated by you, is the only cause for a permanent separation.

According to Canon 1131, § 1, a temporary separation may be granted for these causes: If the other party has joined a non-Catholic sect, has educated the offspring in a non-Catholic manner, has led an ignominious life or a criminal life, has become physically or morally dangerous to you, made the common life too difficult because of quarrels and cruelty, and other causes of this nature have existed.

1. With this in mind explain the canonical cause which would warrant an ecclesiastical separation in your case.
2. Kindly give the names and addresses of at least two witnesses, preferably Catholics, who could substantiate your allegations.

G. *In re*: *Reconciliation*

1. Is reconciliation with the respondent possible at this time? If not, why not?
2. When did you see the respondent last?
3. Has (he) (she) remarried?
4. Have you any intentions of remarriage?
5. Did you ever speak to a priest outside of the confessional regarding your marital difficulties?
   (a) When?
   (b) What is the name of the priest?
   (c) What is the address of the priest?
   (d) His relationship to you, i. e. parish priest, friend, etc.
   (e) Does this priest fully understand your case?
   (f) Did this priest confer with the respondent?
6. If the answer to n. 5 is negative, please give the name and address of a priest who is acquainted with both you and the respondent and can be interrogated concerning your request.
7. Have you ever presented a petition similar to this in any chancery before?
8. Do you realize that an ecclesiastical separation will not permit you to marry again?
9. Do you realize that even company-keeping would be wrong for you?
10. Do you realize that a separation for any cause but formal adultery is temporary, and that as soon as the cause ceases you will be expected to return to your spouse?
11. Do you apply for a separation under these conditions?

H. Civil Action

1. Have you to date undertaken any action in the civil courts against your spouse?

2. What is the nature of this action?
3. Give the name, address and religion of any lawyer you have consulted and his recommendations in the matter.
4. Do you desire to undertake any civil action?

   The policy of this chancery in the matter of civil action is the following: ....

5. With this in mind, what type of civil action do you desire?
6. What are your reasons for desiring this action?

---

1. Do you have anything further to add to this testimony?
2. (Here the testimony should be read to the deponent.) Do you wish to add to, amend or correct any of the foregoing statements?
3. Please take the following oath:

   "I do solemnly swear that the testimony I have just given is correct and that I have told the truth, the whole truth and nothing but the truth. So help me God and these His Holy Gospels which I touch with my hand."

Date: ....

Priest Notary: .... Petitioner

Parish: .... Parish Seal

(The priest notary is requested to present a statement of his opinion from either personal knowledge or investigation of the deponent with regard to: (1) the deponent's credibility; religious character; probity of life; (2) whether the alleged cause is public, notorious or occult; (3) the possibility of scandal if a separation is granted; (4) whether the alleged causes exist; (5) what efforts have been made toward a reconciliation; (6) his personal recommendations in favor of or against the granting of the petition.)

....

Signature

II. Interrogatory for Respondent

CHANCERY OF THE DIOCESE

Num. Prot. ....

PETITIONER .... Subject: INTERROGATION OF RESPONDENT IN CASE OF ECCLESIASTICAL SEPARATION

RESPONDENT ....

The Priest Notary will administer
the following oath:

> "I, the undersigned, recognizing the sacred character of an oath as a calling upon God to witness the truth of what I say, do solemnly swear that in answer to your questions I shall tell the truth, the whole truth and nothing but the truth. So help me God and these His Holy Gospels which I touch with my hand."

A. Information Concerning the Respondent

1. What is your name (maiden name, if wife)?
2. What is your address?
3. Have you any identification?
4. What is your religion?
   - (a) Date and place of birth?
   - (b) Date and place of baptism?
5. What are the names and addresses of your parents?

....	....
Father's name	Address
....	....
Mother's name	Address

6. Have you always been a practical Catholic? Describe.

B. Information Concerning Marriage

1. When and where did your marriage with the petitioner take place?
   - (a) Before whom?
   - (b) Did a civil marriage precede your marriage before a priest?

2. How long did you live together before difficulties arose?
3. What was the cause of your first difficulty?
   Explain in detail:

C. History of Any Previous Separations

1. How often did you and the petitioner separate?
2. When did the first separation take place?
3. What was the cause?
4. After the first separation did you resume marital life?
   - (a) What persons were instrumental in effecting this reconciliation?
   - (b) Explain their role.
   - (c) Give their names and addresses.
5. How long after this first separation did reconcilation take place?
6. How long did you remain together after this first reconciliation?
7. Were there any separations in the intervening period until the present?
8. If so, give the causes, length of time, date of reconciliation and names and addresses of persons instrumental in the reconciliation.
9. When did the final separation take place?
   - (a) What was the cause?
   - (b) How long for the present have you been separated from your (husband) (wife)?

D. Children of the Marriage

1. How many children have been born of your marriage?
2. What are their names and ages?
3. Did your spouse treat and care for the children as a true parent?
4. Were your children educated as Catholics?
5. Were they sent to a Catholic school?
6. Who has their custody at present?
7. Who will have their custody in the event of a separation?

E. Grounds for Separation

1. Your (husband) (wife) has presented the following allegations as causes for a separation: (Priest should here read the complaint

made by the petitioner.) Are these statements true?
If not, please explain.

2. Has your spouse been remiss in fulfilling (his) (her) marital obligations?
If so, please explain.
3. Kindly give the names and addresses of at least two witnesses, preferably Catholics, who are qualified and willing to testify in your defense.

F. In re: Reconciliation

1. Are you willing to co-operate in correcting the present situation and in effecting a reconciliation?
2. When did you see the petitioner last?
3. Has (he) (she) any intentions of remarriage?
4. Have you any intentions of remarriage?
5. Did you ever speak to a priest outside of the confessional regarding your marital difficulties?
    (a) When?
    (b) What is the name of the priest?
    (c) What is the address of the priest?
    (d) His relationship to you, i.e., parish priest, friend, etc.
    (e) Does this priest fully understand your case?
    (f) Did this priest confer with both you and your (husband) (wife)?
6. If the answer to n. 5 is negative, please give the name and address of a priest who is acquainted with both you and petitioner and can be interrogated concerning this matter.
7. Do you realize that an ecclesiastical separation would not permit you to marry again?
8. Do you realize that even company-keeping would be wrong for you?

G. Civil Action

1. Has your (husband) (wife) initiated any civil action against you?
2. Do you intend to plead any case in the civil courts?
3. If the answer to n. 2 is yes, what type of action do you intend to plead?

1. Do you have anything further to add to this testimony?
2. (Here the testimony should be read to the deponent.) Do you wish to add to, amend or correct any of the foregoing statements?
3. Please take the following oath:

> "I do solemnly swear that the testimony I have just given is correct and that I have told the truth, the whole truth and nothing but the truth. So help me God and these His Holy Gospels which I touch with my hand."

Date: ....
Priest Notary: .... Respondent
Parish: .... Parish Seal

(The priest notary is requested to present a statement of his opinion from either personal knowledge or investigation of the dependent with regard to: (1) the dependent's credibility; religious character; probity of life; (2) whether the alleged cause is public, notorious or occult; (3) the possibility of scandal if a separation is granted; (4) whether the alleged causes exist or the respondent's defense overrides them; (5) what efforts have been made toward a reconciliation; (6) his personal recommendations in favor of or against the granting of the petition.)

....
Signature

III. Interrogatory for Witness

CHANCERY OF THE DIOCESE

Num. Prot. ....
PETITIONER .... Subject: INTERROGATION
RESPONDENT .... OF ....,
WITNESS IN CASE
OF ECCLESIASTICAL SEPARATION

You have been named by ...., PETITIONER/RESPONDENT, as a witness in (his) (her) behalf in reference to a petition submitted by ....

for an ecclesiastical separation from the RESPONDENT, which has been presented to His Excellency the Most Reverend Bishop of the Diocese.

The Priest Notary will administer
the following oath:

> "I, the undersigned, recognizing the sacred character of an oath as a calling upon God to witness the truth of what I say, do solemnly swear that in answer to your questions I shall tell the truth, the whole truth and nothing but the truth. So help me God and these His Holy Gospels which I touch with my hand."

A. Information concerning Witness

1. What is your name?
2. What is your present address?
3. What is your occupation?
4. What is your religion?
5. Describe the practice of your religion.
6. How long have you known petitioner/respondent?
7. Did you know (him) (her) before (his) (her) marriage?
8. Are you related to petitioner/respondent?
9. If not related, what is your connection with petitioner/respondent?
10. Do you consider petitioner/respondent a person who is credible?
11. Did you see much of petitioner/respondent after (his) (her) marriage?
12. Do you know petitioner's/respondent's (husband) (wife)?
13. How long have you known (him) (her)?
14. What is your estimation of (his) (her) character?
15. Do you believe petitioner/respondent to have been a true and faithful (husband) (wife)?
16. What is the name of your parish?
17. Are you known to one of the priests of that parish? If so, give his name?
18. If not, give the name and address of a priest who may be able to vouch for your credibility.

B. Information Concerning the Separation

1. Are you aware that a petition for a separation has been made by the petitioner?
    (a) When did you hear of it?
    (b) From whom?
    (c) Have any suggestions or instructions been given you in regard to your testimony? If so, describe.
2. The petitioner has presented the following allegations as grounds for a canonical separation: (Priest notary should here read the allegations of the petitioner.)
    (a) In your opinion are the charges true or false?
    (b) State exactly whatever testimony you can give to prove the truth or falsity of these charges.
    (c) Is this personal knowledge or hearsay knowledge? Please describe.

C. *In re: Reconciliation*

1. Is there a possibility of reconcilation between the parties at the present time?
2. If not, do you think there is any possibility of a reconciliation at any future time?
3. Can you supply the name of anyone, preferably a priest, who may be instrumental in effecting a reconciliation?
4. What are your recommendations toward this end? Describe.
5. Do you think either party will attempt a remarriage if a separation is permitted?

---

1. Do you have anything further to add to this testimony?
2. (Here the testimony should be read to the deponent.) Do you wish to add to, amend or correct any of the foregoing statements?
3. Please take the following oath:

"I do solemnly swear that the testimony I have just given is correct and that I have told the truth, the whole truth and nothing but the truth. So help me God and these His Holy Gospels which I touch with my hand."

Date: ....
Priest Notary: .... Deponent
Parish: .... Parish Seal

(The priest notary is requested to present a statement of his opinion from either personal knowledge or investigation with regard to the deponent's credibility, religious character and probity of life.)

....
Signature

IV. Interrogatory for Priest Consulted

CHANCERY OF THE DIOCESE

Num. Prot. ....
PETITIONER ....
RESPONDENT ....

Subject: INTERROGATION OF PRIEST CONSULTED IN CASE OF ECCLESIASTICAL SEPARATION

Reverend and Dear Father:

You have been named by ...., petitioner/respondent, in a suit for an ecclesiastical separation, as having knowledge of the facts of the case. You are therefore respectfully requested to express an opinion regarding the merits of the case by completing the following interrogatory.

1. What is your name?
2. What is your present address?
3. Is the petitioner/respondent known to your personally?
4. If so, please express your opinion concerning (his) (her)
   (a) religious character
   (b) probity of life
   (c) credibility, especially in this matter
5. How long have you known petitioner/respondent?
6. Are you acquainted with both parties?
7. Where were the parties married?
8. Have they always lived together?

9. If there have been previous separations please tell what you know of these earlier separations.
10. Were any children born of this union?
    (a) Give their names and ages.
    (b) Please describe their Catholic education.
11. Are you aware of any difficulties between the parties?
12. If so, what is the nature of these dissensions?
13. How often were you consulted concerning their marital difficulties?
    (a) What was your advice in each case?
    (b) If you advised a separation, what was your reason?
    (c) Did you speak to both parties?
    (d) If not, why not?
14. Is either party at present undertaking any civil action?
    (a) If so, what type?
    (b) On what grounds?

The causes alleged by the petitioner for a canonical separation are the following: (Here should be supplied the causes as alleged by the petitioner.)

1. Are you morally certain that these causes exist?
    (a) Please explain.
    (b) Is the case occult, public or notorious?
    (c) What is your estimate of the danger of scandal in this case?
2. What provision will be made, to your knowledge, for the children if a separation is permitted?
3. If this arrangement does not seem satisfactory, what are your recommendations?
4. Have serious efforts been made at reconciliation?
    (a) By whom?
    (b) With what result?
5. Do you believe that medical or psychiatric treatment may offer a solution?
6. Is reconciliation of these parties possible at the present time?
7. If a separation is granted, do you believe that either of the parties will attempt another marriage?

8. Do you believe both parties understand the nature of a canonical separation, especially with regard to the impossibility for the contracting of another marriage and the obligation to resume cohabitation upon the cessation of the motivating cause?
9. After having reviewed the facts in this case what recommendations would you offer in reference to the request for a separation?

Date: ....

Parish: .... Signature of priest

Parish Seal

BIBLIOGRAPHY

Sources

Acta Apostolicae Sedis, Commentarium Officiale, Romae, 1909—

Acta et Decreta Concilii Plenarii Baltimorensis Tertii, A. D. MDCCCLXXXIV, Baltimore: John Murphy & Co., 1886.

Acta et Decreta Sacrorum Conciliorum Recentiorum, Collectio Lactencis, 7 vols., Friburgi Brisgoviae: Herder, 1870-1892.

Acta Sanctae Sedis, 41 vols., Romae, 1865-1908.

Analecta Iuris Pontificii, Romae, 1855-1869; Parisiis, 1872-1891.

Annuario Pontificio per l'Anno 1948, Città del Vaticano: Tipographia Poliglotta Vaticana, 1948.

Bullarum Diplomatum et Privilegiorum Romanorum Pontificum Tauriensis Editio, 24 vols. et Appendix, Augustae Taurinorum, 1857-1872.

Bruns, H., *Canones Apostolorum et Conciliorum Saeculorum IV-VII,* 2 vols., Berolini, 1839.

Codex Iuris Canonici Pii X Pontificis Maximi iussu digestus, Benedicti Papae XV auctoritate promulgatus, Romae: Typis Polyglottis Vaticanis, 1917. Reimpressio, 1933.

Codex Theodosianus, ed. P. Krueger, Berolini: Apud Weidmannos, 1926.

Codicis Iuris Canonici Fontes cura Emi Petri Gasparri editi, 9 vols., Romae (postea Civitate Vaticana): Typis Polyglottis Vaticanis, 1923-1939 (Vols. VII-IX ed. cura et studio Emi Iustiniani Serédi).

Collectanea S. Congregationis de Propaganda Fide, 2 vols., Vol. I, ann. 1662-1866, Nn. 1-1299, Vol. II, ann. 1867-1906, Nn. 1300-1317, Romae: Typographia Polyglotta, S. C. de Propaganda Fide, 1907.

Concilium Tridentinum Diariorum, Actorum, Epistolarum, Tractatum, Nova Collectio 13 vols., Friburgi Brisgoviae: B. Herder, 1901—; Vol. IX, *Actorum Pars Sexta,* collegit, illustravit, edidit Stephanus Ehses, 1924.

Corpus Iuris Canonici, Editio Lipsiensis II (E. Richter-E. Friedberg), 2 vols., Lipsiae, 1879-1881.

Corpus Iuris Civilis, 3 vols., Vol. I., *Institutiones,* quas recognovit P. Krueger, ed. stereotypa 15., 1928; *Digesta,* quae recognovit T. Mommsen et retractavit P. Krueger, ed. stereotypa 15., 1928; Vol. II, *Codex Iustinianus,* quem recognovit et retractavit P. Krueger, ed. stereotypa 10., 1929; Vol. III, *Novellae,* recognovit Rudolphus Schoell, opus Schoelli morte interceptum absolvit Gulielmus Kroll, ed. stereotypa 5., Berolini, 1928-1929.

Corpus Scriptorum Ecclesiasticorum Latinorum, Vindobonae, 1866—.

Decretales D. Gregorii Papae, una cum glossis restitutae, 2 vols., Romae, 1582.

Decretum Gratiani emendatum et notationibus illustratum una cum glossis, 2 vols., Romae, 1582.

Didascalia et Constitutionibus Apostolorum, ed. F. X. Funk, 2 vols., Paderborn, 1905.

Fonti del Diritto Romano, per cura di P. Cogliolo, 2. ed., Torino, 1911.

Epstein, I., *Babylonian Talmud, The*, 13 vols. in 8, London: Soncino Press, 1938.

Hardouin, J., *Acta Conciliorum et Epistolae Decretales ac Constitutiones Summorum Pontificum*, 12 vols., Parisiis, 1714-1715.

Jaffé, J., *Regesta Pontificum Romanorum ab condita Ecclesia ad annum post Christum natum MCXCVIII*, 2. ed. (F. Kaltenbrunner, P. Ewald, S. Loewenfeld), 2 vols. in 1, Lipsiae, 1885-1888.

Liber Sextus Decretalium D. Bonifatii Papae VIII suae integritati una cum Clementinis et Extravagantibus eorumque Glossis restitutus, Romae 1582.

Mansi, J. D., *Sacrorum Conciliorum Nova et Amplissima Collectio*, 53 vols. in 59, Parisiis, 1901-1927.

Monumenta Germaniae Historica, 188 vols., incompleta, Hannoverae—*Leges*, 5 Vols., Vol. I-IV, ed. G. Pertz; Vol. V, edd. G. Pertz, G. Waitz, H. Brunner, Hannoverae, 1835-1889; *Legum Sectio I*, Tome I, *Lex Visigothorum*, ed. K. Zeumer; II, pars 1, *Leges Burgundionum*, ed. L. R. de Salis; V, pars I, *Leges Alamannorum*, ed. K. Lehmann; V, pars 2, *Lex Baiwariorum*, ed. E. von Schwind, Hannoverae, 1888-1927; *Legum Sectio II, Capitularia Legum Francorum*, tom. II, pars 1, edd. A. Boretius, V. Krause, Hannoverae, 1890.

Potthast, A., *Regesta Pontificum Romanorum inde ab anno post Christum natum MCXCVIII ad annum MCCCIV*, 2 vols., Berolini, 1874-1875.

S. Romanae Rotae Decisiones Recentiores, edd. Pr. Farinacius, Petrus Rubeus et Ioannes Baptista Compagnus, pro annis 1518-1684, 25 vols., Romae 1618-1703.

S. Romanae Rotae Decisiones seu Sententiae ab anno 1909, Romae, Typis Polyglottis Vaticanis, 1912—.

Schroeder, H. J., *Disciplinary Decrees of the General Councils*, St. Louis: Herder, 1937.

Theodosiani Libri VI cum Constitutionibus Sirmondianis, ediderunt Th. Mommsen et Paulus M. Meyer, 3 vols., Berolini, 1905.

Thesaurus Resolutionum Sacrae Congregationis Concilii, 167 vols., Urbini 1739-1740; Romae, 1741-1908.

Zamboni, J., *Collectio Declarationum Sacrae Congregationis Cardinalium Sacri Concilii Tridentini Interpretum*, 4 vols., Atrebati, 1860-1868.

Authors

Alford, C., *Ius Matrimoniale Comparatum*, Romae: Anonima Libraria Cattolica Italiana, 1938.

Altaner, Berthold, *Patrologie*, Freiburg in Breisgau, Herder, 1938.

Augustine, C., *A Commentary on the New Code of Canon Law*, 2. ed., 8 vols., St. Louis-London: Herder, 1918-1922.

Ballerini, A., *Opus Theologicum Morale,* absolvit et edidit Dominicus Palmieri, 7 vols., Prati, 1889-1893.

Bengen, I., *Instructio Practica de Sponsalibus et Matrimonio,* 4 vols. in 1, Monasterii, 1858.

Barbosa, A., *Collectanea Doctorum tam Veterum quam Recentiorum in Ius Pontificium Universum,* 6 vols., Lugduni, 1656.

Barrett, J., *A Comparative Study of the Plenary Councils of Baltimore and the Code of Canon Law,* the Catholic University of America Canon Law Studies, n. 83, Washington, D. C.: The Catholic University of America, 1932.

Benedetti, I., *Ordo Iudicialis Processus super Nullitate Matrimonii Instruendi,* ed. nova., Taurini; Marietti, 1938.

Berutti, C., *Institutiones Iuris Canonici,* 5 vols., Vol. II, Pars I, Taurini-Romae: Marietti, 1943.

Beste, U., *Introductio in Codicem,* Collegeville, Minn: St. John's Abbey Press, 1938.

Bouix, D., *Tractatus de Curia Romana,* Parisiis, 1859.

———, *Tractatus de Judiciis Ecclesiasticis,* 2 vols. in 1, Parisiis, 1855.

Bouscaren, T.-Ellis, A., *Canon Law,* Milwaukee: Bruce, 1947.

Bucceroni, I., *Institutiones Theologiae Moralis,* 4 ed., 2 vols., Romae, 1900.

Buckland, W., *A Manual of Private Roman Law,* 2. ed., Cambridge: University Press, 1947.

Cappello, F., *Summa Iuris Canonici,* 3 vols., Vol. I and II, 4. ed., 1945; Vol. III, 3. ed., 1948, Romae: Apud Aedes Universitatis Gregorianae.

———, *Praxis Processualis,* Taurini-Romae: Marietti, 1940.

———, *Tractatus Canonico - Moralis de Sacramentis,* 5 vols., Vol. V, *De Matrimonio,* 5. ed., Romae: Marietti, 1947.

Cerchiari, E., *Capellani Papae et Apostolicae Sedis Auditores Causarum Sacri Palatii Apostolici seu Sacra Romana Rota, ab origine ad diem usque 20 septembris, 1870,* 4 vols., Romae: Typis Polyglottis Vaticanis 1919-1921.

Chelodi, I.-Ciprotti, P., *Ius Canonicum de Matrimonio,* 5. ed., Vicenza: Società Anonima, 1947.

Chrétien, *De Matrimonio,* Metis: Hocquard, 1937.

Cicognani, A., *Canon Law,* 2. ed., English Version by J. O'Hara and F. Brennan, Westminister: Newman, 1934.

Cocchi, G., *Commentarium in Codicem Iuris Canonici,* 8 vols. in 5, Vol. II, 4. ed. Taurinorum Augustae: Marietti, 1937.

Corbett, P. E., *Roman Law of Marriage, The,* Oxford: Clarendon Press, 1930.

Coronata, Matthaeus Conte a, *Institutiones Iuris Canonici,* 2. ed., 5 vols., Taurini: Marietti, 1939-1947.

———, *Interpretatio Authentica Codicis Iuris Canonici,* 2. ed., Torino: Marietti, 1948.

Cosci, C., *De Separatione Tori Conjugalis,* Florentiae, 1855.

Costello, J., *Domicile and Quasi-Domicile,* The Catholic University of America Canon Law Studies, n. 60, Washington, D. C.: The Catholic University of America, 1930.

Coyle, P., *Judicial Exceptions,* The Catholic University of America Canon Law Studies, n. 193, Washington, D. C.: The Catholic University of America Press, 1944.

Daudet, P., *Études sur L'Histoire de la Jurisdiction Matrimoniale,* Paris: Recueil-Sirey, 1933.

De Becker, I., *De Sponsalibus et Matrimonio, Praelectiones Canonicae,* Lovanii, 1893.

De Guise, L., *Le Promoteur de la Justice dans les Causes Matrimoniales,* Universitas Catholica Ottaviensis, Series Canonica, n. 8, Ottawa, Ontario: Les Editions de l'Université d'Ottawa, 1944.

De Smet, A., *De Sponsalibus et Matrimonio,* Brugis, 1909.

———, *Tractatus Theologico-Canonicus de Sponsalibus et Matrimonio,* 4. ed., Brugis: Car. Bayaert, 1927.

Doheny, W., *Canonical Procedure in Matrimonial Cases,* 2 vols., Vol. I, *Formal Judicial Procedure,* 2. ed., 1947; Vol. II, *Informal Procedure,* 1943, Milwaukee: Bruce Publishing Co.

Dugan, H., *The Judiciary Department of the Diocesan Curia,* the Catholic University of America Canon Law Studies, n. 26, Washington, D. C.: The Catholic University of America, 1925.

Durantis, G., *Speculum Iuris,* 4 vols. in 3, Venetiis, 1577.

Esmein, A., *Le Mariâge en Droit Canonique,* 2. ed., 2 tomes, par R. Génestal et Jean Dauvillier, Paris: Recueil-Sirey, 1929-1935.

Feije, H., *De Impedimentis et Dispensationibus Matrimonialibus,* 3. ed., Lovanii, 1855.

Forbes, E., *Canonical Separation of Consorts, The,* Universitas Catholica Ottaviensis, Series Canonica, Tom. 15, Ottawa, Ontario: The University of Ottawa Press, 1948.

Gasparri, P., *Tractatus Canonicus de Matrimonio,* 3. ed., 2 vols., Paris, 1904.

———, *Tractatus Canonicus de Matrimonio,* ed. nova ad mentem Codicis Iuris Canonici, 2 vols., Romae: Typis Polyglottis Vaticanis, 1932.

Genicot, E., *Institutiones Theologiae Moralis,* 6. ed., 2 vols., Bruxellis, 1909.

———, *Institutiones Theologiae Moralis,* 10. ed., 2 vols., quam recognovit I. Salsmans, Bruxellis, 1922.

Gibbons, M., *Domicile of Wife Unlawfully Separated from Her Husband,* The Catholic University of America Canon Law Studies, n. 249, Washington, D. C.: The Catholic University of America Press, 1947.

Glynn, J., *The Promoter of Justice,* The Catholic University of America Canon Law Studies, n. 101, Washington, D. C.: The Catholic University of America, 1936.

Goldsmith, J. W., *The Competence of Church and State Over Marriage - Disputed Points,* The Catholic University of America Canon Law Studies, n. 197, Washington, D. C.: The Catholic University of America Press, 1944.

Hefele, C. J., *Histoire de Conciles,* traduction française par Dom. H. LeClerq, 11 vols. in 20, Paris: Latouzey et Ané, 1907-1949.

Hines, V., *De Coniugum Separatione ac de Civili Divortio in Iure Canonico et in Iure Civili Statuum Foederatorum Americae Septrionalis,* Pontificium Institutum Utriusque Iuris, Theses ad Lauream, n. 62, Romae: Officium Libri Catholici, 1949.

Hostiensis, Cardinalis (Henricus de Segusia), *Commentaria in Quinque Libros Decretalium,* 5 vols. in 3, Venetiis, 1581.

———, *Summa Aurea,* Lugduni, 1568.

Hümmelauer, F. von, *Commentarius in Deuteronomium,* Paris, 1901.

Ioannes Andreae, *Commentaria Novella in Sex Decretalium Libros,* 6 vols. in 5, Venetiis, 1581.

Iorio, T., *Theologia Moralis,* 3 vols., Vol. III, 3. ed., Neapoli: D'Auria, 1947.

Jemolo, A., *Il Matrimonio nel Diritto Canonico,* Milano: Vollardi, 1947.

Joder, *Formulaire Matrimonial,* 3. ed., Paris, 1891.

Joyce, G. H., *Christian Marriage,* London: Sheed and Ward, 1933.

Kantorowicz, H., *Studies in the Glossators of Roman Law,* Cambridge: University Press, 1938.

Karlowa, O., *Römische Rechtsgeschichte,* 2 vols., Leipzig, 1901.

Kay, T., *Competence in Matrimonial Procedure,* The Catholic University of America Canon Law Studies, n. 53, Washington, D. C.: The Catholic University of America, 1929.

Kearney, R., *The Principles of Delegation,* The Catholic University of America Canon Law Studies, n. 55, Washington, D. C.: The Catholic University of America, 1929.

Kennedy, E., *The Special Matrimonial Procedure in Cases of Evident Nullity,* The Catholic University of America Canon Law Studies, n. 93, Washington, D. C.: The Catholic University of America, 1935.

Kenrick, F., *Theologia Moralis,* 2. ed., 2 vols., Mechliniae-Baltimorae, 1866.

Knabenbauer, J., *Commentaria in Evangelium secundum Matthaeum,* 2 vols., Paris, 1922.

Konings, A., *Theologia Moralis,* Boston, 1874.

Lega, M., *Praelectiones de Iudiciis Ecclesiasticis,* 4 vols., Romae, 1896-1901.

Lehmkuhl, A., *Theologia Moralis,* 12. ed., 2 vols., Friburgi, 1914.

Le Picard, R., *La Communauté de la Vie Conjugale,* Paris: Recueil-Sirey, 1930.

Loeb Classical Library, edd. E. Capps, T. Page, W. Rouse; Juvenal, *The Satyra,* transl. by G. G. Ramsey, London, 1918.

Lombardus, Petrus, *Libri IV Sententiarum,* studio et cura PP. Collegii S. Bonaventurae 2. ed., 2 vols., ad Claras Aquas, 1916.

McClunn, J., *Administrative Recourse,* The Catholic University of America Canon Law Studies, n. 240, Washington, D. C.: The Catholic University of America Press, 1946.

Mansella, J., *De Impedimentis et de Processu Iudiciali in Causis Matrimonialibus,* Romae, 1881.

Merkelbach, B., *Summa Theologiae Moralis,* 3 vols., Vol. III, 5. ed. De Brouer: Desclée, 1947.

Migne, J. P., *Patrologiae Cursus Completus, Series Graeca,* 161 vols., Parisii, 1857-1866.

———, *Patrologiae Cursus Completus, Series Latina,* 221 Vols., Parisiis 1844-1855.

Môra, M. von, *Die Frage des Zivilprozesses und der Beweislast bei Gratian,* Pécs, 1937.

Muirhead, J., *Historical Introduction to the Private Law of Rome,* 3. ed., London, 1916.

Muñiz, T., *Procédimientos Eclesiásticos,* 3 vols., Vol. III, 2. ed., Sevilla, 1926.

Noldin, H.-Schmitt, A., *Summa Theologiae Moralis,* 3 vols., Vol. III, 26. ed., Oeniponte-Lipsiae: Rauch, 1940.

Noval, J., *Commentarium Codicis Iuris Canonici,* Lib. IV, De Processibus, Pars I, *De Iudiciis,* Augustae Taurinorum-Romae: Marietti, 1920.

Oesterle, G., *Praelectiones Iuris Canonici,* Vol. I., Romae: Collegium S. Anselmi, 1931.

Ojetti, B., *Commentarium in Codicem Iuris Canonici,* 4 vols., Romae: Apud Aedes Universitatis Gregorianae, 1927-1931.

Ottaviani, A., *Institutionibus Iuris Publici Ecclesiastici,* 2 vols., Vol. II, 2. ed., *Ius Publicum Externum,* Romae: Typis Polyglottis Vaticanis, 1936.

Panormitanus, Abbas (Nicolaus de Tudeschis), *Commentaria in Quinque Libros Decretalium,* 5 vols. in 7, Venetiis, 1588.

Payen, G., *De Matrimonio in Missionibus ac Potissimum in Sinis Tractatus Practicus et Casus,* 2. ed., 3 vols., Zi-ka-wei: Typographia T'ou-Sé Wé, 1935-1936.

Pellegrino, C., *Praxis Vicariorum,* Venetiis, 1743.

Perrone, J., *De Matrimonio Christiano,* 3 vols., Romae, 1858.

Pirhing, E., *Ius Canonicum in V Libros Decretalium,* 5 vols., Dilingae, 1674-1678.

Prat, F., *Theology of St. Paul, The,* translated from the 11. French edition by J. Stoddard, 2 vols., London, 1926.

Prümmer, D., *Manuale Theologiae Moralis,* 3 vols., 4. et 5. ed., Friburgi Brisgoviae, 1928.

Raymundus de Pennafort, St., *Summa,* ed. nova, Veronae, 1744.

Regatillo, E., *Institutiones Iuris Canonici,* 2 vols., Santander: Sal Terrae, 1941-1942.

———, *Ius Sacramentarium,* 2 vols., Santander: Sal Terrae, 1945-1946.

Reiffenstuel, A., *Ius Canonicum Universum,* 5 vols. in 6, Romae, 1831-1834.

Rivier, A., *Précis du Droit de Famille Romaine,* Paris, 1891.

Roberti, F., *De Delictis et Poenis,* Vol. I, Pars 1, *De Delictis in Genere,* 2. ed., Romae: Libraria Pontificii Instituti Utriusque Iuris, 1938.

———, *De Processibus,* 2 vols., Vol. I, 2. ed., Romae: Apud Custodiam Librariam Pontificii Instituti Utriusque Iuris, 1941.

Roby, H., *Roman Private Law,* 2 vols., Cambridge, 1902.

Rufinus, *Die Summa des Magister Rufinus,* ed. Heinrich Singer, Paderborn, 1902.

Sabetti, A., *Compendium Theologiae Moralis,* concinnatum a Timotheo Barrett, 19. ed., Ratisbonae, 1906.

Sanchez, T., *Disputationum de Sancto Matrimonii Sacramento, Tomi Tres,* Antverpiae, 1626.

Santi, F., *Praelectiones Iuris Canonici,* 5 vols. in 2, Ratisbonae, Neo-Eboraci et Cincinnati, 1886.

Sartori, C., *Enchiridion Canonicum,* 8. ed., Romae: Pontificium Athenaeum Antonianum, 1947.

Savigny, F. K. von, *Geschichte des Römischen Rechts im Mittelalter,* 6 vols., Heidelberg, 1815-1831.

Schmalzgrueber, F., *Ius Ecclesiasticum Universum,* 5 vols. in 12, Romae, 1843-1845.

Seneca, *De Beneficiis,* ed. C. Hosius, Teubner Text, Lipsiae, 1900.

Sherman, C., *Roman Law in the Modern World,* 2. ed., 3 vols. New York: Baker Vorhees, 1924.

Smith, S., *The Marriage Process in the United States,* New York, 1893.

Strack, H., *Introduction to the Talmud and Midrash,* Philadelphia: The Jewish Publication Society of America, 1931.

Stitt, A., *De Promotore Iustitiae eiusque Munere in Curia Dioecesana,* Romae: Apud Ed. Scientifica Internazionale, 1939.

Tobin, T., *De Officiali Curiae Dioecesanae,* Romae: Apud Aedes Pontificiae Universitatis Gregorianae, 1936.

Torre, I., *Processus Matrimonialis,* 2. ed., Naples: D'Auria, 1947.

Toso, A., *Ad Codicem Iuris Canonici . . . Commentaria Minora,* 5 vols. in 2, Liber II, *De Personis,* Tom. I, Taurini-Romae, 1922.

Van Hove, A., *Commentarium Lovaniense in Codicem Iuris Canonici,* Vol. I, tom. 1, *Prolegomena ad Codicem Iuris Canonici,* 2. ed., 1945; Vol. II, *De Legibus Ecclesiasticis,* 1930, Mechliniae-Romae: H. Dessain.

Vaughan, W., *Constitutions for Diocesan Courts,* The Catholic University of America Canon Law Studies, n. 210, Washington, D. C.: The Catholic University of America Press, 1944.

Vermeersch, A. - Creusen, J., *Epitome Iuris Canonici,* 3 vols., Vol. I, 7. ed., 1949; Vol. II, 6. ed., 1940; Vol. III, 6. ed., 1946; Mechliniae-Romae: H. Dessain.

Vlaming, T., *Praelectiones Iuris Matrimonii,* 2 vols., Vol. II, 3. ed., Bussum, 1919-1921.

Wernx, F. X., *Ius Decretalium,* 6 vols., Vol. I, 3, ed., 1913; Vol. II, 3. ed., 1915; Vol. III, 2. ed., 1908; Vol. IV, 2 ed, 1911; Vol. V, 1914; Vol. VI, 1913; Romae et Prati.

Wernz, F. X. - Vidal, P., *Ius Canonicum,* 7 vols. in 8, Vol. I, 1938; Vol. II, 3. ed., a P. Aguirre recognita, 1943; Vol. III, 1933; Vol. IV, pars 1, 1934, pars 2, 1935; Vol. V, 3. ed., a P. Aguirre recognita, 1946; Vol. VI, 1927; Vol. VII, 1937, Romae: Apud Aedes Universitatis Gregorianae.

Zabarella, F., *Commentarium in Clementinas,* Venetiis, 1504.

Articles

Cappello, F., "De Separatione Coniugum," *Periodica,* XXI (1932), 286-288.

Hannan, J., "Marriage after Civil Divorce," *The Jurist,* VII (1947), 311-312.

Kelly, J., "Separation and Civil Divorce," *The Jurist,* VI (1946), 187-238.

———, "Divorce—Some Practical Canonical Considerations," *The Jurist,* IX (1949), 187-204.

Kinane, J., "Regarding the Acquisition of Domicile," *Irish Ecclesiastical Record,* 5. series, XX (1922), 408-409.

Kuttner, C., "The Father of the Science of Canon Law," *The Jurist,* I (1941), 2-19.

Manucci, U., "Annotazioni ad alcune ultime risposte della Commissione per l'interpretazione autentica del Codice, can. 93," *Il Monitore Ecclesiastico,* 4. series, IV (1922), 339-340.

Planchard, J., "Divorce Civil," *Nouvelle Revue Théologique,* XXIII (1891), 664-679.

Roberti, F., "De Separatione Coniugum," *Apollinaris,* V (1932), 294-296.

Toso, A., in *Ius Pontificium,* II (1922), 84.

Waffelaert, C ,."Question du Divorce," *Nouvelle Revue Théologique,* XVII (1885), 231-254.

Periodicals

Apollinaris, Romae, 1928—

Irish Ecclesiastical Record, Dublin: Browne & Nolan, 1864.

Ius Pontificium, Romae, 1921-1940.

Jurist, The, Washington, D. C., 1941—

Monitore Ecclesiastico, Il, Romae: Desclee, 1876-1948.

Nouvelle Revue Théologique, Paris, 1869—

Periodica de Religiosis et Missionariis, Brugis, 1905-1919; from 1920: *Periodica de Re Canonica et Morali utilia praesertim Religiosis et Missionariis,* Brugis, 1920-1927; *Periodica de Re Morali, Canonica, Liturgica,* Brugis, 1927-1936, et Romae, 1937—

Abbreviations

AAS—Acta Apostolicae Sedis.

ASS—Acta Sanctae Sedis.

Bruns—*Canones Apostolorum et Conciliorum saec. IV-VII,* ed. Bruns.

C.—*Codex Iustinianus* or Causa.

c.—canon or caput.
C. Th.—*Codex Theodosianus.*
Collectanea—*Collectanea S. C. de Propaganda Fide.*
D.—*Digestum Iustinianum* or Distinctio.
Fontes—*Codicis Iuris Canonici Fontes*—cura Gasparri editi.
Hardouin—*Acta Conciliorum, etc.*
J E—Jaffé, *Regesta Pontificum Romanorum* (edited by P. Ewald; for the years 590-882).
J K—Jaffé, *op. cit.* (edited by F. Kaltenbrunner; to the year 590).
J. L—Jaffé, *op. cit.* (edited by S. Loewenfeld: for the years 882-1198).
Mansi—*Sacrorum Conciliorum Nova et Amplissima Collectio.*
MGH—*Monumenta Germaniae Historica.*
MPG—Migne, *Patrologia, Series Graeca.*
MPL—Migne, *Patrologia, Series Latina.*
Nov.—*Novellae Iustinianae.*
NRT—*Nouvelle Revue Théologique.*
P.C.I.—*Pontificia Commissio ad Codicis Canones Authentice Interpretendes.*
Potthast—*Regesta Pontificium Romanorum, etc.*
S. C. C.—Sacra Congregatio Concilii.
S. C. de Prop. Fide—Sacra Congregatio de Propaganda Fide.
S. C. de Sacramentis—Sacra Congregatio de Disciplina Sacramentorum.
S. C. S. Off.—Sacra Congregatio Sancti Oficii.
S. R. R.—Sacra Romana Rota.

ALPHABETICAL INDEX

Actions, 90
actio de spolio, 91
actio ex novi operis nuntiatione, 91
Administrative Process
definition of, 123
Introductory and probatory stages of, 127
nature and character of, 121
pre-Code, 26, 38
proper authority in, 123
Adultery
as cause for separation, 17, 55, 69
compensation of, 20, 29
cause of, 31
condonation of, 32
consent to, 21, 29, 31
formal, 21, 29, 49, 93
in Glossators, 17
in Gratian, 17
notorious, 55, 69
presumptions of, 17, 33, 50
spiritual, 23, 37, 53
suspicion of, 17, 50, 54
Affectio maritalis, 2
Alimony, 35, 51
without divorce, civil action of, 139
Appeal, 114
Appellate stage in administrative process, 135
Assesores, 84

Bishop,
and marriage cases, 11
and separation cases, 18
Boards for administrative hearing of separation cases, 85, 126

Causa favorabilis, 106
Cause,
of adultery, 31, 93
of separation, 45, 53, 77
just, in Canon Law, 64
Civil action, 138
Civil divorce, 140
Civil separation, 45, 140
and decree of Ordinary, 134
causes for, 140
and *libellus,* 98
permission for, 110
petition to initiate action for, 98
Collegiate tribunal, 83
in appellate stage, 115
Compensation for adultery, 20, 29, 93
Compentency,
determination of, 80
in separation cases, 47, 80
quasi-domicile as a determinant of, 49
Competent authority for separation,
in administrative process, 124
in Code of Canon Law, 66, 78
in Decretals, 29, 44, 46
in early Church, 11
in Gratian, 25
Competent Tribunal, 27, 47, 49, 80
Condonation of adultery, 32, 94
Confessions,
judicial, 100
Consent,
to adultery as an exception in a separation suit, 29, 31
word as used regarding marriage in Canon Law and Roman Law, 2
Consultors,
as assistants to the judge, 84
Council of Trent, 41
Court of second instance,
and newly discovered delict, 118
number of judges, 115
Court,
organization of, 80
in second instance, 116
Custody of offspring, 35, 51, 111

Danger in delay, 55, 70, 73
Decree,
of separation, 133
recourse against, 135
Decretals of Gregory IX, 23
Defensor vinculi, 28, 47, 86
Delegate,
of Ordinary in separation suits, 79
Departure,
legitimate, 66, 69
opinion regarding it and legitimate separation, 69
Divorce,
among the new nations, 9
among the Jews, 1
causes for, 141, 156
in Roman Law, 1, 3
in the various American states, 140
pre-Code period, 143, 147
Tridentine period, 142
Divortium, 3, 9
Domicile,
as determinant of competency, 48, 69, 80
of wife unlawfully separated from husband, 69, 73
Dowry, 111

Exceptio spolii, 20, 196
Exceptions,
judicial, 29, 79, 93
Excommunication,
for divorce and remarriage, 144

Formal procedure,
in separation cases, 25, 45, 75

Germanic age, 9
Gratian, 15

Informal process, 26, 38, 57, 75
Ivo of Chartres, 13

Judge,
competent, 80, 83
number of for separation suit, 83
number of in appellate stage, 115
Judicial Exceptions,
cause of adultery, 31, 93
compensation for adultery, 20, 29, 93
condonation for adultery, 32, 93
consent to adultery, 29, 31, 93
exceptio spolii, 20, 96
in decretals, 29
in Gratian, 20
nature of 79, 90
Judicial process, 78, 80
Juridical effects of canonical separation, 111
Jurisdiction,
for administrative hearing of separation cases, 124
Just cause,
for separation, 64

Libellus,
in separation case, 32, 196
rejection of, 98
Litis contestatio, 96

Marriage,
among the Jews, 1
and the Frankish kings, 9
in Roman Law, 1

Officialis,
in administrative process, 125
power of, 85
Ordinary,
as competent authority in separation cases, 78
decree of, 133
in administrative process, 123
in formal process, 83
redress against decree of, 135
Ordinary procedure,
among Glossators, 17
in Code, 75
in Decretals, 25
in Gratian, 16

in Tridentine law, 45
Parties,
actions allowed to, 90
in separation case, 28, 49, 79, 88
legal compulsion to plead a separation suit, 89
parity of rights to plead a separation suit, 89
right to appeal, 116
recourse in administrative process, 135
Permanent separation, 65, 73
Personnel,
in appellate stage, 116
of court in first instance, 27, 80
Petition,
for separation in administrative process, 128
Physical harm, 55
Plaintiff,
in separation suit, 49
Power,
Judicial and voluntary, 123
Presumptions,
definition of Alexander III, 33, 103
in administrative process, 131
in *libellus,* 97
of adultery, 17, 33, 50
of law in condonation of adultery, 94, 102
norms presented by Rota, 103
personal presumptions, 101, 102
presumptions of law, 101
regarding notorious acts of spouse, 102
violent, 33, 104
Probatory stage of the trial, 99
Procedure,
administrative, 119
first reference to in ecclesiastical law, 8
formal, 25, 45, 75
in decretals, 23
in divorce cases of Jews, 2
in divorce cases of Romans, 2
in early Church, 5
in Germanic age, 9
in Glossators 17
Ivo of Chartres and, 13
in informal cases, 26, 38, 57, 75, 119
ordinary in decretals, 25
ordinary in Gratian, 16, 19
summary, 26, 38, 59, 120
Process,
nature of, 73
Promoter of Justice,
ecclesiastical jurisprudence regarding, 87
his activity in separation suit, 87
his presence in separation suit as necessary, 87
in administrative process, 132
in appellate stage, 116
nature of his office, 87
right to appeal, 116
Proofs,
by testimony, 97
confessions, 100
documentary, 97
Propria auctoritate separation, 22, 36, 54, 68, 70
Psychiatrists,
as aides to Ordinary in separation cases, 130
Public good, 64, 87

Quasi-domicile
as a determinant of compentency, 49, 80
special instruction concerning, 82

Reconciliation of the spouses, 98
in administrative process, 129
in decree of separation, 134
provision for in law, 113
Recourse,
against the decree of the Ordinary, 135

Remarriage,
after civil divorce, 158
Repudium, 3, 9
Res Iudicata, 34
Restoration of common life, 52
Right to appeal, 116

Sentence of Separation,
format of, 107
general notions concerning, 27, 34, 71, 105
in administrative process, 133
publication of, 110
Separate maintenance, 139
Separation,
as a penalty, 22, 25
cause of, 45, 53
competent authority for, 11, 25, 29, 45, 46, 66
first reference to procedure for, 8
obligation to separate, 5, 28
permanent, 65
propria auctoritate, 22, 36, 54, 68, 70
right to, 2, 14, 18, 28
temporary, 65
Spiritual adultery, 23, 37, 53
Spiritual harm,
as cause for separation, 55
Summary process, 26, 38
in separation suits and Code of Canon Law

Temporary separation, 65, 73

Unity of marriage, 63

Vicar-General,
in administrative process, 125
in judicial process, 83
Vice-Officialis, 85
Witnesses,
as evidence in trials, 50, 97, 103
of adultery, 50, 103

BIOGRAPHICAL NOTE

James Patrick King was born August 8, 1920, in Manhasset, New York, and there attended St. Mary's Parochial School. He graduated from Cathedral College High School in 1938, and from Cathedral College in 1940. In September of that year he entered the Diocesan Seminary of the Immaculate Conception, Huntington, New York. He was ordained to the Holy Priesthood on June 15, 1946, by His Excellency, the Most Reverend Thomas E. Molloy, S.T.D., Bishop of Brooklyn. He was engaged in parochial work until the fall of 1948, when he entered the School of Canon Law of the Catholic University of America, Washington, D. C., where he received the Baccalaureate degree in Canon Law in June, 1949, and the Licentiate degree in Canon Law in June, 1950.

CANON LAW STUDIES *

322. Gaffigan, Rev. Aloysius J., O.S.F.S., J.C.L., Residence of Religious.
323. Cappiello, Rev. Linus V., O.F.M., J.C.L., De Ordinariorum Dispensandi Facultate ad Normam Canonis 81.
324. Conway, Rev. Walter J., J.C.L., The Time and Place of Baptism.
325. King, Rev. James P., J.C.L., The Canonical Procedure in Separation Cases.
326. Wrzaszczak, Rev. Chester F., J.C.L., The Betrothal Contract in the Code of Canon Law.

* A complete list of the available numbers in the series will be found in earlier studies. All the published numbers are available from The Catholic University of America Press, 620 Michigan Avenue, N.E., Washington 17, D. C., except the following: Nos. 1-114 inclusive, 116, 118-123, 128, 136, 153, 162, 166, 178, 182, and 198. But the following numbers now reissued, are obtainable from *The Jurist*, The Catholic University of America, Washington 17, D. C., namely: Nos. 5, 7, 11, 17, 18, 19, 26, 28, 30, 31, 34, 42, 44, 51, 52 and 61.